GENERATION UNBOUND

Drifting into Sex and Parenthood without Marriage

Isabel V. Sawhill

BROOKINGS INSTITUTION PRESS
Washington, D.C.

The Brookings Institution is a private nonprofit organization devoted
to research, education, and publication on important issues of domestic
and foreign policy. Its principal purpose is to bring the highest quality
independent research and analysis to bear on current and emerging
policy problems. Interpretations or conclusions in Brookings publications
should be understood to be solely those of the authors.

Library of Congress Cataloging-in-Publication data
Sawhill, Isabel V.
 Generation unbound : drifting into sex and parenthood without marriage /
Isabel V. Sawhill.
     pages   cm
 Includes bibliographical references and index.
 ISBN 978-0-8157-2558-9 (hardcover : alk. paper)—ISBN 978-0-8157-2635-7
(pbk. : alk. paper) 1. Unmarried mothers—United States. 2. Unmarried
fathers—United States. 3. Youth—Sexual behavior—United States. 4. Family
planning—United States. 5. Marriage—United States. I. Title.
 HQ999.U6.S35 2014
 306.874'32—dc23   2014016992

9 8 7 6 5 4 3 2 1

Printed on acid-free paper

Typeset in Sabon and Ocean Sans

Composition by Cynthia Stock
Silver Spring, Maryland

To

JOHN, JAMIE, AND JOHN

Three Generations Bound

Contents

Preface

Writing a book is hard. So one better have some good reasons for doing so.

One reason I wrote this book is because I began my career studying family issues and wanted to revisit them with the benefit of more years of experience. Although trained as an economist rather than as a scholar of the family, my first serious research job was working on a Ford Foundation–sponsored project devoted to assessing whether the increasing number of female-headed families in the black community was as problematic as Daniel Patrick Moynihan had contended in his famous report "The Negro Family." This project led to my first book, *Time of Transition: The Growth of Female-Headed Families,* coauthored with Heather Ross and published by the Urban Institute in 1975.

Nearly forty years later, I am still drawn to the issue of how changes in the family have affected child poverty, inequality, and social mobility in the United States. The issue is no longer just high rates of unwed parenting in the black community. It is high rates for whites as well. I have come to believe that social policy faces an uphill battle as long as families continue to fragment and children are deprived of the resources of two parents.

The issue has recurred in my work, both as a researcher and as a government official. As an associate director of the Office of Management and Budget (OMB) during the Clinton administration, I worked on the president's welfare reform legislation. The question of what to do about the breakdown of the American family was an important part of the legislative debate at that time. The reform law, enacted in 1996 on a bipartisan basis, contained two new messages. To women, it said full-time motherhood at public expense is no longer an option. To men, it said if you father a child you will be expected to contribute to that child's support.

I encouraged the president and other members of his administration to focus more on the prevention of teen pregnancy, something both he and the first lady actively supported. After leaving the administration, I helped to launch a new bipartisan nonprofit organization called the National Campaign to Prevent Teen Pregnancy. This organization, whose board I now lead, later expanded its mission to include not just teen pregnancies but also unplanned pregnancies among single women in their twenties. I am proud to say that we have had considerable success, especially in reducing teen pregnancy. The teen birth rate has declined by over 50 percent since 1991. However, parenting by young unwed women has not declined. It has just moved up the age scale.

Although welfare reform was enacted in 1996, and teen pregnancies and births have declined, the debate about what to do about the growth of unmarried parenthood continues to rage. So I was not particularly surprised when, in 2012, the *Washington Post* asked me to write a piece reflecting on the twentieth anniversary of former vice president Dan Quayle's criticism of single motherhood, in which he used the behavior of a TV sitcom character named Murphy Brown to make his case.

Murphy Brown was an unmarried 40-something journalist who found herself unintentionally pregnant and decided to raise the baby on her own. Quayle criticized the show for sending the wrong message to younger viewers about the importance of marriage. It set off a national debate in the media about family values. In my article, I wrote that Dan Quayle was right. While he may have picked the wrong role model— since most unmarried moms are younger, are less educated, and make less money than the fictional news reporter—his concern about changes in the family were consistent with research showing that children, on average, benefit from being raised by their own married parents.

Although I was not surprised by the *Post*'s interest in these family issues, I was surprised by the intensity of the response to my article. It became the most viewed article of the year in "Outlook"—the newspaper's Sunday opinion section. In a matter of days, more than 2,500 comments were logged on the *Post*'s website, and I received dozens of letters and calls from readers who wanted to share their (often heated) opinions on the matter.

Some readers noted that single parents are not single by choice: "Nobody ever doubted that it's better for a child to have two parents. Nobody who actually cares about the children ever doubted that it is wrong to point fingers at mothers struggling to cope with realities they cannot change, and usually did not choose." Another said, "Most women would want a partner to help them but were never offered that option."

Others agreed with Quayle and stressed the importance of personal responsibility: "If you choose to be a single parent I don't think you should expect help from the government," and "There are ways of preventing such atrocities, you know! Saying no to frivolous close encounters that cause pregnancy and maintaining one's virtue comes to mind here!"

Some said good riddance to marriage: "Marriage is an anachronistic institution that has outstripped its usefulness in modern society." Several readers bemoaned the absence of male responsibility from the discussion: "I've not seen many comments that admonish the men for taking part in creating this child and situation and not taking responsibility for their part." Other readers were concerned about expanding marriage to same-sex couples or about how children fare in such unions: "I would also want to know how the children of gay couples (married and unmarried) stack up," said a letter writer.

How did federal policy fit into the equation, wondered some readers? "Instead of providing financial incentives to married parents, who already have the financial advantage, why not provide meaningful child care subsidies for single parents?" What about access to contraception, asked another: "If the Republicans had consistently supported the availability of birth control over the past two decades, there would be fewer unmarried mothers." But perhaps the most common response was one of ambivalence. Marriage is great—except when it isn't: "Marriage is better for children. That doesn't mean single parents can't succeed or that just because two people are married the children will do better. It does mean that if people would take care with whom they have children, the children will do better as will the adults." This kind of conflicted and nuanced thinking reared its head again and again:

It is . . . better to have two parents for lots of reasons. That's not to say that it is critical. It isn't the right choice to stay with a bozo in order for a child to have two parents. It's preferable to have two parents, but only if those parents are reasonable and can create a loving and supportive environment, which is not always the case.

As someone who by temperament and training prefers grays over blacks and whites, this last set of comments resonated with me. More important, the *Post*'s readers reminded me that these are questions on which almost everyone has an opinion. The questions are difficult, and they go to the very heart of our own lives and identities as partners, spouses, children, and parents. We generally accept as a social good that women now have educational and professional opportunities that free them from dependence on men and that all have new choices about how to manage their lives. But we wonder how this rapid transformation may have affected society both for good and for ill. How do we reconcile the benefits of more personal freedom with some of the social costs? Is the problem single parenthood in and of itself, or is it that single parents tend to have less money and time? Are two parents always better than one? Are unmarried, cohabiting families the new norm, or will a revival of marriage occur? And most important, in the midst of these uncertainties, how can we do right by children who do not get to pick their parents or the circumstances of their births?

Many of these questions will never be definitively settled, but the strongest social science research can shed some light on what we know and what we don't yet know. With that evidence as my guide, I set out to write this book. I wanted to find some answers to these questions, both for myself and for those who, along with me, have been wondering what to think. So I immersed myself, once again, in the research and learned a lot in the process. I have not shied away from adding my own interpretation to the facts. And where the answers are elusive, as they often are, I hope to catalyze a broader debate about social norms and attitudes in this intensely personal arena.

A final note about my own life may be in order since we are all embedded in a web of personal experiences that consciously or unconsciously bias our views. I was blessed with a good marriage and one child. I am now widowed, and from the perspective of my advanced years I believe that these decisions about marriage and childbearing are the most important we ever make. I was an indifferent parent and a sometimes difficult wife (some of my current colleagues will smile knowingly), but I was very lucky to have had a supportive husband. I now have a son and a grandson of whom I am very proud, without being able to take the least bit of credit for any success they have had.

I want to end this preface by thanking the many people whose work and ideas have contributed to this book. At the top of the list is my research assistant, Joanna Venator, whose diligence and patience were nothing short of astounding. She has been a partner in this effort from the beginning, reviewing literature, collecting and analyzing data, and drafting text. I literally could not have written this book without her. Other colleagues who helped in a variety of ways include Stephanie Cencula, Bill Galston, Kerry Grannis, Ron Haskins, Quentin Karpilow, Jonathan Rauch, and Richard Reeves. Haskins, Reeves, and I all share a strong interest in these issues and have benefited from sharing ideas and writing essays, either singly or together, for a variety of outlets. Rauch and Galston, along with Brad Wilcox, have kept me from getting too gloomy about the future of marriage in the United States. The entire team at the Brookings Press has also been a delight to work with, and I especially appreciate the careful editing done by Janet Mowery.

In addition to my colleagues, I am deeply indebted to my friends and colleagues at the National Campaign to Prevent Teen and Unplanned Pregnancies, where I have the honor to serve as president of the board. Sarah Brown, Andrea Kane, Laura Sessions Stepp, and Kelleen Kaye in particular reviewed earlier drafts and offered wise commentary on what they read. Participating in the work of the campaign, and learning from my colleagues there, has given me an especially acute sense of both what is needed and what is possible.

This book builds, I hope, on the work of numerous scholars of the family. Stephanie Coontz, probably the most prolific and articulate writer on this whole topic, has warned us not to compare today's families with some idealized family form from the past, since history shows that families have always been in flux and not all of the recent news is bad. My book is too short to address this longer history, but I hope it does not fall into the nostalgia trap.

Sara McLanahan, Irwin Garfinkel, and Ron Mincy have changed our view of family life by producing new data on what they call "fragile families," those in which the parents are unmarried at the time of their child's birth. They have emphasized the turbulence in the lives of these children: not just the high rates of breakup between their parents, but also the large number of additional partners and half-siblings that enter the household even before the child turns 5. Another invaluable source has been a volume by Lynne Casper and Suzanne Bianchi called *Continuity and Change in the American Family,* whose review of the data and the literature is comprehensive, balanced, and thorough.

I would be remiss to not mention the excellent work of Brad Wilcox and the National Marriage Project, sometimes in collaboration with the Institute for American Values. They have provided a steady stream of good data and interpretation of ongoing trends but have not flinched from taking a stand, believing that marriage is too important an institution to let go quietly into some dark night. (Disclaimer: I am on the advisory board of both organizations.)

Kathy Edin's ethnographies have added enormously to our understanding of the more qualitative aspects of family life as experienced in some of our poorest neighborhoods. Andrew Cherlin has shown how American marriages differ from those in other advanced countries, pointing out that the United States has a marriage-friendly culture combined with higher rates of family formation and dissolution than in other advanced countries. David Ellwood and Christopher Jencks earlier called attention to the fact that marriage was alive and well among better-educated women but that the less-educated, although not marrying, were still having children. This has been a theme in my own work as well, going back to 1999, when I first sounded the alarm about growing class divisions in family formation. It has been reaffirmed by Sara McLanahan, by the National Marriage Project, by Charles Murray in his book *Coming Apart,* and in *Social Class and Changing Families in an Unequal America* edited by Marcia Carlson and Paula England.

None of the aforementioned should be blamed if I have gotten anything wrong. In the end, facts will take us only so far in understanding what has happened to the American family and may not help at all in deciding what kind of world we want for ourselves and our children.

ONE

An Introduction

Understand that the right to choose your own path is a sacred privilege. Use it. Dwell in possibility.

—Oprah Winfrey

Ashley is a 22-year-old single woman from a working-class neighborhood. She is attending community college, hoping to become a medical technician. She gets pregnant and drops out of school. Neither Ashley nor her boyfriend, Eric, has a steady job. They don't believe in abortion. A baby is born; within two years they have split up and Ashley has a new boyfriend, with whom she has a second baby.

Sam and Stephanie met in medical school. Now they are both doctors in their early thirties. They have one child. A full-time nanny from Peru is teaching the child to be bilingual. Sam and Stephanie spend all of their free time on child-oriented activities, including trips to the zoo, home-based science projects, and reading *Cat in the Hat* out loud.

Tom and Sebastian are two gay men with successful careers. They live together and have carefully chosen two different egg donors and surrogate mothers in order to have children. Their two daughters are now 5 and 7 and appear to be flourishing.

These family profiles (but not the names) are real. Families like these dot the contemporary landscape. The variations are endless and no longer seem particularly surprising. Single mothers, divorced couples, two-earner families, and same-sex partnerships are all as common as dandelions in spring. The old model of the family consisting of a breadwinning husband and a stay-at-home wife still exists, but that model is rare.

What is happening here? Will we ever see a return of the old model or has marriage as we once knew it gone forever? What might take its place? Can the needs of children be reconciled with the new freedoms afforded to adults? How can we improve the life prospects of the next generation? And what changes in public policy and private decisionmaking are needed to make this possible?

Let's start with the good news: we have a lot more choices than in the past. You no longer have to be married to have sex pretty much as often as you like. You can marry or cohabit with a "significant other." You can have children in or out of marriage. In an increasing number of states you can marry someone of the same sex. I am old enough to remember when we called a woman who had sex before marriage "loose"; cohabitation "living in sin"; a child born outside of marriage "illegitimate"; and a relationship with someone of the same sex "unnatural." These phrases are a reminder of how the times have changed—and at lightning speed.

We like having choices. If I type "chocolate ice cream" into my supermarket's online search engine, I get 100 varieties to choose from: dark chocolate, milk chocolate, Belgian chocolate, fudge brownie, chocolate swirl—it goes on and on. When I was growing up, ice cream was a rare treat; it came in three flavors: vanilla, chocolate, and strawberry. Although my ice cream choices have expanded, the best one for me now is "none of the above." But whether I eat ice cream or not, or choose the wrong flavor, it will not do any lasting harm. Not so with marriage and childbearing. These are high-stakes decisions. If you marry the wrong person or have a baby you are ill-prepared to support financially or emotionally, those decisions cast a long shadow that may last a lifetime.

The defaults used to be much clearer than they are now. We not only had fewer flavors of ice cream to choose from; we also had fewer acceptable ways to form a family. We were guided by social norms to follow a scripted path. As someone who grew up in the 1950s and formed a family in the 1960s, I followed the same path as many of my friends: some dating and cautious experiments with relationships in college, then marriage, followed by a child—and only later a career. In my generation we departed from that path at our peril. Loose women lost the respect of their friends. Unwed pregnant women were sent to Aunt Hattie's or to a special "home" to have the baby, which was then put up for adoption. Gays hid in the closet. A divorced man could not aspire to be president; a woman could not aspire to be president at all.

Very few of us, I suspect, want to turn back the clock. I certainly do not. But the youngest generation, no longer bound by these restrictions, has a new set of challenges. Lacking a clear script, some are choosing well; others are floundering: I call them "the planners" and "the drifters." Realistically, of course, we are all some of both.

In this book I argue that drifting into parenthood is a bad idea. Too many young adults are sliding into relationships and having babies before they are ready to make the commitments to each other and to their children that parenthood requires. A majority of new mothers under 30 are not married to their children's fathers. And those unmarried parents are unlikely to marry or to stay together for very long. The solution is to change the default from having children to not having them until you and your partner want them and are both ready to be parents. Social norms that used to stigmatize unwed parenting now need to stigmatize unplanned parenting. New low-maintenance and long-acting forms of birth control make changing the default possible. (Imagine being able to eat all the chocolate ice cream you want without gaining weight.) In combination with more education and career opportunities for young adults, newer and little-used forms of contraception have the potential to transform the life prospects of children.

Does it matter if some people drift while others plan? Yes, hugely. It matters for the young adults making these choices, and it matters even more for their children. Children are the heart of the matter. Children are poorly served by adults who drift into parenthood, rather than planning and preparing for it. They deserve to be born to parents who have made good decisions, created a stable family environment, and made a commitment to their welfare for the duration of their childhoods and beyond.

We used to have an institution that provided children with this kind of stable environment. It was called marriage. It was the expected way to raise children. Marriage provided not just a secure environment for children; it meant that the resources of two adults—their time, their money, their emotional support—were potentially available to the child. If we could return marriage rates to their 1970 level, the child poverty rate would be about 20 percent lower. Inequality would be reduced as well. Of course, having married parents was no guarantee that children would do well. They were not always good parents and they did not always stay together. Still, on balance, children benefited from this arrangement. Some still do.

Unfortunately, marriage is on the wane, and as a result, children are in trouble. As someone who was happily married for over forty years, I mourn the loss and wish it could be otherwise. But the genie is out of the bottle. No amount of wishful thinking will put it back. But that doesn't mean we should give up. Civic and religious institutions have a role to play. Government can design policies that are more marriage-friendly. Young adults still say they want to marry someday, and we can encourage them to do so. But right now, among women under 30, the simple fact is that half of all babies are born outside of marriage. Often the mother is living with the father at the time of the birth, but these cohabiting relationships tend to be temporary. About four in ten will have ended before the child is age 5.

What is going on here? First and foremost, women's opportunities have expanded. The sexual revolution has delinked sex from marriage (but not sex from childbearing). Declining economic prospects for men have played a role. But the feminist revolution takes center stage: once women discovered that they could earn a paycheck and take charge of their own destinies, they not only began to raise more children on their own, but also set a higher bar for the kinds of men they were willing to marry, or stay married to. In 2012, 28 percent of families with children were headed by a single mom and a much smaller but growing number by a single dad. Not all of them are single parents by choice, and many are doing a more-than-adequate job of caring for their children. Still, it is a tough road for any lone adult to follow, especially for those with few resources or social supports.

What does it all mean and why does it matter? On balance, marriage appears to have been good for adults. Married people are happier, healthier, and wealthier than their unmarried counterparts—even after adjusting for some obvious differences between the two groups. That does not mean, however, that people should stay together in the face of serious conflicts; divorce is an important safety valve, and making it easier to obtain has been, in my view, the right thing to do. For example, it has reduced depression and suicide, especially among women. However, divorce is no longer the main driver of single parenthood; unwed childbearing is. Divorce rates have declined since the 1980s, in part because people are marrying later than in the past and because those who marry are better educated. And although the *proportion* of all babies born outside of marriage has soared, overall, women are having fewer babies than in the past. Indeed, a rapidly growing number of women are having none at all (18 percent by their early forties). Children are expensive. A child can cost the typical couple the equivalent of around $1 million per child if we include the costs of the mother taking some time off or working less than full-time. And although parenthood can be satisfying in the long run, all the academic evidence, as well as reports from parents themselves, suggests that it is very stressful on a daily basis. Happiness plunges during the child-rearing years.

In response to women's changing roles, men have changed as well, but not nearly enough. A husband may think his wife's working is fine, but not if it requires him to sacrifice his own career. Husbands may regularly wash the dishes, but only if they are thanked for helping out. The gaps between what young men and women expect from their intimate partners are still quite large. To be sure, fathers are doing a lot more than in the past where housework and child care are concerned. But mothers continue to do almost twice as much as fathers. Assumptions about who is responsible for what are still linked to gender. A colleague reports that her husband is happy to do the grocery shopping, but only after she has created the list of things to buy. Some men complain that this is the way women want it. Either way, managing a household can be stressful even if one has help with the task.

But evolving gender roles, while important for understanding the new landscape, are not the main focus of this book. Children are. Children raised in single-parent families typically do not do as well as those raised in married families. Generalizations are dangerous; many single parents are doing a terrific job under difficult circumstances. But on average, children from single-parent families do worse in school and in life. These children are four times more likely to be poor than those with married parents. Two parents have not just more income but also more time and other resources. Today's children are paying a price for the new choices afforded their parents.

Add to this a growing class divide in family formation patterns. It used to be that most children were raised by their married parents. For the children of the college-educated elites, that is still true. But for the rest of America, meaning roughly two-thirds of all children, it is no longer the case. Family structure must be added to a list of other gaps that are opening up, not just between rich and poor but more broadly between the struggling middle class and the more affluent. Everyone talks about the widening income gap between the rich and the rest of America, but there are many other gaps that are also growing: in parenting styles, in elementary school test scores, in college attendance rates, and in the extent of residential segregation between those at the bottom of the income distribution and those at the top. We are, in author Charles Murray's words, "coming apart": separating into tribes who no longer share the same life experiences and whose children no longer have the same opportunities to join the middle class.[1] Add the divide in family formation patterns to the growing gaps in other arenas and the result is a toxic combination that is likely to reduce social mobility and threatens to produce a more permanently divided society in the United States.

At the top of the class structure are what I call, for short, "the planners." They are still marrying and having children within marriage, but only after establishing careers and typically not until they are in their late twenties or early thirties. The women in these families worry a lot about whether they can have it all: careers *and* families. At the bottom, and increasingly in middle America as well, are "the drifters." They are not worried about having it all. They simply want to get by. But their problems are compounded by the fact that they are having children early, increasingly outside of marriage and without the continuing support of a second parent. For the women of this group who lack college degrees and perhaps even professional aspirations, childbearing outside of marriage is now the new normal. Almost 60 percent of women without a bachelor's degree are having children outside of marriage. The women in this group overwhelmingly say they did not want to have a child, at least not at this stage of their life. The pill was supposed to change all of that. It was supposed to usher in a world of children by choice, not chance. That hasn't happened. A surprisingly large number of these women are also having children with more than one partner. The upshot is a degree of household churning and family instability that is not good for children. We used to think unwed childbearing was concentrated among low-income minority families living in the inner city. Racial differences still loom large: two-thirds of black children live in single-parent homes. But unwed childbearing has now crept up the socioeconomic scale and is a widespread pattern that includes all racial groups—in fact, just about everyone except the college-educated elites.

What to do? Those on the political left, a group that I call "village builders," argue for more social supports for families: better education, more and better-paying jobs (especially for men), subsidized child care, paid parental leave, more family-friendly workplaces, and much more assistance for the large number of low-income families headed by a single parent. Those on the right, "the traditionalists," argue for restoring marriage so that more children will have two stable and committed parents. Some conservatives even hope to bring back the old division of labor within the family, arguing that such an arrangement is biologically or religiously ordained.

In the end, I agree with much of what each side is arguing. The traditionalists are right that marriage is the best environment yet invented for raising children. However, government efforts to promote marriage have not worked in practice. And cultural trends, once they gain a certain momentum, are hard to reverse. These facts should give us pause. Government has limited tools with which to restore marriage as the primary institution for raising children. If marriage is to be revived, it will only be because civic and religious institutions are successful in encouraging more young people to marry before having children or because young people themselves see its value and act on these aspirations.

The village builders are right that more social supports are needed. But those added supports are not likely to be forthcoming any time soon in a country where fiscal resources are limited, where higher taxes are unpopular, and where even a Democratic president, Bill Clinton, once noted that "governments don't raise children; parents do."[2] In the meantime, the elderly are claiming a rising share of whatever resources exist. While I have argued elsewhere for a reallocation of resources from the affluent elderly to younger families and their children, recent budget battles give little reason for optimism.[3]

Given these difficulties, the solution is to combine elements of both the traditionalists' and the village builders' agendas and to add a critically important third element that both groups have neglected. That third element is what I call *childbearing by design, not by default.* Put simply, it means preventing unplanned pregnancies and births. Traditionalists have avoided this issue because they believe separating sex from childbearing and marriage is morally wrong or undermines responsible behavior. Village builders have avoided the issue because they are overwhelmingly focused on what happens to children once they are born, ignoring the fact that the circumstances of a child's birth matter, too.

Better social policies are needed, but they need to be combined with greater personal responsibility on the part of would-be parents themselves. In the end, it is not clear that well-educated women can have it all, or that less well-educated women who do not have enough can count on government alone to make things right. One theme of this book is that members of the youngest generation will be better off if they think carefully about their choices. For the well-educated, that means thinking harder about what it takes to be both an effective parent and successful in one's career. It means accepting the idea that there may be trade-offs. For the less well-educated it means not drifting into parenthood before they are ready. For both groups, the old social scripts have disappeared. The reason they need to choose, to plan more carefully, is that there is no longer a clear default. No longer are children typically born inside marriage. No longer do women typically stay home to care for them.

The most important decision by far is the decision to have a child. (You can divorce a spouse but not a child.) Yet slightly more than half of all pregnancies in the United States are unplanned or unintended, and the proportion is 70 percent for single women in their twenties. Close to half of these pregnancies will be terminated by abortion, which is a difficult choice for almost anyone and morally wrong in the eyes of many. The result? The majority of births to unmarried young women under 30 are unplanned. And an unplanned birth means bringing a child into the world whose parents are either ambivalent or unenthusiastic about being a parent. They may—indeed often do—come to accept and love the child; but it is not an auspicious beginning, and is too frequently accompanied by a less-than-favorable environment for the child.

How can we help drifters become planners? The answer is by changing the default. Research from the new field of behavioral economics shows that defaults matter in a big way. When employees are automatically enrolled in a retirement plan but with an option to decline coverage, the proportion enrolled in the plan skyrockets. When I keep chocolate ice cream out of my freezer, I am less likely to indulge. These are forms of soft paternalism or pre-commitment consistent with preserving individual choices while nudging us in a direction that is likely to be in our own best interest over the long run.

What does changing the default mean in the context of childbearing? It means recognizing that what people do in the heat of the moment is often at odds with their own longer-term welfare and that of their children. One clever study found that a young man's willingness to use a condom drops by 30 percent in the heat of the moment. When a government survey asked women why they had an unplanned pregnancy, a common response was "I just wasn't thinking." This is an argument for making LARCs—long-acting, reversible forms of contraception—more widely available. LARCs include intrauterine devices (IUDs) and implants. They change the default from getting pregnant (if you do little or nothing to prevent it) to *not* getting pregnant until you take deliberate steps to do so. The beauty of LARCs is that they do not depend on someone making a rational decision in an irrational state. They do not require remembering to take a pill or to get a prescription refilled. They are forgiving of well-documented human frailties (like a desire for sex). As a result, LARCs have been found, in practice, to be about forty times more effective than condoms and twenty times more effective than the pill at reducing the incidence of unplanned pregnancies. The availability of more effective, low-maintenance forms of birth control is only half of the solution. The other half is convincing people to use them. We need to provide young adults with not just the means but also the motivation to delay having children. Unless young adults believe they have the same kind of educational and job opportunities now available to the well-educated, they will see little reason to delay having children. The village builders are right about this side of the equation. However, it will take decades to improve young people's opportunities and cost billions of dollars. LARCs are available now and will actually save taxpayer dollars. If we succeeded in changing the default, the impact on unwed childbearing and on poverty rates would be large. If all women in America were able to reduce their *unintended* pregnancies to the rate experienced by college-educated women (not an unreasonable goal), the proportion of children born outside of marriage would drop by 25 percent. If we reduced unplanned childbearing outside of marriage, more women would be able to continue their education, gain valuable skills in the job market, and form stable relationships leading to marriage. If we could return marriage rates to what they were in the 1970s, the proportion of children who are poor would drop by about 4 percentage points (more than most safety net programs have accomplished). In short, by turning drifters into planners we would not only help these women achieve their own goals but also create much stronger starts for their children.

The year 2014 is the fiftieth anniversary of the War on Poverty. That war ended in a stalemate. The government's official poverty rate is as high now as it was when the war began. One reason for this stalemate is that whatever we did to raise education levels, fund job training, and provide various forms of cash assistance was offset by the growth of single-parent families. To be sure, once one includes the increased value of some of the noncash benefits that poor families now receive (for example, medical care and food assistance), poverty rates, adjusted to include these benefits, did decline over this period. But the basic conclusion is the same: if the breakdown of the family continues, it will require an ever-growing and more expensive benefit package to achieve victory in this long-standing war. I, along with many others, have written about the need for high-quality child care and early education, school reform, strengthening the safety net, providing jobs, and supplementing the earnings of low-wage workers. I hope that more can be done on all of these fronts. But for every child removed from poverty by some social program, another child will take its place. To keep pace with this demographic trend, the safety net would have to expand continuously. To reduce poverty we must slow down entries into poverty, not just speed up the exits.

Providing women with both the means and the motivation to delay childbearing until they themselves feel ready to be parents is critical. In the process, social norms and attitudes toward children might shift as well. Sarah Brown, the president of the National Campaign to Prevent Teen and Unplanned Pregnancy, says: "Having children is not just about what parents want; it's about what children need."[4] Kathryn Edin, a professor at Johns Hopkins University and a highly respected student of very disadvantaged neighborhoods, talks about the high value placed on children in these communities.[5] But what does being highly valued mean in this context? Does it mean what adults want? Or is it about what children need? At the other end of the spectrum, highly educated and ambitious parents may end up putting their careers before the well-being of their children, or they may instead choose to sacrifice some amount of career success to spend more time with their children. Although their children will probably do just fine either way, given their ample resources, they rightly struggle with the trade-off. A more tempered view of when and under what circumstances it is a good idea to bring a child into the world might serve both groups well. A new social norm about what it takes to raise a child is needed. Although there is a class divide here, it would be a terrible mistake to assume that the problem of children being born to young unmarried adults in unstable relationships is a problem that affects only the poor. It has moved up the income distribution to encompass many in the middle class as well. And struggles with how to balance work and family goals now confront almost everyone in the youngest generation.

The past century has seen an impressive broadening of individual rights—for African Americans, women, religious and ethnic minorities, and most recently, gays and lesbians. But what are the rights of children? Don't they deserve to be born to adults who are ready to be parents and fully aware of the responsibilities involved? To create a world in which more children can flourish, we need a new ethic of responsible behavior, one that changes the default from having children to not having children unless both prospective parents feel ready and are prepared to take the task seriously.

But are we ready for this shift in attitudes? Is there any hope that the default can be changed? I see five reasons to be cautiously optimistic.

First, fertility has fallen in every country where women have gained access to education and no longer look to motherhood alone as a source of identity or validation. Providing less-advantaged women, in particular, with more education and job opportunities so that they can pursue alternatives to motherhood is vital.

Second, parenthood is stressful, time-consuming, and expensive. The proportion of adults opting out of parenthood entirely has risen sharply in the United States. Choosing not to have children, or not to have additional children, will become more desirable in a world where having smaller families brings many benefits, including enabling parents to invest more in each child.

Third, children are highly valued by both men and women in low-income communities, and it is only a matter of time until they figure out that providing their children the same advantages elites now provide theirs means substituting "later for earlier" or "quality for quantity," and that the way to do this is to better align their behavior with their aspirations. *Desired* family size does not vary much, if at all, by socioeconomic status.

Fourth, the less-advantaged are having more children, and having them earlier, than they say they prefer, suggesting that—with both the means to control their fertility and additional motivation to do so—fertility rates will fall further within this group. Unintended pregnancy rates are much higher among the poor, minorities, and the least well-educated (and abortion rates lower) than they are among more-advantaged women. I stress this fact to counter arguments one sometimes hears about the importance of not imposing mainstream values on the poor. If the data are to be believed, these are *their* values, not someone else's.

Fifth, new forms of contraception have made it much more feasible to change the default. From a purely medical perspective, an IUD implanted as soon as a woman becomes sexually active would make her virtually infertile until such time as she explicitly chose to become a mother. The proportion of women using IUDs is four times higher in Norway and France than in the United States, where fewer than 10 percent of women have taken up this low-maintenance option. If the first stage of the revolution in living arrangements was all about delinking sex from marriage, the next stage needs to be about delinking sex from childbearing. Paradoxically, delinking sex from childbearing might actually help to restore the idea of childbearing within marriage, or at least bring back the two-parent family. With fewer early unplanned births, more men and women would wait to have children until they were mature enough to make a serious commitment to another adult, unencumbered by children from a prior relationship.

Families and children have always been more central to the lives of women than men; but men must change as well. If they want children, they must become responsible partners and fathers. That means not having unprotected sex; it means supporting any child that is born; and it means doing a fairer share of work in the home. Many men have not stepped up to the plate. Author and journalist Hanna Rosin speaks of plastic women and cardboard men.[6] By this she means that the lives of women have changed in profound ways and that they have adapted well to the challenges. Men, by contrast, have had a harder time adjusting to the feminist revolution and its aftermath. It is true that men's wages and employment opportunities have declined while women's have improved. But men are still better off than women. They have higher earnings and contribute less time to work in the home. More egalitarian relationships within the family could help to redress the balance. Well-educated men have moved further in this direction than their less-educated counterparts, which is one reason that marriage is still alive and well in the professional class.

So where are we headed? What kind of a future should we hope for? If relationships were chosen not only for their sizzle but also for their durability, especially where children are involved, whether these relationships were called marriage or something else might not matter. In Sweden, there are a lot of cohabiting couples, but unlike in the United States, these relationships tend to be stable.

A social norm that once called for parenthood only within marriage contributed to achieving that goal. But now that that norm has all but disappeared, something else must take its place. Given the decline of marriage, it becomes more important than ever to make sure that adults do not have children unintentionally and drift into relationships that are not likely to survive long enough to provide a secure environment for children. The old norm was "don't have a child outside of marriage." The new norm should be "don't have a child before you want one and are ready to be a parent." If children were wanted and planned for, they would be better off. Each of them would get more time and attention from the parents and more societal resources as well. They all would, as a result, face better life prospects.

What does being ready for parenthood mean? For most people, it means completing their education, securing a steady job, and having a committed partner with whom to share the tasks of both earning a living and raising children. The ideal would be education, work, marriage, children—in that order. The achievement of these benchmarks will, in almost all cases, ensure that any children a couple decides to have are not born into poverty.[7] In most cases, those who have made a conscious choice to have a child are ready to be good or good-enough parents. If a 35-year-old professional woman *decides* she wants a child, it is likely that she will provide a good environment for the child, even if she is not in a committed relationship. If a young couple with two low-wage jobs *decides* that they are jointly prepared to take on the extra burdens of parenthood despite the difficulties, they will likely succeed and should be supported in that task. Readiness norms will and should evolve. At the same time, a fear of being judgmental should not deter us from saying that a teenager is not ready to be a good parent. Neither is a drug-abusing older woman or a young man who already has two children with a previous girlfriend and no means of supporting another child. By and large, however, intentionality and readiness go hand in hand. Empowering people to have children only when they themselves say they want them, and feel prepared to be parents, would do more than any current social program to reduce poverty and improve the life prospects of children.

The ideas in this book may be controversial. In addition to debates about what it means to be ready for parenthood, some will worry about the effects of lower fertility on our ability to support an aging society; others will complain that family planning runs counter to their religious beliefs or that it is a new and more subtle form of eugenics; still others will argue that if we just reduced poverty with a more generous safety net, or made greater efforts to revive marriage, stable families would follow. In the final chapter I address these criticisms and others. Here I will simply note that the failure to address these issues because of the controversy they engender is impeding progress.

I believe government should be doing more to help families cope and children to thrive. However, government cannot do it alone. Individuals must make childbearing a choice and not just an accident, and then take responsibility for their choices. Children have rights, too.

TWO

The End of Marriage?

To marry was to say you believed in the future and in the past, too—that history and tradition and hope could stay knit together to hold you up.

—Paula McLain, *The Paris Wife*

Marriage is a wonderful institution, but who wants to live in an institution?
—Groucho Marx

For most Americans in the generations that came of age in the first half of the twentieth century, marriage was the definitive marker of adulthood. Young adults did not leave their childhood home until they entered their marital home. During the 1950s and 1960s, when I was growing up, there was a single life script for young adults with only limited deviations from that script. You finished school, you got a job, you married, and you had children, all in that order. If you were a young woman, that job was more often than not simply a way station before you found the right guy, got married, and settled down to be a good wife and mother. Even if you had aspirations to a career, it came second on your list of priorities. If you were a young man, you launched your career as soon as you finished school, one that you knew ultimately would have to support a family in your new role as the head of a household. Children usually followed relatively quickly after marriage whether you could afford them or not. By today's standards, your one-earner income was typically modest but sufficient to live on if you were reasonably frugal and did without various comforts and conveniences that today's couples often take for granted. Two cars, a house, a microwave, air conditioning, eating out, cell phones, cable TV, and the like were simply not in the picture. Instead you and your wife faced a period of scrimping and saving that would set the foundation for a better life in the future.

Richard Settersten and Barbara Ray, authors of the book *Not Quite Adults,* describe what I and others in my generation experienced as follows: "Young adults once hit the road on a clearly marked path. The first stop was college, some training, or the military. Next up was a job. Marriage followed, and then children. Between marriage and kids, the new family bought a home. All of this was accomplished by age twenty-five—and often in that order."[1] For this older generation, marriage was not what happened after you had finished school, launched a career, and settled down; it was, in the words of marriage historian Pamela Haag, the "fabric out of which an adult life was cut."[2]

All of this has changed. Today's 20-somethings have many more choices. They may marry, cohabit, or remain single. They may openly form a same-sex relationship and even marry in an increasing number of states. They frequently have children outside of marriage, especially if they do not have a college degree. Those with more education are delaying both marriage and childbearing until they are well established in a career, often until their late twenties or early thirties.

Young women still hope to marry or find a lifelong partner, but it is no longer their primary goal. They expect to work and are leery of becoming dependent on a man for support. Young men have the opposite worry; they fear that they will be unable to support a family on one income in today's economy. They assume that their wives or partners will work. Although they are willing to help out with domestic chores and want to be involved with their children, they often believe that this is still primarily a woman's responsibility. When they pitch in at home, it is often called "babysitting" or "lending a helping hand."

These changes are just the most recent chapter in a long history of profound changes in the American family. Marriage is on the wane. Sex and dating are taking new forms. One-third of all children live in single-parent homes. If there is one statistic that sums it all up, it is that among women under 30 more than half of all babies are born outside marriage.[3] If these trends continue, childbearing without marriage will soon become the new normal.

This chapter dives a little deeper into these trends and what lies behind them.

Marriage: An Endangered Institution?

While most young people say they want to marry someday, the data on their behavior tell a somewhat different story.[4] The proportion of adults over the age of 18 who are married dropped from 72 percent in 1960 to 51 percent in 2010. Most of the decline in marriage rates is related to the fact that both men and women are marrying later—women typically at age 27 and men at age 29, up from 20 and 23 in 1960.[5] Young adults are simply not tying the knot during the first decade of adult life as they once did. If maturity matters in deciding on a lifetime partner, this delay should be welcomed. The problem is that, in too many cases, it has not been accompanied by delayed childbearing. Indeed, the average woman now has her first baby before she marries.[6] This reversal of the normal sequence first occurred in the late 1980s. One report calls it "the great crossover"—the point at which, for the first time, the average age at first marriage exceeded the average age at first birth among American women.[7] This decline in marriage has caused considerable heartburn for many older Americans who hope that it can be restored as the primary way of raising children.

Paradoxically, marriage has a new set of advocates: gays and lesbians who are only now obtaining the right to marry. The 2012 election marked a watershed year for these groups. For the first time in history, an American president called for the end to discrimination against gay and lesbian couples, including the right for them to marry. Two Supreme Court cases expanded marriage rights for same-sex couples by striking down the federal definition of marriage as a union between a man and woman, and by overturning California's Proposition 8 banning same-sex marriage. More and more states have approved this right (nineteen states and the District of Columbia as of May 2014),[8] and public acceptance of same-sex marriage has increased dramatically.

My own view of marriage is that, despite having new champions and despite having many benefits, it will be hard to put the toothpaste back in the tube. The wholesale retreat from marriage is related to changes in social norms, greater affluence, the evolving status of women, and the delinking of sex from childbearing created by the availability of birth control and abortion. These driving forces are not likely to be reversed; with half of all babies being born outside marriage in the youngest generation, we may have reached a tipping point.

That said, here is why I could be wrong: social norms are not immutable. Take the case of teen pregnancies and births, which are no longer as big a problem as they once were. Back in the mid-1990s, when I helped to found the National Campaign to Prevent Teen Pregnancy, many people had given up on trying to reduce teen pregnancies and births. Yet by 2012, the teen birth rate had reached the lowest level reported in over six decades.[9] In the meantime, the problem has moved up the age scale. It is now primarily women and men in their twenties who are having children outside of marriage, many of them unplanned. (This development led the National Campaign to expand its agenda and to adopt a new name, the National Campaign to Prevent Teen and Unplanned Pregnancy.) Once a young single woman has had an unplanned pregnancy, followed by a baby out of wedlock, she is less likely to marry and more likely to have additional children outside of marriage. Among other difficulties that follow, few men are willing to marry a woman who has already had a baby fathered by someone else.[10] Perhaps the solution is not to bring back early marriage but instead to encourage young adults to delay childbearing until they are ready to marry.

Another possibility is that we will evolve toward what might be called "marriage lite"—relatively stable cohabiting relationships. Cohabitation has become very common in Europe, especially in Scandinavia,[11] but in many respects does not differ much from marriage.[12] It can be a long-term, reasonably stable relationship in which adults make commitments to one another and raise children together in the process. Perhaps the United States is only one step behind its European counterparts. Lower rates of marriage in other countries do not mean that women are not forming relationships and having children; they are simply doing so outside of marriage. If cohabitation works for these countries, why wouldn't it work here?

In his book *The Marriage-Go-Round,* Andrew Cherlin notes that marriage is more prevalent in the United States than in most European countries.[13] He goes on to stress that both marriage and cohabiting relationships are more fragile in the United States than in other Western countries. Although Americans are more likely to marry or form partnerships, their relationships break up more quickly. As a result, children in the United States are more likely to spend time on what Cherlin calls the "marriage-go-round," with about half of them experiencing their parents' breakup by age 15.[14] Of course, this may reflect the fact that because marriage is rarer in Europe, those who marry are more committed and their marriages more long-lasting. It may also reflect the fact that American women, although they marry much later than they used to, are still marrying younger than most European women.[15] And early marriages are less durable than later ones.

Given the possibility that cohabitation may be the wave of the future, what do we know about this type of relationship? Will it become a good substitute for marriage?

Cohabitation: A Substitute for Marriage?

The proportion of women who report that they are cohabiting with a man has more than tripled since 1982 and is currently around 11 percent. The proportion of women who have ever cohabited with a member of the opposite sex is much larger; it is closer to one-half.[16]

Not all of these women are young. Some are older adults who cohabit after a marriage breaks up or before they remarry, and many bring children from a previous relationship into the new household. But among the young, there are three primary types of cohabitation. The first we might call ad hoc or "shotgun" cohabitations. As the label implies, these are situations in which a romantically involved couple decides to move in together for reasons of convenience, economics, or the unexpected arrival of a child. A second type of cohabitation is more akin to a trial marriage. The couple hopes to marry but wants to test the relationship first. About 44 percent of adult cohabiters in the United States view cohabitation as a step toward marriage and not a substitute for it.[17] The third type of cohabitation is a more permanent substitute for marriage—an arrangement that, as noted above, could become more prevalent in the United States in the future. So far, however, durable cohabitations are a relatively uncommon pattern here. Although many cohabiting couples enter their relationship with a strong expectation that they will marry each other, their expectations are often disappointed. Some will go on to marry each other, but many will break up within a few years, often leaving a single parent, almost always the mother, to raise the children.[18] In the meantime, we are seeing a great deal of what scholars call "family complexity." Young adults, both men and women, are moving in and out of relationships and having children with multiple partners.

Common sense suggests that cohabitation, viewed as a trial marriage, should help people evaluate their compatibility and make better decisions about whom to marry. Research in the 1990s and early 2000s found the opposite, however: cohabitation resulted in higher levels of marital instability. This failure of trial marriages to strengthen marriages may simply be due to the fact that those who cohabit before marrying have attributes that make them inherently more divorce-prone. In fact, more recent research by sociologists Wendy Manning and Jessica Cohen, using data from 1996 to 2008, found that there was no relationship between premarital cohabitation and marital instability after controlling for other factors.[19] In short, current research on the question neither conclusively proves nor disproves the idea that cohabitation is a good way to test-drive a marriage.

What about the idea of cohabitation as a substitute for marriage? Is it just another form of marriage without a piece of paper or a religious ceremony to back it up? Many people argue that cohabiting relationships are not a substitute for marriage because they lack the legal, religious, or social supports that marriage normally entails. A study by researchers at the RAND Corporation found that cohabiting couples are much less likely than married couples to consolidate their finances in joint bank accounts or to make large purchases together. Cohabiters also report lower levels of intimacy than married couples, though this difference dissipates for longer-lasting cohabitation.[20] Most important, only around 60 percent of cohabiting men report that they are "completely committed" to the relationship even after more than a year of living together, which is significantly lower than the 80 percent of married men who are completely committed.[21]

These lower levels of commitment and intimacy may partially explain why cohabiting parents are much more likely to have separated by their child's fifth birthday than married parents are.[22] The shorter duration of these marriage-like arrangements, even where children are involved, means that they are not an ideal environment in which to raise the next generation. As marriage advocates often note, marriage comes with a set of socially sanctioned expectations, legal (and sometimes religious) strictures, kin networks, and a sense of permanency and commitment that cohabitation currently lacks.

In short, for now, marriage is different from cohabitation, and the big difference is in the degree of commitment that each partner makes to the other and the durability of the relationship.

Dating and Sex: The New Hookup and Online Cultures

The issue of commitment comes up not just in the context of cohabiting relationships but also in the context of sex and dating. Because marriage is increasingly delayed, many young adults spend their twenties in a series of relationships, usually involving sex. There is nothing new, of course, about young adults having sex before marriage, especially within a serious ongoing relationship or with someone they plan to marry.[23] What is new is sex without commitment, or what has been called the "hookup culture."

As the *New York Times* put it in 2013, "It is by now pretty well understood that traditional dating in college has mostly gone the way of the landline, replaced by "hooking up"—an ambiguous term that can signify anything from making out to oral sex to intercourse—without the emotional entanglement of a relationship." The *New York Times* piece entitled "She Can Play That Game, Too" both celebrates the role of women in taking charge of their sexuality and warns of the dangers women face in an atmosphere of casual sex.[24] One of the subjects of the *New York Times* article, a college freshman, says, "It's kind of like a spiral. The girls adapt a little bit, because they stop expecting that they're going to get a boyfriend—because if that's all you're trying to do, you're going to be miserable. But at the same time, they want to, like, have contact with guys . . . [So they hook up and] . . . try not to get attached."

Despite many women saying that they enjoy hookups and prefer them to commitment, there is little question that the hookup culture favors men.[25] There is a lot of oral sex, not always reciprocal. Women are more likely than men to want a hookup to turn into a relationship. They also fear that too much hooking up will damage their reputations, since the double standard still applies. Finally, hookups are very often fueled by excessive alcohol, leading to sex that may be less than fully consensual especially on the part of the women involved. This has created a growing problem of date rape on college campuses.

Laura Sessions Stepp, a former *Washington Post* reporter, spent two years talking at length with dozens of high school and college women about their experiences with sex, love, and relationships.[26] Her in-depth findings echo much of what others have found. First, dating has been replaced by casual sex. Seventy percent of both young men and women have had sex before their nineteenth birthday, although many say they wish they had waited longer. Second, sex has become more like a game or a sport, not part of an ongoing relationship. Young women as well as men see it as a way to make a conquest. Third, because it is devoid of commitment, a hookup need not interfere with, or distract from, one's studies or one's career. In the end, she concludes that for all their bravado, women find the hookup culture less satisfying than men do.

These developments are the tip of a deeper cultural iceberg. Women, who in the past would have limited access to sex as a way to ensure commitment, financial security, or more influence within a relationship, now have other routes to the same ends. But with its scarcity value gone, men no longer have to provide much, if anything, in return for as much sex as they want. If a current partner is not willing to provide it, some other woman will be. As Hanna Rosin puts it, "The result is that sex . . . is cheap, bargain-basement cheap, and a lot more people can have it."[27]

It would be a mistake to conclude that casual sex is rampant. In a study by Paula England, involving 24,000 students at twenty-one universities, England found that by their senior year four in ten students were either virgins or had had intercourse with only one person. About a third had never experienced a hookup.[28] Moreover, studies that have carefully measured the sexual activity of different cohorts of young people find that it has declined a bit for the youngest cohort. College students from the recent "hookup era" did not report having more frequent sex or more sexual partners during the past year than students twenty years earlier.[29] However, they did find that students were more likely to have had sex with a casual date/pickup and were less likely to report having sex with a spouse or regular sexual partner. These findings suggest that what is unique about the most recent generation is not how often they have sex or how many people they have sex with, but rather how serious their sexual relationships are. Recreational sex is more common than it used to be, and women are engaging in it as much as men.

Another interesting finding is that there is a class divide within the hookup culture.[30] Ambitious women from more privileged backgrounds deliberately avoid commitment because it might interfere with their desire to get ahead educationally and professionally. Marriage is a distant goal, at best, and the time required for a serious relationship, together with uncertainty about careers and where they will end up living, makes forging close ties at a young age a potential barrier to achieving these goals. The less-privileged women, those who still aspire to early marriage and children, are very uncomfortable with the hookup culture. However, some later realize that it might free them from early marriage to a home-town boy who no longer meets their standard for a marriageable male.

These findings suggest that sensational media reports about casual sex among millennials are overblown. Casual sex does seem to be more accepted than in the past and less tied to romance or a committed relationship. Although women are participating freely and sometimes aggressively in the hookup culture, men are still the primary beneficiaries. The good news is that, for some women and men, casual sex seems to be part and parcel of giving higher priority to one's education and career. As people in their twenties mature, and especially as they approach their thirties, they become increasingly interested in forming more serious or committed relationships. They may meet a significant other in the workplace or through a friend, but they are also using the Internet in new ways. One thing we know about millennials is that they are not only comfortable with technology but virtually addicted to it. Eighty-three percent sleep with a cell phone by their side.[31] Cell phones and the Internet make long-distance relationships possible (texts instead of sex). More important, an increasing number of people are finding dates and relationships on OKCupid, Match.com, and other dating sites. These sites have become quite sophisticated about identifying people with common interests, values, and backgrounds. To an older generation, it may sound decidedly unromantic to meet via computer, but we are moving in that direction. One successful site, eHarmony, using an allegedly scientific matchmaking system involving a 500-question test, was found to have facilitated an average of 236 marriages a day in the twelve-month period ending in March 2007.[32]

These online dating sites are part of an effort to overcome the difficulty of finding other singles with similar interests and backgrounds. Duke University economist Daniel Ariely calls the singles market "one of the most egregious market failures in Western society."[33] That may overstate the case, but it motivated Ariely to investigate the pros and cons of online dating. In a study of this new form of matchmaking, he and his colleagues found that people spent an average of 12 hours a week simply screening and contacting potential partners online and only 1.8 hours a week actually meeting them. Participants reported that they were not very satisfied with the experience overall. Moreover, the ratio of time spent on the computer to time spent actually interacting with someone in person was about six to one. Personal interaction, it turns out, is critical to determining whom you like and whom you don't. As Ariely says, relying on these websites is like "trying to understand how a cookie will taste by reading its nutrition label."[34]

Whatever 20-somethings are doing to find a soul mate, on- or off-line, they are still managing to have sex. And sex, we know, sometimes leads to children.

Children: In and Out of Marriage

One of my friends recently announced that he was having an "out-of-wedlock" grandchild. This is a man who would have never himself countenanced having a child outside of marriage. But like many of us, he has accepted that times have changed.

In part, unwed births are simply the result of delayed marriage. Bear in mind that the typical woman will be sexually active for roughly a decade before she marries. That means any fumbling for a condom can easily lead to an accidental pregnancy and birth—and often does.

However, this is not a sufficient explanation. In an era when birth control and abortion are both available, a child is not the inevitable outcome of sex. Interviews with young adults indicate that two other things are at work. First, there is no longer much, if any, stigma attached to having a baby outside of marriage. Second, marriage is no longer viewed as a way to climb the ladder of life but rather as what one does once one has achieved a measure of success and can afford such things as a house, a car, and a nice wedding. As Andrew Cherlin puts it, marriage is no longer a cornerstone on which to build a life with another person, but a capstone that symbolizes that one has arrived.[35] Until that day arrives, many unmarried couples prefer to simply live together without getting married. Almost 60 percent of unwed births are to these cohabiting couples.[36] For the youngest generation, unwed childbearing is rapidly becoming the new normal.

These changes in living arrangements have been rapid and dramatic over the past half-century. Take the growth of single-parent families: in 1950, 7 percent of all families with children under 18 were headed by a single parent; by 2013, this had increased to 31 percent (see figure 1 in the appendix).[37] There are large differences by class and by race, with the proportion of families headed by a single parent varying from 27 percent for whites, to 34 percent for Hispanics, to 62 percent for African Americans.[38]

How does a woman (or less frequently a man) become a single parent? One way is through the death of a spouse or through desertion. A century or more ago, this was the most common route into single parenthood. Indeed, welfare or public assistance was originally conceived as a way to support widows and their children. No one foresaw how welfare would evolve primarily into a program for unwed rather than widowed mothers.

A second route into single parenthood is divorce. Divorce drove up the number of single parents in the 1960s and 1970s, as individuals sought new and more satisfying relationships in an environment of relaxed norms about divorce, a more permissive legal system, and new opportunities for women. Divorce rates, although higher than in the past, have leveled off and even declined a bit since the 1980s.

The fact that the divorce rate has declined is a surprise to many people (see figure 2 in the appendix). In the popular press, divorce rates are often measured as the number of divorces per 1,000 married women age 15 or older. This number more than doubled in the 1960s and 1970s and then declined starting in the early 1980s (but remains higher than it was in the 1950s).[39] A somewhat better way to think about divorce is to consider the number of all marriages that will break up before the couple reaches specific anniversaries. If we use their twentieth anniversary as the benchmark, the proportion is currently around half or a little lower.[40] However, since younger couples have not yet had a chance to reach their tenth much less their twentieth anniversary, we can only speculate about the durability of more recent marriages. But the evidence points to their lasting longer than those of their parents' generation. Couples who married in the 1980s are reaching more anniversaries so far than those who married in the 1970s, and the most recent marriages appear to be the most stable of all.[41] Today's young married couples are now a more select group of well-educated individuals who tie the knot almost a decade later than in the past. Their age and education alone make them less susceptible to divorce. The good news here is that waiting until you are mature enough to pick your lifetime partner matters.

A third route into single parenthood is unwed childbearing—women having babies without marrying at all. It is this third source of single parenthood that has led to all of the increase in unmarried parents since the mid-1980s.[42]

The decline of marriage and growth of single-parent families have not been good for children. But before getting to the consequences, let us look at the causes of these wholesale changes in the family.

What Is Driving the Change in Family Structure?

While there is widespread agreement on what has happened to families, there is less agreement on *why* it has happened. The major drivers appear to have been new opportunities for women outside the home, fueled in part by the advent of the birth control pill and legalized abortion; the declining economic prospects of men; increased affluence; and changes in social norms.

New opportunities for women

I believe that the changing status of women is the most important driver of changes in the family. It is impossible to explain the earthquake in the American family without understanding the revolution in gender roles that has occurred over the past century, and especially in the past fifty years. What is in dispute is not so much whether the changing status of women has mattered but rather how much it has mattered and in what ways.

In an earlier book, *Time of Transition,* coauthored with Heather Ross, I argued that as women secured more opportunities outside the home, they increased their bargaining power within marriage and became less dependent on marriage.[43] When husbands did not adjust to women's new expectations or the marriage was an unhappy one, the marriage would end in divorce. Writing in the 1970s, we saw this as a time of transition in two senses. First, most women who divorced usually remarried, so single parenting was typically a transitional state between marriages. Second, we speculated that once the necessary adjustments in gender roles had occurred, the growth of single parents would abate. Divorce rates would flatten out, although at a new and higher level. Although we were prescient in seeing the leveling off of the divorce rate starting in the 1980s, we did not foresee the continued increase in unwed childbearing.[44]

We called the relationship between women's changing status and the growth of single-parent families "the independence effect." How important is this independence effect? The social science literature on the topic is mixed[45] but suggests that gender ideology, as I have always suspected, plays a role in predicting divorce. Couples in which men have more progressive or egalitarian views of marriage are less likely to divorce.[46]

So why is it that well-educated women with good economic prospects continue to marry in the largest numbers? They are delaying marriage but certainly not forgoing it entirely. One possible explanation is that the men they are marrying typically have high incomes and thus high status themselves, making an independent woman with her own earnings less threatening than it would be to men further down the economic ladder.

In short, it may be women who earn more than a potential partner that most threaten men.[47]

Another reason these well-educated women are still marrying is that they are much less likely to have an unplanned pregnancy and birth leading to single motherhood. Like their less-educated counterparts, they are forming romantic relationships in their twenties and may cohabit for a period. But unlike the less-educated, well-educated women are more likely to take full advantage of the availability of reliable contraception and are more willing to choose an abortion in the face of contraceptive failure. It may be their greater ability to control their fertility and their much-improved career prospects that explain why they are delaying marriage and childbearing. These women are still marrying not because they need financial security, but because their marriages bear little resemblance to the marriages of the past. These new marriages are more egalitarian, more selective of men and women with similar interests and capabilities, and more oriented toward a committed partnership forged for the purpose of raising children or enjoying the benefits that come from having shared interests and two professional incomes.[48]

At the other end of the education scale, fewer people are marrying but, as we have seen, still having children, many of them unplanned. Some people believe the welfare system is at fault, but welfare is now only available on a temporary basis and is conditional on the mother's working, often in a low-wage job. A high proportion of these women are living in poverty—43 percent of all single-mother families fall below the poverty line, which was about $19,530 for a family of three in 2013.[49] They very much need a second income to make ends meet.

The declining economic prospects of men

So where are the fathers? Could they do more to support any children? Too often they are unemployed or incarcerated, and even when they have jobs, their inflation-adjusted earnings have declined over the past few decades. Thus many believe that it is the declining economic prospects of men, as much as or more than the greater economic independence of women, that has undermined marriage and led to more unwed childbearing. This view, popularized by the sociologist William Julius Wilson, is often referred to as the "marriageable men" hypothesis.[50] Marriageable men, the argument goes, are in short supply.

The narrative about men's declining fortunes is by now quite familiar. Improvements in technology, in areas such as computing and advanced manufacturing, may have increased the overall productivity of the economy, but they have reduced the demand for less-skilled workers.[51] The outsourcing of many jobs and competition from cheaper imports have added to the problem.[52] As the economy evolved from one in which manufacturing jobs were prevalent and paid enough to support the typical family to one where most new jobs are either in the low-paid service sector or in management or technical fields that require higher levels of education, less-skilled men have found their job opportunities and ability to earn enough to support a family greatly curtailed. The average earnings of young men without a college education are now roughly $30,000 a year, which, after adjustment for inflation, is $5,000 less than it was for their father's generation.[53]

Their situation has been exacerbated by the fact that, starting in the 1980s, men's education stagnated while young women's continued to increase, as measured by years of schooling completed.[54] Men's failure to obtain higher levels of education at a time when the job market requires and rewards it—while their sisters breezed right past them educationally—is one of the great puzzles of our era. The job market is not just biased toward jobs requiring high levels of education; it also favors the kinds of jobs that women have traditionally held (teacher, nurse, administrative assistant, restaurant worker, child care provider).[55]

But can we link these changes in the job prospects of men to the decline in marriage? One obvious piece of evidence is the fact that well-educated men are still marrying in large numbers. Charles Murray, in his book *Coming Apart,* compares white men in two communities, Belmont and Fishtown. Belmont is an upper-middle-class community in which most of the adults have college degrees and work in business or professional occupations such as executive, lawyer, physician, and university professor. Fishtown is a working-class community in which most of the adults have no more than a high school degree. They work in blue-collar occupations such as electrician, plumber, assembly-line worker, construction laborer, and security guard.[56] In 1978, marriage rates in the two communities were high and not very different. But by 2010, marriage rates in the two communities had not only fallen but were also much farther apart.[57]

Murray does not blame economics as much as culture for these divergent trends, but other experts have pointed a stronger finger at the economy. In her book *The End of Men*, Hanna Rosin is especially articulate on this issue. Like Murray, she describes whole communities where factory jobs that pay an annual wage of $70,000 or more are disappearing and where men are either earning less or jobless altogether, making them less desirable as marriage partners.

It is difficult to separate the importance of the decline in well-paid jobs for men from other developments that may have contributed to the decline in marriage. Studies that have tried to look at multiple factors simultaneously find that declining male earnings have played some role, but that role is far too small to explain the magnitude of the changes we have seen.[58] Men's real wages, even at the bottom of the skill ladder, have simply not changed enough over the past thirty years to be the primary driver of the dramatic changes in family formation patterns that have occurred.[59]

In addition, marriage is still one of the most successful routes to a higher income. Millions of families have achieved middle-class status by sending a second earner into the labor force. Those who do not marry or form stable relationships with another adult are depriving themselves of this advantage. If adults are not availing themselves of one of the most effective ways ever invented of raising their household income, something other than pure economics must be involved. I believe that the culprit is gender role attitudes and expectations, including the assumption that men need to be good breadwinners. From a cultural perspective, the solution is to raise male earnings and maintain a wage gap between men and women. That strikes me as inconsistent with the idea that policies should be gender-neutral and not try to preserve, much less increase, such differentials.

The sexual revolution, birth control, and abortion

The invention and release of the birth control pill in 1960, and the subsequent 1973 ruling of the Supreme Court on abortion in *Roe* v. *Wade*, changed the landscape dramatically by enabling millions of women to more easily control whether and when to have children.[60] The pill, combined with abortion, has enabled women to invest more in their own education, to seek professional careers, and to earn higher wages.[61] These advances have made them less dependent on men for support. The gains have been greater for more-advantaged women than for their less-advantaged counterparts. The latter have less to gain from deferring parenthood and are having less success in doing so even when that is their preference.

Greater availability of birth control and abortion, along with a drop in desired family size, has reduced fertility in the United States to its lowest point in recorded history. In 2012, the total fertility rate was 1.9 children per woman, slightly below the replacement level of 2.1.[62] A growing number of women are deciding not to have children at all.[63] Some observers consider this a problem, arguing that we cannot remain strong as a nation or support an aging population with so few children.[64] I disagree. If we want a bigger population there is an easy way to achieve it: admit more immigrants, especially those with the skills we need. In the meantime, lower fertility means more time and money invested in each child and is more compatible with women's new aspirations.[65]

At the same time, research by George Akerlof, Janet Yellen, and Michael Katz shows that access to birth control and abortion may have contributed to high rates of childbearing outside of marriage by reducing the need for "shotgun marriages."[66] With women now presumed to be in control of their fertility, men no longer feel an obligation to marry a pregnant girlfriend.

Growing affluence and its cultural manifestations

Most Americans still believe in marriage. Marriage, they think, is the best way to live one's life; it should ideally last until "death do us part," it should be sexually exclusive, and divorce should be a last resort.[67] This deep belief in the value of marriage is stronger in the United States than in other Western countries. However, as Andrew Cherlin has argued, the cultural ideal of marriage as a lifelong commitment has in recent decades come into tension with another set of values that puts front and center the individual's need for personal growth and self-expression: "This kind of expressive individualism has flourished as prosperity has given more

Americans the time and money to develop their sense of self—to cultivate their own emotional gardens, as it were."[68]

Real-world relationships reflect these tensions—a belief in the cultural ideal of marriage on the one hand, and the need to end a particular relationship that no longer meets one's personal needs on the other. Some people suppress their individual needs to achieve the ideal of marriage, while others suppress that ideal in order to free themselves from a specific relationship.

In the past, marriage was more of an economic necessity for another reason: the lack of good market substitutes for home-produced goods and services. Taking care of the home was more of a full-time job in the past. Thanks to modern technology and markets, most people now have access to household appliances, such as dishwashers and washing machines, and to commercial outlets such as their local supermarket or Wal-Mart, where they can buy prepared dinners and inexpensive, ready-made clothing. Even women who still aspire to be homemakers have been forced to find new outlets for their creativity. Weaving, gardening, creating scrapbooks, and gourmet cooking are a lot more fun than the routine chores that were once a wife's responsibilities.

Affluence also makes it more feasible for people to live alone than in families. Whether they are young adults, divorced individuals, or older people who have lost a spouse, the proportion of the population that live on their own has skyrocketed.[69] That said, the "affluence effect" is probably more about heightened expectations of marriage than it is about the time needed to produce household goods and services or the cost of living alone. With fewer economic constraints, individuals are worrying more about whether a particular marriage meets their need for a soul mate or a playmate and less about whether their spouse is good at bringing home the bacon or bringing up the children.

Changes in social norms

Social norms matter. The economist James Duesenberry once quipped, "Economics is all about how people make choices. Sociology is all about how people don't have any choices to make."[70] Fewer people will divorce if being divorced is socially stigmatized, but if divorce becomes more common for some other reason, it may also become more socially acceptable. This mutual interaction between behavior and attitudes can cause a social trend that starts to slowly gain momentum as behavior feeds back on attitudes, propelling further changes in behavior.[71]

Nowhere has this shift in social norms been more apparent than in views of what is right and proper for men and women to do. In 1977, two-thirds of Americans agreed with the statement "It is much better for everyone involved if the man is the achiever outside the home and the woman takes care of the home and family." By 2012, the proportion who agreed with these traditional gender roles had dropped to less than one-third.[72]

This shift in views about gender roles has been accompanied by greater acceptance of people who are not married or do not have children. In the 1950s, a majority of Americans expressed negative attitudes toward people who did not want to get married and expected that, once married, a couple would have children.[73] Strong disapproval of the single lifestyle and of childlessness gave way to a growing acceptance of these choices in the late 1970s and 1980s. In the course of two decades, the proportion of Americans who disapproved of those who chose to remain single had dropped to about one-third, and only about 40 percent agreed with the idea that those who can have children should do so.[74] These views still hold today; marriage and childbearing are considered individual choices rather than social imperatives.

These changes in norms help to explain the decline in marriage and fertility, but what explains why people are increasingly having children outside of marriage? A partial explanation is that there has been a shift toward more liberal views about premarital sex.[75] But attitudes about sex before marriage shifted long before the changes in family formation we have seen in the past two decades. More recently, the youngest generation seems to have decoupled marriage and childbearing. They place more emphasis on the importance of children and less emphasis on marriage.[76] About 60 percent of Americans approve of or are neutral about an unmarried couple having a child.[77] The couples who were part of the Fragile Families study see childbearing and marriage as totally separate decisions (see chapter 4). None of them believes that having a child is a reason to get married, and none of them sees anything wrong with having a child outside of marriage.[78] These young adults no longer think of the two states as inherently connected, but rather as two separate life events.

The one opinion that has remained constant over the past half-century is that single motherhood is bad for both children and society. Seventy percent of Americans think that the growing number of single mothers constitutes a "big problem" for society.[79] The percentage of Americans who think that children need a home with both a mother and a father has remained fairly constant at around 60 percent since the 1980s.[80] Although this may seem inconsistent with the view that parents do not need to be married, the two can be reconciled if it is assumed that parents do not have to be married to raise a child together. In fact, there is now widespread acceptance of such cohabiting relationships.[81]

In sum, over the past fifty years the American public has become increasingly liberal in its views about sex, gender, and the family. Overall, these shifts in norms represent a vote for personal freedom in the realms of sex and family, although not a vote that will please everyone.

Too many choices?

The disappearance of clear norms about sex, marriage, and childbearing has benefits and costs. People are freer to choose for themselves what type of family best suits their own needs and preferences. But having more choices puts a much bigger burden on individuals to make good decisions and to become actively engaged in the process.

In light of this burden, many people are either making bad decisions or making no decision at all. Scott Stanley, a professor at the University of Denver, uses the phrase "sliding, not deciding" to describe how many young adults are approaching decisions about relationships and having children.[82] Andrew Cherlin has also emphasized that many young adults slide into cohabitations, some of them triggered by an unplanned birth.[83]

In the old days when I was growing up, if a young couple got pregnant, it was often followed by what we called a shotgun marriage. Now what we have are not shotgun marriages but a lot of shotgun cohabitations. The new parents may be romantically involved and committed to each other when their child is born, but rarely stay together to raise the child over the ensuing decade or two.

This seems to me to be the downside of the new ethic of individualism. Because there are no external markers, such as marriage, to structure the lives of young adults, and because society now tolerates a wide range of behaviors, from casual sex to unwed childbearing, there are few if any constraints other than one's own good judgment to keep one's life on track and to prevent the next generation from being born into less-than-ideal circumstances. The explosion of choices—if combined with good decisionmaking—could be viewed as an unadulterated good. But when individuals are unable to cope with the overload of so many choices, the consequences are far less benign.

Young adults in the early twenty-first century have much less direction than their parents did on what paths they should follow. As Settersten and Ray put it in their book, *Not Quite Adults,* "To be at the corner of such profound change and without a road map is both scary and exhilarating."[84] Having more choices should be liberating, particularly in America, where we so highly value freedom and autonomy in all aspects of our lives. But in reality, it is more of a mixed bag. Too many choices can leave a person paralyzed and unable to choose. Psychologist Barry Schwartz names this phenomenon the "paradox of choice" in his book of the same name.[85] He argues that having more choices can actually make a person less happy. Economists Betsey Stevenson and Justin Wolfers have found that women are less happy than they were before the women's movement took off.[86] Perhaps with more choices, women are suffering from Schwartz's paradox. Previously, being happy with one's life might have only meant being happy with your home and family. Now a woman must make the right choices in the home, in the workplace, in school, and in relationships if she wants to "have it all."

Economic instability only exacerbates the difficulty of navigating the many choices that Americans are faced with as they transition into adulthood. Decisions about relationships and parenthood affect decisions about education or employment—which in turn affect the choices one makes about relationships. The interlocking nature of these choices means that uncertainty in any one sphere makes the choices in another sphere that much more difficult. In interviews with 100 working-class Americans, sociologist Jennifer Silva found that "the unpredictability, insecurity, and risks of everyday life come to haunt young people within their most intimate relationships . . . transforming commitment into yet another risky venture."[87] Many of the young Americans to whom Silva spoke expressed a fear that commitment to a relationship would limit their independence and their already shaky control over the path their lives were taking.

Most choices involve trade-offs. In making any complex decision, a person must consider all the pros and cons, a process that is cognitively difficult and can reduce one's well-being.[88] Marriage and children involve making profound commitments to others that limit one's own autonomy, but also provide a sense of connection and close ties whose value, to most people, is hard to overstate. Still, no matter what someone chooses, he or she will forever be aware of what had to be given up in the process. For this and other reasons, Schwartz argues that having more choices is not always a blessing.[89]

Conclusions

Our grandparents would not recognize today's American family. In fact, there is no longer *an* iconic American family; there are *many* types of families. On the one hand, this kind of diversity gives people more freedom to choose how to live their lives. On the other, it requires more careful decisionmaking than in the days when almost everyone followed the same script. Those decisions have consequences, especially for children.

Diversity brings with it both good and bad news. One piece of good news is that divorce rates have declined. But they have declined primarily because the people who are still marrying are well-educated men and women in their late twenties or early thirties who are the most likely to succeed at it. At the other end of the economic spectrum, families are falling apart. Most children are born outside marriage.

A second piece of good news is that teen birth rates have plummeted, although they are still higher than those in other advanced countries. The twenties, it seems, are the new teens, a period when young adults appear to be adrift, not ready to settle down but having sex and babies nonetheless.

Finally, it is probably good that individuals are less constrained by social opinion than in the past. It appears that the well-educated and well-situated are using this freedom to make reasonable choices. A much larger group of the less-privileged, including many members of the middle class, is drifting into relationships they did not plan and frequently cannot maintain. While the economic challenges they face are real, these "choices" are not helping them or their children move up the ladder. This class divide and its implications for social mobility are new.

How young adults, both men and women, are coping with the stresses of combining work and family life, and how children born of not-yet-committed parents are faring, is the subject of the next chapter.

THREE

Why Should We Worry?

. . . to bring a child into existence without a fair prospect of being able, not only to provide food for its body, but instruction and training for its mind is a moral crime, both against the unfortunate offspring and against society.

—John Stuart Mill, *On Liberty*

When all is said and done, why do changes in family life in the United States matter? The family, after all, is a voluntarily chosen set of arrangements, codified in laws about marriage, divorce, and the benefits available to different kinds of families, but still primarily a private affair. From a libertarian perspective, there is a powerful argument that we should let a thousand family flowers bloom.

The problem with the purely libertarian perspective, however, is that family living arrangements and behaviors do have consequences for individuals within the family and for society. In particular, the growth in the number of single-parent families has had consequences for children. Children do not get to pick their parents or their living arrangements. And society pays a high price for supporting children in single-parent families or for using schools and other extra-family institutions to substitute for what struggling parents cannot provide. What should be a private institution has in the process been partially socialized: instead of distributing resources within the family via private and voluntary transfers of time and money, we must now redistribute more resources between households, necessitating higher taxes and less personal forms of care.[1] Some of this collective action is surely warranted and beneficial, but how far do we want to go with the substitution of public institutions for what we used to assume would occur within the family? And even if we are willing, how effective would these substitutions be if adults neglect their own responsibilities?

From the perspective of the individual, there are few decisions in life that are more important than those involving marriage and childbearing. Whether and when to commit to one person for life—and who that person is—could not be more consequential. Similarly, deciding whether and when to have children, and how many, is life-altering. Never before have these decisions been so much under the control of the individual. In the past, such matters were left to the dictates of religion, custom, and biology. In her comprehensive and insightful history of marriage, Stephanie Coontz explains how marriages were primarily motivated by economic or political considerations up until the late eighteenth century.[2] Gradually, they evolved into the companionate and romantic institutions we know today. These reached their peak in the 1950s and 1960s, when they were still normatively prescribed for almost everyone. Now those norms are weakening, and young adults, whatever they may say about their hopes to marry one day, are abandoning the institution in droves.

The main exceptions are the very well-educated. Men and women with at least a bachelor's degree are still marrying and, as Hanna Rosin points out, are beginning to treat marriage more like a business partnership than an enduring love affair. Or, as my colleague Richard Reeves likes to say, it is becoming "a commitment device" for raising children together.[3] Still another view, articulated by Betsey Stevenson and Justin Wolfers, is that it is a purely hedonic way for two people to enjoy the good things in life together, to be best friends for life.[4]

Consequences of Changes in Family Life for Adults

Before deciding whether to marry or have children, today's young adults might want to know what research on these topics says. What exactly are the advantages of marriage that young adults might want to consider before making a lifetime commitment to another person? And what are the benefits of having children?

The answers to these questions are not always clear. Studies that show that married people are happier than unmarried people, or that growing up with their biological parents is good for children, cannot prove that it is marriage or the child's living arrangement that matters most. It could be that the kind of people who marry are just different from the kind that do not. Researchers call these differences "selection effects." While they try hard to adjust for such differences, their efforts are rarely if ever 100 percent successful. The problem is that we cannot do clinical experiments under controlled conditions to decide what is the best environment for an adult or a child. Still, the research tells a story that is worth knowing.

Whether to marry

In an address to the Population Association of America, Linda Waite reviewed all of the social science and medical evidence on how marriage affects adults. Later she and Maggie Gallagher wrote a book in which they argue that married women and men live longer; they are less likely to be disabled; they are physically and mentally healthier, and when they are in poor health, they are more likely to remain at home under the care, or with the support of, a spouse. Married couples have better sex than the unmarried and they are less likely to be lonely.[5] Most of this seems obvious, but some of the results are surprising.

Consider for a moment just one of these benefits: a lower mortality rate among those who are married than among those who are not. In the mid-1990s, one study looked at a national sample of more than 6,000 families and tracked all of the major events that occurred in their lives between the ages of 48 and 65.[6] After accounting for a host of other factors that might affect one's probability of dying, they found that roughly 4 out of 10 of the never-married men and almost as many of the divorced and widowed men had died before the age of 65. This contrasted with 1 out of 10 for married men. These are huge differences. Married women were also less likely to die before 65 than their unmarried counterparts, but the gap was not nearly as large as it was for men. Widows, in particular, did not die earlier than married women.

What can we infer from these striking differences? Some of them are likely due to selection effects. Those who marry or stay married are likely to be healthier, less likely to be the victims of disabilities or chronic diseases, and more likely to choose a healthy lifestyle, independent of their choice to marry. But several other pieces of evidence suggest that marriage actually confers some protection against poor health and mortality. For one thing, individuals tend to adopt healthier life styles *after* they marry. For another, these differences in mortality exist even after taking initial health status into account. And finally, men in poor health are actually more rather than less likely to marry than those who are healthy. Perhaps all of the jokes about men who are hopelessly irresponsible when it comes to taking care of their own health and about wives forever nagging them to go to the doctor or take their medications are true. Maybe having a "nurse-in-residence" has real benefits.

Still another reason that marriage may be good for adults is that the presence of a spouse enhances a sense of responsibility. That sense of responsibility, in turn, may lead to fewer problem behaviors such as excessive drinking. It appears to produce higher earnings, at least for men.[7] Indeed, some observers believe that for men, marriage serves as a socializing influence, taming their greater inclination to be violent, promiscuous, or socially irresponsible.[8]

At the same time, high rates of divorce suggest that there are plenty of unhappy marriages. Even when a marriage survives, it can be unfulfilling or even stultifying, preserved more out of a sense of obligation than of personal preference. Greater affluence has created greater demands for autonomy or the freedom to live one's own life as one wishes. In the trade-off between the greater security that comes with having "ties that bind" and the freedom to make one's own decisions, freedom and autonomy are increasingly on the winning side. The decisions to marry or stay single, to stay together or to split, are now almost entirely private ones. As Hillary Clinton put it in a context with which we are all too familiar, "I have learned a long time ago that the only two people who count in any marriage are the two who are in it."[9]

Social and legal pressures to marry or stay married are abating, freeing more people to tilt in the direction of remaining single or splitting up when a relationship proves troublesome. Marriage is not always an ideal state. The rapid rise in divorce rates that followed the earlier shift in norms about the acceptability of divorce suggests that many people in the past were trapped in unhappy—even abusive—marriages. The courts adjusted, too; it used to be that a spouse had to prove wrongdoing by the other spouse in order for a judge to grant a divorce; many states have since adopted "no-fault" systems that allow couples to end their marriages more simply. Stevenson and Wolfers have shown that the replacement of fault-based divorce with unilateral or no-fault divorce reduced suicide, domestic violence, and the murder of husbands by wives.[10] In the short run, the shift to a regime in which either spouse can exit a marriage "at will" provides an opportunity for the unhappiest spouse to leave. Over the longer term, the effects of unilateral divorce laws on divorce rates tend to fade, as spouses renegotiate their positions under the new bargaining regime that no-fault makes possible. The spouse who most wants out of a marriage suddenly has much greater ability to demand changes within the marriage. This side of the story should not be forgotten. Still, if marriage is a commitment device, then some limits on free exit and entry may be desirable. Prenuptial counseling or agreements, and waiting periods for divorce, can still make sense as a way of putting some brakes on overly hasty and ill-considered decisions.

When to marry

The fact that people are marrying at older ages is good news. Later marriages are more durable than early ones. The most recent data suggest that it is best to wait at least until your mid-twenties, and better still until your early thirties, if you want to reduce the risk of divorce.[11] After that age, the probability of divorce levels off or may even increase a bit owing to the increasing difficulty of finding a suitable partner and the corresponding likelihood of making compromises that imply a less-than-ideal match.[12]

The reasons that later marriages are more durable are not hard to understand. Older adults have greater maturity, more experience with relationships, a better sense of their own goals and preferences, and often, more education and resources. Of course, waiting too long also has its downside. The market shrinks, especially for women, and people get set in their ways. There is something to be said for "growing up" in tandem with another person, melding one's interests and values in the process. In any case, the youngest generation, the so-called millennials, seems to have received the message that marrying later has many advantages. The bottom line is that the delay of marriage has been a very positive development, on balance. The problem is that the majority of young adults are not simultaneously delaying childbearing.

What about having children?

The failure to delay childbearing is the critical element in this story. After all, one can divorce a spouse, but not a child. So why are so many people having children before they marry and before they are arguably mature enough to take on this responsibility? To be sure, children are a source of great satisfaction to many people, and some go to great lengths to conceive a child or adopt one when infertility is a problem. However, the scholarly evidence, as well as the tales told by parents, suggests that raising kids is expensive and not that much fun.[13]

The Department of Agriculture estimates that the cost to middle-income parents of raising one child from birth to college age is $241,080 for a child born in 2012.[14] This estimate only includes money spent on education, child care, clothing, housing, food, transportation, health care, and miscellaneous goods and services. It does not include the "free" child care provided by a stay-at-home parent. Take, for example, a husband and wife who each make $45,000 and decide that one parent will stay home with the child until the child is school-age, and then work part-time once the child is in school. The estimated cost of such an arrangement is over $800,000, which would make the total cost of raising a child more than $1 million.[15] Under what is probably a more realistic set of assumptions about how quickly most mothers now return to work and their likelihood of working full-time when they do, the total cost of raising a child would be closer to half a million.[16] Still, it is an expensive proposition.

Two costs loom especially large: child care and college. Families with children under 5 years old paid an average of over $9,300 a year for child care.[17] Families below the poverty level pay almost one-third of their income for child care, on average.[18] The other big-ticket item, college, is now a virtual prerequisite to joining the middle class; for 2013–14, average annual tuition was $8,898 at an in-state four-year public college and

$30,094 at a private four-year college (without room and board, which can add $10,000 dollars per year).[19] Parents need to put away a lot of money to make this affordable. For these reasons, we have seen what economists call (even in this most personal domain) a gradual substitution of quality for quantity—that is, fewer children but more investment per child.

But isn't having children such a joyous experience that the benefits exceed the costs? Not necessarily. Multiple studies have found that, in the aggregate, parents report lower levels of happiness, life satisfaction, and mental well-being than non-parents.[20] In addition, having children is associated with less marital stability and satisfaction, especially for the youngest generation and among higher-income and better-educated parents.[21] Highly educated individuals in fulfilling careers have to give up more as parents. In addition, as people have delayed parenthood until later in life, they have had the time to build up a more fulfilling childless life in the years before bringing a child into their lives. In past generations, people began having children right after moving out of their parents' households and were less likely to feel they were "giving up" the freedom of unfettered adulthood.

Two researchers at the University of California at Berkeley, Philip Cowan and Carolyn Pape Cowan, note that the drop in marital satisfaction after childbirth is almost entirely accounted for by couples who slid into being parents, disagreed about it, or were ambivalent about the conception. Those couples who planned a child together were likely to maintain or even strengthen the marital bond after the child was born.[22]

Although having children may not improve people's well-being on a day-to-day basis, many people who look back on their child-rearing years express great satisfaction with the experience.[23] On a day-to-day basis, parenting means nagging your child to do his homework or to clean up the mess she has made of your living room. Measures of day-to-day happiness do not take into consideration the joy of seeing your child ride a bike for the first time or the pride you feel when she gives the valedictory speech at her high school graduation ceremony. When studies look at how rewarding parenting is as opposed to how pleasurable it is, they find that people rate parenting as one of the most rewarding activities in which they have been involved, even if it is not always pleasurable.

Parenting is more like work in this regard, which most people rate as high in reward but low in pleasure. Contrast parenting with watching television, which gets high marks for pleasure and low marks for reward.[24]

What should adults consider when making the choice to have children (or additional children): day-to-day happiness or the overall sense of purpose that they give to your life? Happiness psychologist Daniel Gilbert describes this conundrum as follows: "When you pause to *think* what children mean to you, of course they make you feel good. The problem is, 95 percent of the time, you're not thinking about what they mean to you. You're thinking that you have to take them to piano lessons. So you have to think about which kind of happiness you'll be consuming most often. Do you want to maximize the one you experience almost all the time [moment-to-moment happiness] or the one you experience rarely?"[25] People do, and should, weigh these two different sources of lifetime satisfaction differently.

Women vs. men: different perspectives

Marriage and childbearing have always been more central to the lives of women than to the lives of men. As women's opportunities have expanded, gender differences in attitudes toward marriage and child-bearing may have narrowed. But they have not disappeared. In particular, women are still subject to social pressures that make it harder for them than for men to make a decision to forgo marriage or children. They may also be biologically oriented in this direction, although there is still a lively debate over the issue.[26] Even assuming that there is a biologically based maternal instinct, it is likely to vary widely from one individual to another and to be shaped by social context as well as the extent of early bonding with a child. During the seventeenth and eighteenth centuries, high rates of infanticide and child abandonment by mothers, even among the European middle classes, and high rates of child abuse and neglect in our own day, suggest that whatever role biology plays, it cannot always be counted on to secure the well-being of children.

Contemporary debate has centered less on whether women are biologically primed to be mothers and more on whether they can combine motherhood with a career. The popularity of Sheryl Sandberg's book *Lean In,* and of Anne-Marie Slaughter's *Atlantic* article on "having it all," is testimony to the conflicts many young women feel in the face of these pressures.[27] As I discuss later, there are policies, such as paid leave, that could reduce these conflicts. But young women who have not yet married or had children need to know that "having it all" may indeed be difficult. There are trade-offs that cannot be denied. For an ambitious, well-educated woman, children can be a barrier to entering the executive suite. For the less well-educated, a sick child can spell the difference between holding on to a job and ending up dependent on government assistance. By the same token, women intent on having it all may find that getting ahead comes at the expense of not devoting enough time to children and family. Maybe having it all should not be the goal. Maybe being happy with what you *do* have should be the goal.

When women marry, and especially when they have children, they pay a price in the labor market that men do not. According to a number of good studies, the wage penalty for having children seems to be around 7 percent in lost earnings per child.[28] Many possible reasons for this penalty have been posited. Mothers may opt out of the labor force for periods of time when their children are young or work part-time; they may be less productive at work, given their family responsibilities; they may be discriminated against by employers who perceive them to be less productive even when they're not; they may choose more family-friendly but lower-paying jobs; or they may simply be less work-oriented than women who are not mothers. About one-third of the penalty appears to be related to the fact that mothers with children at home spend less time working than women without children, but the remaining two-thirds appears to be due to some combination of employer-based discrimination and lower productivity. Studies have largely ruled out other possible explanations, such as the tendency of mothers to select more family-friendly occupations. We have direct evidence about discrimination from an audit study that found that employers were less likely to hire women with children than identically described women without them (the existence of children made no difference in the case of men).[29] However, the fact that the penalty rises with the number of children (for example, it is twice as high for women with two or more children as for those with only one), even after adjusting for other potential sources of the motherhood penalty, suggests that there could be some differences in productivity related to time demands at home.[30] The penalty is also greatest for the most-educated women.[31] The less-educated, although they obviously face many challenges, encounter a smaller wage penalty for motherhood, probably because the wages they earn are much lower and the jobs they hold are not as open-ended in their demands. Perhaps because of these penalties for motherhood, high-achieving women are much more likely than high-achieving men to simply forgo parenthood or marriage entirely. For example, according to a survey conducted by Sylvia Ann Hewlett, almost half of very high achieving women (those earning more than $100,000 a year) who were age 41–55 in 2001 were childless. That compares with 19 percent for very high achieving men in the same age bracket.[32] Some of these career-oriented women intend to marry and have children in their forties but then slide into childlessness because it becomes increasingly difficult for them to find a partner and have a child as they age. This is what Hewlett calls a "creeping nonchoice."[33]

In this book, I emphasize the downside of not choosing well, and in particular the consequences of not planning one's childbearing. But here is an example not of drifting into parenthood, but of drifting out of it—unintentionally. It is also an example of the class divide, another theme of this book. If less-educated women are opting in to childbearing without meaning to, their more privileged sisters are opting out without meaning to. Based on their research on high-achieving women, Hewlett and Sandberg counsel young women who want both a career and a family to become "highly intentional" about what they want their life to look like at age 45. That means that if they want to marry, they should find a partner while they are still in their twenties or early thirties; if they want children, they should have their first child before age 35; and if they want a career, they should choose one that, while it may not enable them to have it all, will enable them to have more. Be an entrepreneur rather than a lawyer, Hewlett advises, and avoid corporate jobs with rigid career ladders.[34] In the end, she argues that having it all is a myth. My reading of the research on these questions is that she is right. Yes, society and employers could do much more to ease the trade-offs that women face (and I return to this topic in chapter 5). In the meantime, a dose of reality, based on how the world works now, is needed.

I would add that the problem for women is much deeper than a lack of family-friendly workplaces, paid parental leave, or subsidized child care. It is embedded in cultural assumptions about what men and women normally do. In insightful research on how these cultural assumptions shape one's identity or self-image and how that self-image, in turn, affects behavior, George Akerlof and Rachel Kranton have shown that deviating from one's prescribed role can be costly.[35] Men do not wear dresses (at least in Western countries). Those who do don't just upset women; they make other men uncomfortable as well. Or consider a less rigidly prescribed rule: young black men growing up in the ghetto are not rewarded by their peers for mastering math in high school but for playing basketball and joining gangs, even when such behavior is self-destructive.

Marianne Bertrand and her coauthors use this framework to explain what might otherwise seem like anomalies in the behavior of women who are torn between their desire to achieve in male-dominated spheres and maintain their feminine identity at the same time.[36] She starts with two specific behavioral prescriptions: first, that "men work in the labor force and women work in the home," and second, that "a man should earn more than his wife." Since deviating from these prescriptions threatens identity for both men and women, they engage in behaviors that make no sense from a purely economic perspective. Specifically, she finds that marriages are much more likely to occur when men earn more than women and are less likely to occur if a woman earns more than the man, even if the latter is what we would expect in an "efficient marriage market" where personal characteristics but not the distribution of income between the two mattered. Since women are now better educated than men and increasingly slated to earn more as a result, this creates a problem for highly educated women. There will not be enough high-earning men to go around unless these attitudes change. Professional women within the black community are already facing this problem.[37] Bertrand further finds that in order to not threaten her husband's identity, a married woman with high earning potential often pulls her economic punches by working less, or if she does earn more, works even harder at household tasks to compensate for the implicit threat signaled by her financial success.[38] The finding that women who earn more than their husbands also do the bulk of the work in the home, especially the household chores (not just child care), has now been found in at least two different studies.[39]

In this context, a closer look at current attitudes about gender roles among young men and women is revealing. Male attitudes are still less egalitarian than women's. Men are more likely than women to agree with the statement that it is better for everyone involved if men are the achievers outside the home and women take care of the family. While both young men and young women have more egalitarian attitudes than their parents' generation, the number of young men who still believe in the breadwinner-homemaker model is close to 40 percent.[40] These attitudes are not just a problem for elites. Among the least well-educated, such attitudes about men's and women's roles are even more traditional than they are among the professional classes. The proportion of both men and women who think that men should be breadwinners is more than twice as high among high school dropouts as it is among the college-educated. As Richard Reeves puts it, "The bitter irony is that those most likely to disdain female breadwinners (the least-educated men and women) would be helped the most by dual-earner households. The men who want to be breadwinners are very often the ones least able to fill that role. . . . Our central problem is not the slow retreat of the idea of traditional marriage. It is the stubborn persistence of the idea of traditional marriage among those people for whom it has lost almost all rationale."[41]

In her book *The Unfinished Revolution*, Kathleen Gerson writes that young adults from all backgrounds understand the conflicts that now exist between work and family life, and the difficult choices that they are being asked to make.[42] In interviews, most of her respondents talked about their parents' generation as looking much like my description of those growing up in the 1950s and 1960s; they also described the fundamental ways in which their own aspirations differed from those of their parents. They are hopeful of finding a lifetime partner but wary of marriage, especially the kinds of traditional marriages that many of their parents had. They understand, and often admire, the traditional breadwinner/homemaker roles played by their parents, but have overwhelmingly rejected those roles as outmoded and less than desirable. Four-fifths of the women and two-thirds of the men see egalitarian relationships as ideal. However, since the difficulties of combining a career with child rearing are clear to them, they are also able to articulate a fallback strategy should equal sharing prove infeasible. The compromises they are willing to make are still very gendered.[43]

The fallback position among young women if they are unable to find a mate willing to share equally in work and family tasks is self-sufficiency or going it alone. Over 70 percent of the young women said that they preferred this outcome to a more gendered division of labor. These women, many of whom were still young, unmarried, and childless, spoke about wanting to postpone marriage and childbearing until they have enough education and career experience to live independently if necessary. Some of the women had already left marriages or relationships because the man involved expected them to put themselves second to his needs. A few who were already single mothers had chosen single parenthood over dependence on an unreliable husband or boyfriend. Only a minority (about 25 percent) said that they were willing to sacrifice their own desire for a career or other kinds of autonomy if that should prove necessary.

The young men in Gerson's sample had a different set of views. They, too, wanted to find a lifelong partner and expected there to be some sharing of work and family responsibilities. However, they worried about their ability to both earn a good living and help out at home. Under these circumstances, they saw two fallback positions. The first, favored by 70 percent, was a more traditional division of labor in which they became the primary breadwinners and their wives, even if working, took primary responsibility for child care and other domestic tasks. The other view, less prevalent than the first but articulated by a significant subset of the men, was to escape the time bind by avoiding formal family responsibilities entirely. These men saw freedom from a wife and children as a real option. There was surprisingly little variation by race and class, although a somewhat higher fraction of the less well-off and of minority men held the view that the best fallback position was not to tie the knot at all.

The Gerson interviews are fascinating for several reasons. First, both genders, but women more strongly than men, believe that the days when women can, or should, take primary responsibility for child rearing are over. Second, they also understand that even were women willing to play a more traditional role, the ability to support a family on only one income is rarely feasible. Third, they understand that "doing it all"—being both breadwinner and caretaker—is extremely difficult. If necessary, almost three-quarters of the men but only one-quarter of the women would resolve the conflict by tolerating a more traditional arrangement in which men make earning a living their primary responsibility and women bear more of the caretaking responsibilities, even when both have jobs. In the end, these data suggest that unless young men and women can find more accommodation between their divergent views, there will be either more discontented couples or simply less childbearing and marriage overall as men and women of the current generation mature and find no other way to reconcile their differences in light of the arguably unrealistic demands on their time.

A 2013 Pew Research Center report on modern parenthood reinforces Gerson's findings on the difficulties of doing it all, finding that about half of parents, both mothers and fathers, feel stressed about juggling work and family life.[44] Pew did find some blurring of gender roles within the family. In 1965, mothers spent almost seven times as much time as fathers on child care and housework (42 hours vs. 6.5 hours). By 2011, the gap had narrowed, but mothers still spent almost twice as much time as fathers (32 hours vs. 17 hours). And although fathers reported that they wished they could spend more time with their children, they were more focused on having a high-paying job while mothers gave more weight to having a flexible schedule.[45] Whatever progress has been made in sharing work-family tasks in practice, public attitudes have lagged behind. Almost half of all adults (42 percent) still say the best situation for a child is if the mother works part-time, while one-third say it is best if the mother does not work at all while her children are young.[46] In the meantime, couples with children are putting in more total hours than ever to fulfill their dual roles as workers and parents. Between paid work, housework, and child care, both mothers and fathers report spending almost sixty hours a week on those combined tasks, more than in the 1960s. Women in dual-income families spend slightly more time per week on those tasks than their male partners.[47]

This conflict between work and family life—which is so salient in the minds of today's young women—could influence not just their decision about whether to marry, but also their willingness to have children. Especially among those with high levels of education who have the most to lose by sacrificing progress in a career to the demands of child rearing, "having it all" can mean marrying but not having children. Freed from the most demanding task embedded in the old package deal of marriage and children, they could potentially reap the benefits of marriage without the costs associated with having children.

This seems to be happening already. A growing number of women are choosing not to have any children at all.[48] By 2008, the proportion nearing the end of their reproductive years without having children had risen from 10 percent in 1976 to 18 percent.[49] The bulk of this increase is related not to involuntary infertility but to voluntary childlessness—or as advocates of this lifestyle call it, a child-free adulthood. Still, roughly half of those in this group are women who are not childless by choice.

The reasons for falling fertility and rising childlessness are many. The economic costs of motherhood are much higher than in the past; the ability to control one's fertility is much improved; and women's identities and social status are less tied to parenthood. (Recall what happened to Henry VIII's wives when they failed to bear children.) In the more recent past, a woman without a child was at best a social enigma and at worst a person to be pitied, on the grounds that she either could not have children or did not want them. Elizabeth Badinter has written eloquently about these social pressures. As she notes, no one ever asks "Why did you have children?" But they always wonder, whether they articulate it or not, why someone did *not* have children.[50]

Consequences of Changes in Family Life for Children

New choices for adults, and the diversity of family types they have spawned, have enabled many people to escape from conflict-ridden or troubled marriages and to forge more satisfying relationships or living arrangements. However, these new choices for adults have not, by and large, been good for children. Children born to couples who never marry, or who divorce, did not ask to be born into such circumstances. Marriage is, of course, no guarantee that children will do well, and single parenthood is no guarantee that they will do badly. But marriage has, on the whole, helped to provide stable environments in which children have access to more resources of all kinds than those in single-parent families.

As noted earlier, the proportion of single-parent families has grown rapidly over the past half-century, from 7 percent of all families with children in 1950 to 32 percent in 2013.[51] It is important to remember that not all of these so-called single parents are living alone. Many are cohabiting with a partner, often the biological parent of their child, but because these relationships are fragile and break up at a much higher rate than marriages, they can still be problematic for the children.

Both married and cohabiting parents benefit from what economists call "economies of scale" in maintaining a household. They pay only one rent, can make do with one TV, and require fewer of the many other things needed to maintain two separate households. Even more important, they can combine their individual earnings to provide a far higher income for the household than either could provide alone. And if one spouse stays home or works less than full-time, although their earnings will be lower, their costs for child care and other "do-it-yourself" goods and services will also be lower. In addition to pooling their earnings and their work in the home, two parents can also pool their assets to, for example, buy a home or send a child to college.[52]

For these reasons, among others, the incomes (and wealth) of married and cohabiting parents are higher than those of single parents (see figure 3 in the appendix). In 2012, the median income for married-parent families was $81,520, while the typical single female parent earned only $29,539, less than half as much. Cohabiting parents fell somewhere in between, with incomes of $48,937.[53]

On the basis of these figures, it is tempting to conclude that single parents would be much better off if they married or at least found a live-in partner. In particular, there would be much less child poverty. Poverty rates for children growing up with a single parent are high. Forty-seven percent of children living in single-mother families were living below the poverty line in 2012. This is more than four times as high as the 11 percent poverty rate for children living with their married parents.[54]

Not only do children living with a single parent face a high risk of being poor, but the decline in marriage and growth of single parenthood has tended to push up the poverty rate at the same time that other factors, such as a more generous safety net and higher earnings for women, have reduced the risk that these families will be poor. In 1970, 12.8 percent of families were headed by a single mother. If there had been no growth in single-parent families after 1970, so that the proportion of children living in single-parent families in 2012 was the same as it was in 1970—before divorce and out-of-wedlock childbearing dramatically increased the proportion of children living with a single parent—then the child poverty rate would be only 15 percent, six percentage points lower than the actual child poverty rate in 2012 (21 percent).[55]

One problem with this conclusion is that it may confuse correlation with causation. Put differently, married parents have more income than single parents because the kinds of people who marry tend to be more successful to begin with. If, for example, highly educated adults are more likely to marry than their less-educated counterparts, then the higher incomes among married couples reflect both their two incomes and their higher level of education.

In an attempt to adjust for these selection effects, Adam Thomas and I identified a group of single mothers in annual Census data and arranged "virtual marriages" between these mothers and a group of single men who looked like good marriage partners for each other on the basis of their age, race, and education level. We "married off" enough single mothers to replicate the marriage rates that had prevailed in 1970 before the big spurt in divorce and unwed childbearing had occurred. After creating these virtual marriages, we recalculated the household incomes of the sample and found that child poverty rates fell by 3.4 percentage points, roughly 20 percent.[56] In comparison with the outcomes of most other anti-poverty policies, this is a huge effect. Government policies to offset an increase in child poverty of this magnitude would be extraordinarily expensive. For example, we would have to triple welfare benefits to have as large an effect.[57]

My conclusion is that the growth of single-parent families has pushed up the child poverty rate a lot. In fact, this demographic trend has completely offset the poverty-reducing effects of the growth of cash assistance programs over the past four decades or so. The government is doing more, but the official poverty rate has remained stubbornly high because of the decline in marriage.[58]

The consequences of living in single-parent homes extend beyond the effects on household incomes and poverty rates. Children in such homes also suffer from cognitive, social, and emotional deficits relative to children raised in two-parent homes. No one contends that every child is affected adversely, only that the best research suggests that, on average, growing up with a single parent is not the best environment for a child. Every family and every child's circumstances differ enormously, making generalizations both difficult and potentially misleading.[59]

Given these caveats, what do we know from the research, beginning with the effects of divorce? In several syntheses of many different studies, Paul Amato, a professor at Pennsylvania State University and one of the most knowledgeable researchers in this field, has found that the children of divorced parents are worse off than those in continuously married families on a range of measures, including academic success, appropriate behavior, psychological well-being, peer relations, and emotional bonding with parents.

Although every case is different, the research on these issues suggests that, for the typical child, the consequences can include acting out in aggressive ways, becoming depressed or withdrawn, doing less well in school, or having problems relating to others. Although the shock of divorce can lead to immediate problems in adjusting to a new life that may dissipate with time, research also suggests these adverse consequences can flare up during adolescence and extend into adulthood, leading to lower earnings or less stable relationships later in life (for example, more troubled marriages, more divorces, more unwed births). Somewhat surprisingly, remarriage and living in a step-parent family, while adding important financial and social resources that can benefit a child, does not seem to produce any better outcomes for that child. Finally, experiencing the death of a parent as a child appears to put children at a disadvantage, but not as much as a divorce or being born to an unwed mother.[60]

Although divorce was the most frequent route into single parenthood in earlier decades, in recent years a more common pattern of family formation is for a woman to have a baby before marriage, either on her own or with a cohabiting partner. In comparison with children born into two-parent married families, these children are more likely to fare worse on a number of dimensions, including school achievement, social and emotional development, health, and success in the labor market. They are at greater risk of parental abuse and neglect (especially from live-in boyfriends who are not their biological fathers), more likely to become teen parents, and less likely to graduate from high school or college.[61]

What could account for these differences? Why are the children of divorced or unwed parents at greater risk of experiencing poor outcomes? There are a number of possibilities, including the disruption and instability that accompany divorce or other household transitions, stress or poorer mental health on the part of the mother, strained relationships between the parents, poorer-quality parenting of the child, or the lack of an involved father. To these should be added the more central fact that such families typically have less income and less time to devote to their children. Indeed, the three most common explanations for poorer outcomes among children in single-parent homes center on changes in the material circumstances of the family (loss of income, living in a poorer neighborhood), changes in the quality of parenting after a breakup, and the fact that individuals who have difficulty forging healthy relationships with their marriage partners may also be less-adequate parents.

In the last case, it is not the divorce or unwed birth that causes the problem but the underlying personal attributes, mental health, or competencies that produce both a broken family and worse outcomes for the child—selection effects, again. For example, a depressed mother, or one who is an alcoholic, may find her marriage in trouble but also have difficulty being a reliable or engaged parent. Similarly, a violence-prone man may face problems in his marriage but also be the kind of father that provides harsh or inconsistent discipline to his children. In these cases, it is the violence or the depression or the substance abuse that is responsible for relationship failures between the two adults involved and also between parents and their children. The bonds between parent and child and between two adults are drawn from the same psychological well. Adults who have drunk deeply from this well are likely to be both good parents and good partners. Similarly, adults who make strong commitments to a marriage may also make bigger commitments to their children. Thus it would not be surprising if the two were closely related and if the adverse consequences for children *after* divorce result from some of the same underlying conditions, attitudes, behaviors, or interpersonal skills that so often tip a couple *into* divorce. Death, by contrast, is more likely to be a random event, not connected to the attributes or temperaments of the parents. The lesser disadvantages for children end-ing up in a single-parent family as the result of the death of one parent may reflect this fact and point to the importance of taking unobserved attributes, temperaments, and behaviors into account when talking about the consequences of single parenthood for children.

Even where there are real causal effects, one cannot say too often that not all children who grow up in single-parent families are adversely affected by the experience. Moreover, no two cases are alike. In cases of divorce, the child's response may vary with the extent of conflict in the family prior to the breakup, the way in which the custodial parent (usu-ally the mother) handles the stresses involved, and compensatory changes in parenting styles by both parents. For example, a common pattern is a shift from a more adult-directed and authoritative style of parenting to a more child-oriented and permissive type of parenting as parents compete for a child's affection or try to replace their own loss by strengthening ties with their child. This is a shift that is understandable but not helpful to a child that needs consistent direction and discipline. The effects of divorce may also be buffered if the father stays involved in the child's life; if the single parent has strong supports from other family members or friends; or if the loss of income experienced by the new single-parent household is not too great, as the result of remarriage or child support from the father. Potentially important as well are the length of time the child spends in a single-parent household and the child's own sensitivity to the loss of a parent. Some children feel abandoned by their fathers or are especially susceptible to the changes necessitated by a divorce, such as a move to a new house, a new school, and a new set of friends. Others cope with such challenges reasonably well. Although there seem to be few differences related to the timing of the divorce in the child's life, there are some inter-esting gender differences; boys usually fare worse than girls, presumably because of the loss of a male role model in the family.

This finding that boys are more affected than girls has raised the pos-sibility that the growing share of single-parent families may be one reason that men are trailing women in educational achievement and slowly los-ing some of their traditional advantage in the job market. The declining economic prospects of men, in turn, have made them less desirable as marriage partners, producing still more single-mother families in what could become a vicious circle.[62] It is well established that, regardless of the type of family in which they are raised, boys do less well throughout their school years in reading and in various measures of behavior; they are more likely than girls to be disruptive, fight, argue, act impulsively, and not pay attention. And boys raised in single-parent families do worse than those raised in two-parent families. In addition to the lack of a male role model and the kind of preferential treatment that mothers sometimes give to daughters, the research suggests that boys are far more sensitive than girls to the kind of parenting they receive and thus are more likely to be affected by the fact that a single parent has less time to devote to child-oriented activities.[63] Working mothers, including those in two-parent families, also have less time to spend in child-oriented activities; but after the first year of life, maternal employment unlike single parenthood does not seem to adversely affect child development.[64]

Taken together, all of these findings indicate that there is something about the absence of a biological parent that causes children to have greater difficulty adjusting to life's challenges. In addition, family stability matters. The research community has spent years trying to untangle these issues, and especially the role played by selection effects. Most scholars now believe that divorce and unwed childbearing do have real effects on children's well-being. The fact that children raised in step-parent families do worse than those raised by their own parents suggests that it is not just the absence of sufficient income or of a male role model that leads to poorer outcomes for children. Biology matters as well. Ties between a step-parent and a child are often weaker or more fraught than those between a parent and his or her own offspring. On the other hand, the fact that children who lose a parent through death fare better than those who lose a parent through divorce suggests that selection is part of the story, even if not the whole story.[65] Finally, there is no evidence that children with cohabiting biological parents in long-term relationships fare worse than those in married families; but such long-term cohabitations without marriage are quite rare.[66]

But how large are these effects? Is this much ado about almost nothing? Amato has provided one set of interesting estimates. He finds that the proportion of teens who repeat a grade, who are suspended from school, who are delinquent or violent, who require therapy, or who have attempted suicide are all lower in two-parent families and that increasing the proportion being raised in two-parent families to, say, 1970s levels would reduce the incidence of such problems, although usually by a small amount. He notes that although these effects are small at the individual level, when aggregated across the entire population of children at risk, the social impacts are sizable. He uses an analogy from medicine, pointing out that lowering cholesterol levels among men has a small impact on an individual's risk of dying from a heart attack but a large impact on the society-wide number of heart attacks that occur over a decade's time and thus on the costs to society.[67]

In sum, poorer outcomes for children in unmarried or single-parent families have been found in many different studies, and the sheer accumulation of evidence from different sources has produced a near-consensus among social scientists that, except in cases where the relationship between parents is highly conflict-ridden, a long-term marriage is best for children.[68]

Same-Sex Parents

There is little doubt that marriage is good for children in traditional families, but it is perceived by some as bad for children when the parents are of the same sex.[69] Although the jury is still out, so far there is little evidence to support such concerns.

Opponents of same-sex marriage believe not only that marriage should be between one man and one woman but also that same-sex couples are less capable of raising well-adjusted children or are less stable than their heterosexual counterparts. Because this issue is new both to the public and to academics, there is disagreement among social science researchers about whether there is any truth to these claims. While some researchers, most notably Mark Regnerus and Douglas Allen, claim that children of LGBT (lesbian, gay, bisexual, and transgender) parents fare less well than children with two opposite-sex parents,[70] the American Sociological Association has criticized their findings, noting, in particular, flaws in their characterization of what constitutes being raised by a parent with same-sex inclinations.[71] Many other studies have found no difference in the outcomes of children being raised by same- and opposite-sex parents.

In a 2005 review of fifty-nine published studies of gay and lesbian parents and their children, the American Psychological Association (APA) found that "not a single study has found children of lesbian or gay parents to be disadvantaged in any significant respect relative to children of heterosexual parents."[72] However, critics of the APA's pronouncement argue that the findings of "no difference" are based on studies with small, nonrepresentative samples.[73] Research on this topic continues to be hampered by the lack of data on same-sex parents.

On balance, my reading of current research does not support the assertions of the critics of same-sex marriage about its effects on children. Rather, the societal stigmas that have caused lesbians and gays to stay in the closet and disallowed same-sex marriage have also resulted in the majority of their children being born as the result of a prior heterosexual relationship. When these individuals later form a same-sex relationship, the children from a prior marriage are then often raised by a cohabiting same-sex couple.[74] But cohabiting relationships are much less stable than marriage, regardless of sexual preference.[75] This means that most children of LGBT parents are being raised in situations similar to those in divorced or unmarried parent families. Contrasting them to children being raised in continuously married families, as Regnerus does, is not a fair comparison. Assuming marriage equality eventually becomes the law of the land, then we will be able to see more clearly how the children of such couples fare.

Consequences of the Changing Family for Society

All of these changes in the family have not been good for society. The problem in a nutshell is that, as noted earlier, single parents are much more likely to be poor than those who are married, and thus to need income support and other forms of social assistance.

The relatively low incomes of these families stem from several sources. First, most single parents are women (77 percent), and women still earn less than men with similar qualifications.[76] More important, there is no second earner in the family, and there are often extra costs for child care or other work-related expenses for the family's sole breadwinner. Finally, single parents are not drawn equally from all segments of society; for example, they are more likely to be less educated, black, and young, and they often face other impediments such as physical, mental, and emotional problems or a lack of assets with which to cushion economic shocks. Many of these single mothers (34 percent) started their childbearing as teens, and they are more likely than their married counterparts to have problems due to a partner's violence, drinking, or drugs.[77]

Single mothers rely on support from a variety of sources, including their own earnings, public benefits, child support from the father, and help from relatives and friends. Public benefits loom large. These benefits include welfare; food stamps (now called the Supplemental Nutrition Assistance Program, SNAP); housing assistance; the Women, Infants and Children (WIC) nutrition program; school lunch subsidies; the earned income tax credit (EITC); and housing assistance. In 2001, one year after the birth of a child, 94 percent of single and cohabiting mothers were at least partially dependent on public benefits.[78] About a third received Temporary Assistance for Needy Families (TANF), more colloquially known as welfare. In 2010, the above-mentioned list of benefits averaged $4,522 per family.[79] But the biggest cost to the government is Medicaid, which cost an additional $4,225 per single-parent family.[80] This means that the average level of benefits paid per single-parent family is approximately $8,750 and the total cost of these benefits to the government is about $107 billion. To be sure, these costs are small compared to what government spends on, say, Social Security, Medicare, or defense, but they are still significant.

Assuming that the number of single parents continues to rise, these costs will increase. Extrapolating from data for the past thirty years, I estimate that there will be more than 16 million single-parent families in 2030. If benefit levels remain at around $8,750 per family, this will cost the U.S. government approximately $116 billion per year in benefits to these families. If, however, benefits continue to increase at rates similar to the increases seen over the past ten years (as the result of rising health care costs in particular), the average benefit level per family could increase to about $9,300 by 2030, and the total costs to the government will be upwards of $123 billion.[81]

In addition to the need for these forms of cash and noncash assistance, single-parent families are disproportionate users of other services for themselves and their children, including special education, child care subsidies, Head Start, and child welfare services. No one should assume that reducing the growth of single-parent families would reduce spending on these kinds of services dollar-for-dollar, but it would reduce the need somewhat.

Child support payments from absent parents are intended to help single parents maintain their families or defray some of the costs now borne by government. However, their ability to do either is limited by incarceration, poor employment prospects, and low earnings of many fathers, and because it is difficult to collect court-awarded payments even from employed fathers. Recent years have seen stepped-up efforts to establish and collect child support from absent fathers, but the amounts are still quite modest, totaling about $32 billion a year.

In sum, too many young families with children are dependent on the rest of society to help make ends meet. If this were a small group, such dependence might not be a problem. But if such families continue to grow in numbers and become the majority, other families may rebel against the level of taxation needed to support them along with a growing number of elderly Americans.

Conclusions

The evidence cited in this chapter suggests three conclusions. First, marriage, on average, seems to increase adult happiness and welfare. At the same time, adults, especially women, have benefited from more choices about whether and when to marry or to have children, and from their greater ability to leave an unhappy marriage. Whatever the merits of marriage for the typical couple, the choice to marry or stay married should depend on individual circumstances. The shift from fault-based to no-fault divorce and the reduced stigma associated with divorce has, in my view, been good for adults.

Second, what is good for adults is not necessarily good for children. They have lost the stability and the commitment to their welfare that long-term marriages between their biological parents encouraged. There is a near-consensus about this in the academic and practitioner communities.

Third, these trends are imposing significant costs on taxpayers, costs that must be addressed in the context of thinking about where we are headed as a nation. Put most simply, if unwed childbearing and unstable relationships become the new norm, and if these produce a very large group of parents who cannot provide adequately for their own children without government assistance, the costs of socializing these new arrangements may prove to be unacceptable to the average taxpayer.

The resulting dilemma should be clear. How do we reconcile the needs of children with the desire of adults to leave an unhappy marriage or to never make a long-term commitment to the child's other parent in the first place?

Some people will look at these facts and call for a much more robust governmental effort to support single parents. Others believe that government has a role to play but that without more personal responsibility it will be impossible to turn the tide. For reasons that will become clearer in the following chapters, I count myself in the latter camp.

FOUR

A Growing Class Divide

It is the privileged Americans who are marrying, and marrying helps them stay privileged.

—Andrew Cherlin

Let me begin with a story about the diverging destinies of two young women.

The first young woman, Christina, graduated from high school and went on to attend community college, where she earned a certificate that enabled her to get a job with a beauty salon in her hometown. Robert, her boyfriend since high school, is a clerk at Target. Both are in their early twenties and very much in love. They have been spending much of their free time together, and when his lease expires he moves into her one-bedroom apartment to save on rent. Christina had been taking the pill but neglects to refill her prescription, partly because she is comfortable with their relationship and partly because she is convinced that it is the cause of those extra five pounds she's put on. When she accidentally gets pregnant, they agree that an abortion would be the wrong thing to do. They are worried about how they will manage with a baby, but at the same time a little excited about becoming parents. Although they hope to marry someday, they do not feel that they can afford to do so quite yet.

When Brendan is born, Christina prevails upon her sister to help look after him so that she can return to work.

Fast forward a few years. As they near 30, Christina and Robert now have a 4-year-old, a new baby, and a big stack of credit card bills. Christina is juggling her job with taking care of two young children. She pays a neighbor $100 a week to watch the children while she is at work. That $5,000, along with other work-related expenses, takes a big chunk out of her $25,000 annual earnings. Robert has had a series of low-wage jobs as well as some periods of unemployment, but contributes what he can toward paying the rent. He is discouraged, but is also spending more time than Christina would like watching television and hanging out with his friends. Just before Brendan's fifth birthday, they split up. Life is not easy, but Christina, Brendan, and the new baby try to make do on her modest salary. Christina worries that the long hours she has to spend on her job do not let her spend enough time with the children. Her sister has moved away, and she is trying to do the best she can with little or no help from Robert.

Compare this story with that of another young woman, Allison. When Allison enters high school, her mother has already begun researching colleges for her. When her junior year rolls around, they take an East Coast road trip to visit more than ten colleges, and Allison applies to seven of them. She ultimately chooses a private liberal arts college where she majors in computer programming. Upon graduation, she applies for many jobs and accepts a job at a start-up in California.

Her college boyfriend, Carlos, gets a job in Connecticut. They stay together for a year and a half, but living on different coasts is hard, and they eventually realize they need to make a decision about the future of their relationship. Carlos grew up in a large family with a stay-at-home mom and wants to have several children. Allison soon realizes that if they were to marry and have kids, she is the one who would have to sacrifice her career goals to accommodate becoming a parent. They mutually agree to break up. Allison later goes back to school for her master's degree and meets Jim in her second year of graduate school. He proposes upon graduation, and they get married shortly before her thirtieth birthday. They decide to have children before her biological clock reduces their chances of success. By the time Allison is 35, they have one toddler and a newborn infant. Allison is teaching at the local university now, which enables her to spend some time at home, and their two salaries make it feasible to afford high-quality child care.

The different trajectories of these two young women are shaped by different opportunities, but also by different choices. These different choices are creating a great diversity of family formation patterns and lifestyles for the youngest generation. And they are leading to a new class divide in America.

It used to be that most children, whether rich or poor, grew up in intact families.[1] That is no longer true. Nowadays the children's family environments and the kinds of parenting they receive are more likely than in the past to be determined by class. As the journalist Jonathan Rauch explained in a 2001 essay, "Marriage is displacing both income and race as the great class divide of the new century."[2]

Members of the youngest generation have more choices than ever where marriage and childbearing are concerned. Some of them are making wise choices both for themselves and for their children. Others are not. They are drifting into relationships and into childbearing. Unfortunately, the line that most often divides the two is social class.

In 2004, Sara McLanahan spoke to the Population Association of America about what she called "the diverging destinies" of children. She argued that the children of well-educated women were benefiting from the fact that their mothers were devoting both more time and more money to the task of raising the next generation, while the children of the less-educated were without such resources as a result of the kinds of changes described in chapter 2: delays in marriage and childbearing among the more-advantaged and an increase in cohabitation, divorce, and unwed childbearing among the less-advantaged.

Charles Murray sounded a similar alarm in his book *Coming Apart,* where he argued that the decline in marriage is at the heart of the problem.[3] Another researcher sounding the alarm is sociologist W. Bradford Wilcox, who writes, "Marriage is an emerging dividing line between America's moderately educated middle and those with college degrees."[4]

My own work has also focused on diverging destinies and a society that appears to be coming apart. I have argued that the bifurcation in children's early environments—defined by income, by education, and by family structure or home environment—implies larger economic and social divisions a few decades hence.[5] These inequalities in the circumstances of a child's birth are so highly intertwined that it may be more realistic and accurate to just call them differences in social class.[6]

A new book by June Carbone and Naomi Kahn on what they call "marriage markets" further reinforces the new class divisions in family formation patterns. The book was published just before my own went to press, so I cannot do it full justice here. I would simply note that it includes one of the best explanations of what has transpired as a combination of growing inequality in male earnings, women's new autonomy, and the way in which these have together affected cultural scripts and are reshaping the American family.[7]

Family Breakdown: No Longer Just about Race

In 1965, Daniel Patrick Moynihan wrote a report, "The Negro Family: The Case for National Action," that became a lightning rod for a contentious debate about the state of the black family.[8] Moynihan's thesis was that these families were highly unstable and that the absence of a father from so many was a recipe for social disorder. "The white family has achieved a high degree of stability," the report said; "By contrast, the family structure of lower class Negroes is highly unstable, and in many urban centers is approaching complete breakdown."[9]

Critics charged Moynihan with racism and blaming the victim, despite the fact that he had identified joblessness among young black males as the primary source of family instability. Few social scientists, however, have questioned his facts. By the 1960s, large proportions of black children were being born outside marriage, and single parenthood was far more common in the black community than among white Americans.

In retrospect, the Moynihan report seems almost prescient. What happened to the black family in earlier decades is now happening to white families. By 2000, the proportion of white children living in single-parent families was 22 percent—identical to the proportion of black children living in such families in 1960. Moreover, the reasons for the breakdown of marriage among whites are similar to the reasons for the breakdown among blacks. In both cases, joblessness among less-skilled men and relatively greater opportunities for women than for men appear to have played a role, along with changes in social norms that create a self-perpetuating cycle once certain behavioral patterns become commonplace.[10]

Although whites are following a marriage path similar to that of blacks in an earlier time, I do not want to overstate the similarities. Despite substantial racial progress since the 1960s, the gap between the marriage rates of blacks and whites has not narrowed much, if at all. In 2012, the proportion of black children born outside marriage was 72 percent; for whites the figure was 36 percent.[11] The deeper sources of the problem, rooted in a history of slavery and now massive incarceration, and the scars these have left, have been identified elsewhere but should not be forgotten.[12]

Whatever the causes, these differences in family structure are a major source of the continuing income gap between black and white families and help to explain the high poverty rates among black children. Part of the problem is what William Julius Wilson calls a lack of "marriageable males" in the black community, by which he means there are too few young men who are not incarcerated, dead, or jobless. When Adam Thomas and I tried to figure out how much of the child poverty gap was due to this lack of marriageable men, we found that Wilson was partially right. Using Census data, we tried to identify potential marriage partners for young African American women with children and discovered a dearth of suitable young men.[13]

Still, the fact that marriage rates have not converged despite considerable progress in providing greater opportunities for black men suggests to me that once marriage disappears, it is very hard to bring it back. What might have begun as an adaptation to discrimination and joblessness has now become at least partially embedded in the culture. Something similar may now be happening among working-class and lower-middle-class white Americans.

The New Class Divide

The story about racial differences in family structure is an old one. The new divide in American society is less about race and much more about class (although, of course, the two overlap).[14] Back in the 1950s and 1960s, most adults married, and most children could count on being raised in a two-parent family. In the twenty-first century, however, childbearing outside of marriage is not only common; it is close to being the new normal for young women without a college degree. Very disadvantaged women (those without a high school degree) have always had high rates of childbearing outside marriage. What is new is that middle America, meaning women with at least a high school degree, and often some college as well, are now having children outside marriage. In 2010, 58 percent of first births to women with either a high school degree or some college were out of wedlock, while for those with a college degree, the comparable statistic was only 12 percent.[15] The group of women without a college degree is large; it includes about two-thirds of the population.[16]

Musical Partnerships

Most of the research on how children fare when they grow up in a single-parent family was done during a period when the major source of single parenthood was still divorce and when children born outside of marriage ended up in a reasonably stable single-parent home. This research typically did not differentiate between children with well-educated, mature mothers who might have actually chosen to become a single parent and those who became mothers without planning to, and whose financial and personal resources were insufficient to raise a child on their own. When Vice President Dan Quayle criticized Murphy Brown, a TV character in a professional job, for having a baby outside of marriage, he stirred up a major controversy. But if all single parents looked like Murphy Brown, it is hard to imagine that single parenthood would be particularly worrisome. What is worrisome is the number of children who, besides being born outside marriage, are being subjected to a degree of relationship chaos and instability that is hard to grasp. Equally important, this is no longer just the small group of largely minority families concentrated in the inner city that so alarmed Senator Moynihan back in 1965 when he was writing about the black family.

These new patterns of family formation have now been detailed in a major survey, The Fragile Families and Child Wellbeing Study.[17] The Fragile Families survey began in 1998 and covered a representative sample of about 5,000 newborns in large and mid-size U.S. cities.[18] Both the mothers and fathers were interviewed at the time of their children's birth, and the mothers were re-interviewed when the children were ages 1, 3, 5, and 9.[19] Their children's health and well-being are assessed as well. The study includes both married and unmarried parents, but focuses especially on the latter. Keeping in mind that over 40 percent of all births now occur outside of marriage (and more than half of all births to women under 30 occur outside of marriage), I focus on the children born to these unmarried parents.

At the time the children were born, half of the parents were living together and another one-third were dating or were romantically involved. Only a small number of births resulted from a "one-night stand" or some other form of casual hookup. Many of the parents hoped to marry each other one day, but these good intentions were rarely realized. By the time their children were age 5, only one-third of these unmarried couples were still together, in contrast to 80 percent of their married counterparts.[20]

Most of these mothers went on to form new relationships and to have children with other men, sometimes with a series of different men. The fathers did the same with other women.[21] By the time their children were age 5, almost half of these mothers had split with the children's fathers and gone on to have another baby with a different man.[22] Strikingly, 23 percent of these unmarried mothers had children by two different fathers, 16 percent by three different fathers, and 8 percent by four or more fathers. Researchers call this "multiparent fertility" or "family complexity" or "the family-go-round" and are beginning to pay far more attention to its prevalence and its consequences for children.[23] Even if these mothers did not have children with another man, many of them had new live-in boyfriends, adding to the large amount of household instability in their children's lives. Adding together the proportion of these children whose mothers had new boyfriends and the proportion whose parents have had additional children with new partners, the study found that more than three-quarters (78 percent) of all the children initially born to unmarried parents experienced a major change in their household by the time they were age 5.[24]

This game of musical partners affects children in various ways. In comparison with parents in stable relationships, cohabiting couples invest less time and money in their children.[25] Mothers are likely to find the changes in their own relationships or household living arrangements stressful. This leads to harsher parenting and less time devoted to learning activities in the home.[26] The children end up with lower test scores and poorer physical and mental health than children in intact families, even after adjusting for other differences between the two groups.[27]

The loss of a biological father or substitution of a "social" father for a biological one may also be upsetting to the child. Some of these children have not just nonresidential fathers, but fathers they rarely see or do not even know. Fathers sometimes gravitate toward children they have parented most recently or who are the offspring of their current girlfriend, depriving their older biological children of any meaningful contact. There are residential moves and changes in routines and discipline to cope with. Relationships with friends and extended family members may be disrupted as well. Boys appear to be more adversely affected than girls.[28]

In recent years, as musical parenthood or the family-go-round has become more common, the focus has been less on the absence of a father and more on how family instability affects children. In fact, a stable single-parent family in which a child does not experience the constant comings and goings of new boyfriends (or girlfriends) or the addition of new half-siblings has begun to look like a better environment than musical parenthood.[29] When the adults involved end up with multiple children by different partners, they may have a larger number of children to support than if they had stuck with just one relationship. How this much change, complexity, and spreading of parental time and resources among different children will affect these children remains to be seen, but most experts are concerned that their life chances will be adversely affected. Children need not just financial security but also a certain amount of stability in their lives and their relationships if they are to develop secure and trusting ties with others.

Every time I read or hear about the data from the Fragile Families study, I have the same reaction: this cannot be a widespread set of behaviors. But I would be wrong. Here is the rough arithmetic: over 40 percent of all children in America are born outside marriage. Of those, about three-quarters will experience the kind of instability just described. That means that roughly one-third of all babies born in America are experiencing the "family-go-round." These data leave me hoping that children are far more resilient than we think.

Parenting in Poor Neighborhoods

If the Fragile Families group is having problems, they pale in comparison with what is happening in the poorest communities in America. Focusing on a much more disadvantaged group of families, Kathryn Edin and her colleagues have given us a richer and more granular picture of these families. These researchers have lived among and studied women and men in poor and working-class neighborhoods in Philadelphia and in Camden, New Jersey. Their findings have been reported in several spell-binding books that describe how young men and women in these neighborhoods meet, form casual relationships, have a baby together, and then typically break up after a short period to go their separate ways or establish new relationships.[30] Even when children are not planned or expected, once born they provide a great deal of meaning or sense of purpose to those whose opportunities are limited and whose lives are otherwise troubled. These young men and women say that they would like to marry someday, but they see marriage as something that you do after you have obtained the trappings of a middle-class life. It is a luxury that comes only after one has been successful in other domains. In the meantime, they do not see anything wrong with having children outside of marriage.

It would be easy to label this as a story about the poor economic prospects of those living in such communities, and economics is part of the story. But it may not be the biggest part.[31] After all, from a strictly financial perspective, these couples would be much better off if they pooled their earnings and shared household living expenses. Women do want to marry someone who has a regular paycheck. But their biggest worries center more on infidelity, domestic violence, substance abuse, and criminal behavior, and given the number of bad actors in their lives, their worries are not unfounded. Even when the men who father their children are not engaged in the more egregious forms of bad behavior, women want sufficient resources of their own to put them in a position to be able to bargain for the kind of respect and authority within the household that middle-class couples often take for granted. In professional circles, men have adapted in varying degrees to the new reality that women want to be viewed as equal partners in a marriage, but the feminist revolution seems to have bypassed low-income men. Women living in poor neighborhoods say they are not willing to marry until they have the personal resources to leave a marriage if it should turn out badly.[32] In the meantime, by insisting on maintaining their own households, these women are able to exert more control over their and their children's environment. Indeed, they often act as gatekeepers by denying a father access to his own children. This is not only a story about economics and the quality of relationships; it is also a story about the centrality of children in these poor communities. More-advantaged couples tend to put their own relationship first, with children being added after they have cemented that tie. In low-income communities, for both men and women, it is the other way around. The primary tie is between parent and child. The adult relationship is secondary and more readily put aside if it turns out badly. Because their prospects are limited to begin with, and unlikely to change very much with the birth of a child, the costs of early childbearing to poor women are not nearly as high as they might be for their better-educated counterparts. But beyond that, they attach great value to their role as mothers. Children are the one bright spot, and the human connection they most cherish, in their otherwise depressing or troubled lives.[33]

Somewhat surprisingly, this is true not just for the women in these communities, but for the men as well: "Men are drawn in—usually after the fact of conception—by the rare opportunity for a profound connection to another human being, a child of their own." The women who bear their children are not the lodestar of the story: "The old-fashioned 'package deal'—where the adult relationship takes priority and men's relationships with the children come second—has been flipped." The mother has become a conduit to a child. These men say that fatherhood gives them a chance to redeem themselves in the face of a variety of deviant behaviors, including crime, drug abuse, and other antisocial behaviors, or in some cases as a chance to do right by their children in contrast to what they experienced in their own childhoods, where fathers were often distant or unknown. "Doing right" does not necessarily mean being a successful provider. Indeed, they reject the idea that they should be treated as just a paycheck.[34] Instead, they appear to be resigned to the reality that it is the child's mother who is the chief breadwinner in the family. Their role is to pay a few of the household bills and to try to forge a relationship with the child on the side. However, since most of them have multiple children and rarely live with them, whatever their intentions, these children are growing up with only tenuous connections to their fathers. Put differently, for many, fatherhood is a symbolic role, not a day-to-day reality.

These highly distressed neighborhoods are a small slice of the population. For this reason they should not be viewed as broadly representative in the same way as the Fragile Families data cited earlier. Still, they represent a tragedy in the making. I come away from reading this literature believing that the men and women in these very poor urban communities are caught up in relationships that are, at best, shaky and lacking in depth, and at worst, conflict-ridden and toxic. Whatever the reasons for their behavior, one cannot help worrying about the impacts on the next generation, the children who are growing up without knowing any kind of stable family life. Will they be able to form stable relationships themselves when they have not experienced stability in their own lives?

The irony here is that children are highly valued in low-income neighborhoods, and one might expect them to benefit from this, despite a lack of material resources. Eventually I think this will redound to their benefit. But right now, given the hopelessness of their parents' environments, children in such communities are too often perceived as a source of adult validation, rather than a vulnerable group who need parents who can provide them with a stable environment.

Implications of the Divide for Social Mobility

The wider divide in American society between more- and less-educated young adults is significant. It adds family formation patterns to a whole host of other factors that advantage the children born to more successful parents. To be sure, better-educated adults with higher incomes have always been able to provide a leg up to their children. Now, the college-educated are not only earning more than the less-educated but are often delaying marriage until they are in their late twenties or early thirties. They are marrying other successful people, having children within marriage, and typically having one or two children. One recent study finds that the tendency of the well-educated to marry each other (what social scientists call "assortative mating"), combined with the ability of married women to earn far more than in the past, has increased income inequality by 25 percent.[35] It used to be that doctors married nurses and CEOs married their secretaries, and even when a highly educated man married a highly educated woman, the woman was unlikely to work. Now their combined incomes from work propel them into the upper ranks of the income distribution. Finally, these couples are investing heavily in their children and divorcing less frequently than in the 1970s and 1980s.

The other group—the majority of young adults—is having children outside of marriage, often in a cohabiting relationship. Sometimes members of this group marry after a few years, but more often they break up, form new relationships, and have children with a new partner.

In sum, family formation is a new fault line in the American class structure. When added to the existing fault lines of income and education, and all of the differences that these imply for access to information, connections to the broader community, parenting styles and expectations, and what social scientists call "cultural capital," it suggests that we may be headed for a more permanently divided society, one in which class lines are less flexible than in the past and upward mobility harder to achieve. Americans have always valued providing children with an equal opportunity to succeed in life. But these new patterns of family formation, and growing inequalities of income and education, are threatening that long-held principle.

I and others at the Brookings Institution have created a lifecycle model that we call the Social Genome Model.[36] The model incorporates a child's circumstances at birth, including whether that child is born to married parents, whether the mother is educated, and what is the family's income. We can then ask the model, "If more children were born in more favorable circumstances, how would this affect their life chances?" When we do this, we find that the children of continuously married mothers would do better on a whole host of later outcomes than those with discontinuously married mothers, who would do better, in turn, than those with never-married mothers (see figure 4 in the appendix).[37] For example, the probability that children born into the bottom fifth of household income will remain there as adults is 50 percent for those with never-married mothers, 32 percent for those with discontinuously married mothers, and 17 percent for those with continuously married mothers. These results should not be interpreted to mean that all we have to do is change family structure if we want to improve mobility. Marriage is correlated with many other factors that affect a child's life prospects. When we adjust for as many of these other factors as possible, family structure still has an effect on intergenerational mobility, but it is much smaller and we cannot exclude the possibility that it is spurious, since we cannot control for all of the unobserved differences between married and unmarried parents.

In a similar effort to look at what determines the social mobility of children living in different areas of the country, Raj Chetty and his colleagues found that family structure was one of the most important variables explaining mobility.[38] Geographic areas with low levels of upward mobility tend to have more children being raised by single mothers, even after adjusting for other factors. Not only are those who grow up in a single-parent household less upwardly mobile; those who grow up in *communities* with many single-parent households are also less mobile.

Still others have looked at the role of different parenting styles in producing unequal chances for children.[39] Well-educated mothers are more likely to be the helicopter moms, the ones who read and talk to their children, take them to museums, buy them educational toys, limit their TV time, and engage them in conversation. They tend to adopt a warm and responsive style of parenting, comforting their children when necessary and challenging them to be inquisitive and learn new things. They see their role as not just caring for the physical safety and well-being of their children but also teaching them strategies for success. They involve them in a multitude of stimulating experiences outside the home, from dance and music lessons to sports and scouting. Well-educated parents spend more time with their children than the less well-educated. Even after adjusting for employment or hours of work, mothers with a college degree spend twice as much time with their children as mothers with less than a high school degree.[40] Moreover, educated moms are more likely to tailor what they do with their children to the child's interests and readiness to learn; they appear to have absorbed the message that the early years are the most important and are especially likely to invest time in child-oriented activities during this period.

Less-educated parents, in contrast, are more laissez-faire, more likely to believe that beyond caring for the physical needs of their children, little else is required for the children to thrive. Working-class parents tend to be more authoritarian, drawing brighter lines between what children should and should not be allowed to do, but they are also more content to let children just be children. Their children tend to be more obedient, less bored, and less likely to whine than those from more-advantaged homes.[41]

The gap between time and resources devoted to children by more-educated and less-educated parents has increased since the 1980s.[42] In part because of these differences in parenting styles, gaps in children's competencies open up very early in life, as early as 9–18 months of age. For example, a 2013 study found gaps in language skills even in infancy. At 18 months, children from high-income households recognized the meaning of common words such as "dog" or "ball" much more readily than children from lower-income households. These gaps grow over time—in the period between 18 months and 2 years, children in more affluent families learn 30 percent more words than children from lower-income families.[43]

Using the Social Genome Model, we have looked at the impact of parenting on children's later success. We use a well-validated measure of parenting called the HOME scale. It captures both the amount of learning materials and activities in the home, and how emotionally responsive parents are to their children, based on the mother's answers to a series of questions and interviewer observations in the home. We divide parents into two groups: the 25 percent with the weakest parenting skills and the 25 percent with the strongest skills. We find that parenting skills are strongest among those with the highest incomes and the most education, and among parents who are older, white, and married. Forty-four percent of single mothers fall into the weakest category and only 3 percent in the strongest category.[44]

The weak parenting skills found among single parents are related not only to the lack of a second parent but also to their lack of income and education. Education, in particular, stands out as the most critical factor in explaining poor parenting. But it is not clear that we should look at these variables in isolation from one another. In real life, single parents tend to be poorer than married parents (because there is not a second earner in the family) and less well educated (in part because early childbearing interrupts or discourages education). To be sure, one can find good and bad parents in any social stratum. Nonetheless, the research suggests that the class-based (and relatedly the race-based) divide is real and that its implications for social mobility are large. As Reeves and Howard note, "the parenting gap is a contributor to the opportunity gap."[45]

By the end of adolescence, three out of four children with the strongest parents in our study graduated from high school with decent grades and without having been convicted of a crime or giving birth. The corresponding proportion for the children who experienced weak parenting during early childhood was 30 percent. When we simulated the effects of turning weak parents into average parents, holding other things constant, we estimated that 9 percent more of their children would have graduated from high school and have had fewer teen births and fewer run-ins with the law.[46]

It will never be possible to break the link between parental advantages and those that accrue to their children. Some of the linkage is related to the fact that parents and children share the same genes. Even were it possible to compensate for genetic advantages, interfering with the rights of parents to provide their children with the best possible environments would be an inappropriate intrusion into a very private realm. That said, parents are a child's first teachers, and the growing gaps in opportunity caused by the breakdown of the family and the different parenting styles of different types of families, if left unaddressed, will likely make any effort to equalize opportunity less than fully successful.

Conclusions

The growing class divide in family formation patterns is now well recognized. At one end of the spectrum we have well-educated men and women delaying the process of family formation, marrying each other, having children within marriage, and investing heavily in their children. At the other end of the spectrum, we have less-educated men and women who are doing just the opposite: having children early and outside of marriage, frequently with more than one partner, and remaining stuck at the bottom of the ladder.

The most troublesome aspect of the divide is not just the rise in childbearing outside of marriage, but the lack of stability in the resulting families. They typically break up relatively quickly, and the adults in them go on to form new partnerships and have additional children with their new partners. Although this pattern is not yet universal, it is widespread enough to spark alarm among most observers. Among the college-educated members of the youngest generation, the success sequence is still intact. First you finish school (and for the most advantaged that now includes college, not just high school), then you settle into a job or a career. Later you marry, and only then do you have children.[47] The important point is that the success sequence no longer applies to the majority of 20-somethings in the United States. It is still alive and well only among the one-third of the population that has a college degree. Middle America has taken a different path on the journey to adulthood.

I have defined class in terms of income, education, family structure, and parenting, since the four are so intertwined. Current inequalities in all four of these domains threaten to turn the United States into a more permanently divided society. As the rungs on the socioeconomic ladder grow farther apart, it becomes harder for children at the bottom to climb the ladder. Children born at different levels experience very different life trajectories that have dramatic implications for their chances of adult success. The research on this topic is not dispositive, since we cannot predict the future. But all of the research summarized in this chapter suggests that the circumstances of a child's birth affect the child's eventual success, and that as these circumstances diverge, so will children's chances of upward mobility.

These predictions would have much less validity if they had not been supplemented by an outpouring of more detailed research on unmarried parents. This research from the Fragile Families study has provided new insights into what is happening to childbearing and relationships—in both poor America and middle America. Young adults are no longer constrained by social strictures that once condemned childbearing outside of marriage, but many—the drifters—appear to lack some of the basic decisionmaking competencies that these new freedoms require for success. The planners—primarily well-educated elites—in contrast, have adopted family patterns and competencies that are well suited to what a modern economy requires. These competencies include the ability to plan, to defer gratification, and to develop the interpersonal skills that make relationships work at home as well as on the job. The outward manifestations of that planning include getting a good education, finding and keeping a steady job, and delaying childbearing.

Liberals will label these conclusions "blaming the victim" and chalk up self-defeating behaviors to a lack of opportunity. Conservatives will attribute all or most of the problem to deficits of character and culture. My own view is that each individual case is different, but usually both economics and culture play a role.[48] Brink Lindsey and David Brooks have both written in an insightful way about how the two factors interact, but each argues that, in the end, culture matters.[49] As Lindsay notes,

> We are uncomfortable acknowledging this truth precisely because we realize that a person's norms, beliefs, values, and habits are a constitutive part of her identity. And so, when we criticize cultural traits on the ground that they undercut socioeconomic achievement, we can't help but feel abashed that we are disrespecting people by denigrating things that matter to them on a deeply personal level.

He goes on to say that this discomfort stems from a healthy liberal respect for pluralism and for "a humble aversion to telling people that we know their true interests better than they do."[50] Amen. That is the dilemma.

I end this chapter with a few additional observations. First, the decline in manufacturing and other jobs for less-skilled men has surely played some role. But as noted earlier, it cannot explain more than a small fraction of the behaviors described here. Male earnings have declined a bit, but women are earning more. Together, less-advantaged couples are still financially better off than any prior generation. Scholars who point to joblessness or men's earnings as the main source of the problem for the half of the population that is no longer marrying before having babies are putting too big a burden on this explanation. If today's young men are not marriageable, it is not just because well-paid jobs have dried up. Their difficulties reflect a host of other changes in the culture, including the fact that men have lost their positions of authority and status as women have asserted theirs.[51]

Second, social norms have undergone a dramatic transformation. Premarital sex and unwed births are no longer stigmatized. Although people still disapprove of women raising children on their own, even this norm is no longer operative among a broad swath of the population. Two people having children together outside of marriage is simply no big deal. It is what many people now do—even in the middle class.

In much poorer communities, having a child adds meaning to one's life. Relationships between adults, by contrast, are more fragile and expendable—a sad fact and one that is inconsistent with what is best for their children. The problem is not a lack of desire to do well by their children; the problem is a failure to turn that aspiration into a reality. By appealing to the desire among low-income parents to give their children a chance for a better life, we might still turn the tide.

It may not be feasible to bring back marriage as the normative standard for raising children. The next chapters examine why efforts to restore a marriage culture have not worked, and why we are, in my view, beyond the tipping point at which a social trend of this magnitude can be easily reversed. I am more hopeful that efforts to improve education and reduce unplanned pregnancies and births—along with the drift into multiple relationships that unplanned pregnancies produce—can be tackled. My hope is for a future in which far more children are brought into the world *after* their parents have formed a stable relationship and are prepared to be the kind of parents they seem to want to be. At that point, but not before, marriage or something like it might well come back into favor.

FIVE

Traditionalists and Village Builders

The truth is, the greatest tool to lift children and families from poverty . . .
isn't a government spending program. It's called marriage.

—Marco Rubio

It takes a village to raise a child.

—African Proverb

Almost everyone is surprised to learn that unwed childbearing is the new normal. The great crossover sums up the situation: the average age of marriage is now later than the average age at which women have a first baby. The baby carriage now comes before the ring. And fewer and fewer people are even bothering with the ring. With the exception of college-educated elites, young adults are drifting into relationships and into childbearing without marriage.

Some believe this trend is benign, but most people—including most experts—find it troubling. As Ron Haskins and I put it in our book *Creating an Opportunity Society,* "Some claim that anyone who is concerned about these trends is simply out of touch with modern culture; we respond that if that be the case, then 'modern culture is out of touch with the needs of children.'"[1] New choices for adults have not generally been helpful to the well-being of children, and in too many cases have

83

been harmful. In this chapter, I consider the role government has played in shaping these trends, and what it could do to deal with the unintended consequences for both adults and children.

In the debate over these questions, people tend to fall into one of two camps: the "traditionalists" or the "village builders." The first group, the traditionalists, wants to bring back marriage, believing that it is a historically tested and successful institution for raising children. The second group, the village builders, believes that single parents are here to stay and that the most appropriate response is to provide them with greater assistance in the difficult job of raising children on their own. The question, in the end, is how far we should go as a society in taking collective responsibility for the raising of children.

Both the traditionalists and the village builders make good arguments and have proposed sensible solutions. But as the review in this chapter suggests, their solutions may not fully achieve the goals they have set.

The Traditionalists

Traditionalists believe that without strong families, societies crumble. Senator Rick Santorum says that "the family is the foundation of our civilization."[2] As a corollary, many conservatives believe that government does more harm than good, because in too many instances it tries to replace the family instead of strengthening it.

Traditionalists run the gamut from religious conservatives and politicians, such as Richard Land and Rick Santorum, to secular writers and experts, such as Wade Horn, Kay Hymowitz, David Blankenhorn, Charles Murray, Mitch Pearlstein, Barbara Dafoe Whitehead, Bradford Wilcox, and Ron Haskins. There are important differences among them, but what they all share is a deep concern about the fragmentation of the family and its implications for adults and especially for children. Government must take care, in this view, not to undermine the family's role by replacing it with welfare programs or other supports that enable parents to avoid taking responsibility for themselves and their children. It should not liberalize divorce laws or allow family planning and abortion policies to undermine the values of caution and delay, or the institution of marriage itself.

New York Times columnist Ross Douthat has nicely articulated this view. The social revolutions of the 1970s, he says,

> [stripped away] the most explicit cues and rules linking sex, marriage, and childrearing, and nudging people toward the two-parent bourgeois path. No longer would the law make any significant effort to enforce marriage vows. No longer would an unplanned pregnancy impose clear obligations on the father. No longer would the culture industry uphold the "marriage-then-childbearing" script as normative or endorse any moral script around sexuality save the rule of consenting adults.[3]

Less moderate and more religiously oriented conservatives (or at least their leaders), including many Roman Catholics, Evangelical Protestants, Mormons, and Orthodox Jews, not only support traditional families but often the more patriarchal forms of the family. They urge not just procreation within marriage, and marriage as a sacred commitment between one man and one woman, but also restoring men as leaders, protectors, and sources of authority within their families. As one leader of Promise Keepers, the 1990s movement to reinvolve men in their families, put it:

> The primary cause of this national crisis [the decline of the family] is the feminization of the American male. . . . The first thing you do is sit down with your wife and say something like this: "Honey, I've made a terrible mistake. I've given you my role. I gave up leading the family, and forced you to take my place. Now I must reclaim that role."[4]

In his fascinating book about this culture and the role of religion in encouraging or tolerating certain behaviors such as stricter parenting or less egalitarian gender roles, Bradford Wilcox finds evidence that churchgoing conservative Protestant men are what he calls "soft patriarchs." Soft patriarchs have resisted the social changes occurring in the rest of society, especially where gender equality and more permissive parenting is concerned. They hold strong and religiously based views about the sanctity of a marriage between one man and one woman, in which the man is the breadwinner and the head of the family while his wife subordinates her own interests to her domestic responsibilities as a wife and mother.

However, they also engage in less domestic violence and are often very involved in their families.[5] This group tends to be concentrated in the South, to be of lower socioeconomic status, and to be part of a community that, ironically, experiences high rates of divorce and unwed births.

Indeed, the paradox is that conservative attitudes may have contributed to more single-parent families. Conservatives' belief in abstinence from sex until marriage, discomfort with discussing or providing contraception, and strong opposition to abortion has likely led to more unplanned pregnancies and more births outside of marriage. The paradox is documented in a book by Naomi Kahn and June Carbone, *Red Families v. Blue Families*.[6] They describe it as the "Bristol Palin effect," citing vice presidential candidate Sarah Palin's teenage daughter's pregnancy as an example of how these views play out across the political spectrum. Conservative women praised the Palins for sticking to their values and not arranging a quiet abortion to prevent an out-of-wedlock birth to Bristol—a decision that was sure to roil her mother's political campaign. Liberals, in contrast, were shocked that it was considered a good idea for a 17-year-old to be raising a child on her own. They also fail to understand why pro-life conservatives have not embraced contraception as the most effective way of preventing abortion.

The coupling of traditional gender roles and marriage in the values of some religious conservatives has, of course, caused heartburn among most feminists. In response, some of the more moderate defenders of marriage are careful to avoid sounding like they are turning back the clock on women's new roles and the more egalitarian relationships that these have spawned.

Nonetheless, these mainstream traditionalists argue fiercely, and often very effectively, for marriage as an institution. A good example is a report put out by the National Marriage Project and the Institute for American Values in 2012.[7] It states, "Marriage is not merely a private arrangement; it is also a complex social institution. Marriage fosters small cooperative unions—also known as stable families—that enable children to thrive, shore up communities, and help family members to succeed during good times and to weather the bad times."[8] The report goes on to offer a set of recommendations to America's leaders, including the president, on how to restore marriage. Their marriage agenda includes eliminating marriage penalties and disincentives in tax and benefit programs, and tripling the child tax credit. They argue for making young men more marriageable by offering them apprenticeships or job training, and also for marriage education and relationship strengthening programs in the military and the criminal justice system. It is a thoughtful and serious set of proposals. But how does this agenda contrast with that of the village builders?

The Village Builders

In her book *It Takes a Village,* Hillary Clinton argues that children are too important to be raised only by their parents. The book's title is drawn from an African proverb and reflects the fact that in many societies, children are raised by many adults, not just by their parents. In Clinton's words, "children are not rugged individualists. . . . All of us, whether we acknowledge it or not, are responsible for deciding whether our children are raised in a nation that doesn't just espouse family values but values families and children."[9] While calling for such policies as paid family leave, an increase in the child tax credit during a child's first year of life, early childhood education, more subsidized health care for children, and more family-friendly workplaces, Clinton does not shy away from balancing this public agenda against the importance of parents' own responsibility for children and the role that they can play, for example, in preventing substance abuse, encouraging sexual abstinence among teens, and providing positive role models to their children. But families exist within a larger society that must take some responsibility for helping parents to raise their children. Families cannot do this alone. Without the right supports from the larger community, whether in the form of jobs, health care, child care, or other assistance, families will not flourish. Single parents, in particular, need the support of the larger society if they and their children are to make ends meet.

Feminist economist Nancy Folbre has written extensively on the need for liberals to embrace family values. She does not mean the traditional conservative definition of family values, but rather "love, obligation, and reciprocity"—the work of caring for others. The task of caring for families has traditionally been done by women on a voluntary and unpaid basis. As a result, it has not only been devalued in the marketplace (child care workers are notoriously low-paid) but has reinforced the dependence of women on men within traditional families. The solution, according to Folbre, is to both recognize the high value of the work of raising the next generation and socialize more of the costs. Though she recognizes the pitfalls of moving too far in this direction, Folbre argues that the government needs to take a larger role in valuing care work through policies such as providing paid parental leave, extending public education to the youngest children, and eliminating the so-called marriage penalty in the tax code along with creating a more steeply progressive income tax.[10]

Village builders also differ from traditionalists in their diagnosis of the causes of the class divide and the reasons for such behaviors as childbearing outside of marriage. They argue that individual choices are shaped and constrained by a lack of opportunity, that you cannot change people's choices significantly unless you change the village they live in. As sociologist and liberal pundit Melissa Harris-Perry puts it, "Poverty is evidence of a deficit of resources, not a deficit of character."[11] This view of the world suggests that poverty and joblessness are what lead to poor choices, not the other way around. The solution, then, is to do something about these issues, not wring our hands about the decline of marriage.

The public is divided on the right balance between public and private responsibility for families. Sixty-four percent believe that government should provide more support for single-parent families and help these mothers and their children to succeed. Fifty-one percent think that government should set a goal of reducing the number of children born into single-parent families and use its resources to encourage marriage or two-parent families.[12]

As I discuss below, each of these philosophies plays out more concretely in such policy arenas as welfare, taxes, and education. Moreover, each has a mixed record of success.

Welfare Reform

Traditionalists view welfare and other government assistance programs as being anti-family, providing an incentive for, or enabling, women to have babies outside of marriage, and leading to the growth of single-parent families. For these reasons, marriage and unwed childbearing were a major focus of welfare reform in 1996 and a key impetus for the conservative push to limit or deny benefits to single parents, especially to unwed teens.

The Aid to Families with Dependent Children (AFDC) program was originally enacted in the 1930s and was designed primarily for widows. But beginning in the 1950s, the dramatic increase in single-parent families, most of whom were not widows but women who were divorced or had children out of wedlock, led to a public backlash against the program and fed the conservative argument that public aid was undermining the family. Conservative voices, such as that of Charles Murray, contended that welfare was an important cause of the growth in single-parent families and that the solution was to deny assistance to young unwed mothers.[13] President Clinton, sensing that the public wanted to see something done to curtail assistance to these mothers, campaigned in 1992 on a plan to "end welfare as we know it" and to move people from welfare to work. A bill reforming the system along these lines was enacted in 1996 with bipartisan support. Conservatives did not get everything they wanted, such as the elimination of aid for unwed teen mothers, but the legislation went a long way toward establishing the principle that welfare should be what Clinton called a "way station" and not "a way of life." Welfare (now called Temporary Assistance for Needy Families, or TANF) would be coupled with time limits on the number of years a family could receive assistance and work requirements for the mother. The law also included provisions that required greater efforts to collect court-ordered child support from absent fathers, to strengthen marriage, and to reduce unwed births.[14] Especially controversial was a section of the law promoting abstinence for teenagers and requiring states to abide by its guidelines if they wanted federal funds for sex education in their communities.

This debate and the ensuing legislation spawned a flood of research on the effects of welfare on the growth of single-parent families. The results were by no means definitive but tended to show that any effects of welfare benefits on divorce or unwed childbearing were modest at best.[15] It is doubtful that many women made a calculation that they should have a child or seek a divorce because of the government benefits they would then receive. It is more likely that the availability of that assistance enabled them to make the choice to leave a troubled relationship or continue a pregnancy that they wanted or deemed appropriate for some other reason. The fact that single mothers are now required to work and the fathers of their children are required to provide more child support may have made both think twice before bringing a child into the world. For these reasons, I would not rule out the possibility that this change in government policy has had some modest effects on family formation patterns.[16] All in all, however, it is hard to see strong evidence of this in the data.

Child Support Enforcement

Men as well as women face perverse incentives to have children outside of marriage. If you can father a child and not be responsible for its support, there is little reason to avoid paternity. Traditionalists are inclined to crack down on "deadbeat dads." Liberals, by contrast, tend to be more sympathetic to the fact that, in the words of Kathryn Edin and Timothy Nelson, fathers are usually "doing the best they can."

Low-income inner-city fathers may be doing the best they can, but they are not often doing a lot. Many are irregularly employed or incarcerated. Some have fathered multiple children with different mothers. They may be supporting some of their children but not providing for all of them. Edin and Nelson describe a man who "freely admits he hasn't paid a penny in official child support to the mothers of either of his two older children. . . . Still, he insists, he provides. Occasionally, he'll give his seventeen-year-old son 'little dollars or fives' or, more rarely, spring for a pair of sneakers or jeans the boy may need."[17] Most of the fathers Edin and Nelson talked to believed that fathers ought to play a role in their children's lives. But the consensus among these men was that the mothers of their children were the primary providers, with the fathers providing supplemental income when they could.

The haphazard nature of unofficial child support is what led to federal and state involvement in establishing paternity and enforcing child support payments from absent fathers back in 1975. The 1996 welfare reform law included a large push to improve child support enforcement, and these improvements, particularly in paternity establishment procedures, significantly increased child support payments to low- and middle-income mothers.[18] Between 1995 and 2012, child support collections more than doubled from $12 billion per year to $32 billion per year, almost certainly reflecting provisions in the 1996 law.[19]

Nonetheless, the situation remains dismal. In 2011, only 35 percent of all single mothers received any child support, and among single mothers living in poverty, the proportion was lower: only 29 percent. The payments to these mothers are typically small; even excluding mothers who get no payments, the average payment to an unmarried mother is around $4,500 per year (see figure 5 in the appendix), and the average payment for low-income mothers is even smaller.[20] Obviously, this is a drop in the bucket of what it takes to raise a family.

The current child support system does appear to have had some positive impacts. Stronger efforts to establish paternity and meet state guidelines on the amount of support that should be paid by an absent parent have reduced unwed birth rates by one or two percentage points, according to one study.[21] At the same time, there are limits to how much additional money can be collected given the unstable job histories, low earnings, and high levels of incarceration among many of these fathers.

Marriage Education

In 2002, the George W. Bush administration launched the Healthy Marriage Initiative, which funded programs to encourage or sustain marriage among low-income families. One of these programs, the Building Strong Families program, was aimed at low-income unwed couples who had had a baby together. They received relationship skills education and family support services, such as help with employment or health problems. Supporting Healthy Marriage was a similar program, but targeted at already married couples rather than unwed parents.

Now more than ten years later, the verdict is in. These programs have not been very effective. A rigorous evaluation of Building Strong Families found that, after three years, it had no effect on the quality of couples' relationships and did not make couples more likely to stay together or get married. Not only did it not improve co-parenting, it had a slightly negative effect on fathers' involvement both in terms of time spent with the child and financial support.[22] The Supporting Healthy Marriage project's evaluations were slightly more encouraging: the program resulted in small positive effects on relationship quality (for example, maternal happiness, warmth, and support) and less psychological or physical abuse. But the program had no significant effect on whether a couple was still together at the end of one year.[23] Given the high costs of the program ($9,100 per couple), these small effects are not very impressive. Village builders argue that spending the same amount of money on other anti-poverty programs, such as the earned income tax credit or child care, would have greater benefits. Based on this evidence, my view is that government does not know how to produce stable marriages. That doesn't mean marriage isn't important. Indeed, I have long argued that to stay out of poverty, individuals need to follow three steps: graduate from high school, work full-time, and wait until after age 21 to get married and have children (in that order). In *Creating an Opportunity Society,* Ron Haskins and I called this "the success sequence" and suggested embarking on a social marketing campaign to encourage young people to finish school, get a job, marry, and only then have children.[24] We showed that if people followed these three simple guidelines, only 2 percent would be poor.[25] The National Marriage Project's 2012 "State of Our Unions" report called for similar guidelines. When Mitt Romney started using our message and data in his 2012 presidential campaign, I knew we had struck a nerve. But where I part company with traditionalists is in thinking that marriage education programs are an effective strategy for reviving marriage. I am much more sympathetic to government leaders using the bully pulpit or funding nonprofit organizations to produce new messages about the value of the success sequence.

Marriage Penalties

Because the personal income tax is based on a family's total income rather than how much each individual earns, and because tax rates are progressive (rising as total income rises), individuals sometimes find that their tax bill rises when they marry. That is, they pay more, in total, to Uncle Sam once married than they did when they were single because the addition of a second income puts them in a higher tax bracket. In addition, when two people marry and combine their incomes, they may lose eligibility for some benefit programs, such as the earned income tax credit, Medicaid, food stamps (SNAP), or housing assistance. These disincentives to marry in the tax and benefit system are called "marriage penalties." For low- or moderate-income single parents these penalties can be large.[26]

While these marriage penalties and subsidies can, in principle, affect people's decisions about whether to marry, in practice they likely have minor effects at best. Research on the topic has not been able to find a smoking gun proving that such penalties have adverse effects.[27] Still, marriage penalties and subsidies embedded in law do signal what the government values, and for this reason there have been legislative efforts to reduce the penalties. In addition to reducing marriage penalties, traditionalists like the idea of providing benefits to families with children through the tax system. They doubled the child tax credit from $500 to $1,000 per child in 2001. But they resisted making the child tax credit refundable so that families at the bottom of the income scale who pay little or no income tax might benefit. Despite their resistance, a partially refundable child tax credit was included in the 2001 tax law, along with the doubling of the regular child tax credit and an attempt to reduce marriage penalties.

The Joint Committee on Taxation estimates that the cumulative cost of marriage-penalty-directed tax cuts in the three Bush-era tax bills over the period 2001 to 2011 was $114 billion.[28] As this figure makes clear, such efforts are seriously constrained by the cost of eliminating penalties, since reducing them means extending benefits or tax relief much further up the income scale. And given a lack of evidence that these changes in tax law have had any significant effect on behavior, they must be justified primarily on the grounds that married families, as a matter of equity, should not pay higher taxes than those who are unmarried—and that those with children should pay lower taxes than those without. In other words, almost no one believes these tax provisions will restore the institution of marriage.

My own view is that, over the longer run, a better way to reduce marriage penalties is to base taxes and benefit programs less on total family income and more on the income or earnings of the individual.[29] This policy would be better aligned with the kind of constantly shifting household arrangements that have become so prevalent in recent decades and are likely to be ever more common in the future.

Making Men More Marriageable

As noted earlier, men's employment and earnings have stalled or declined over the past three decades, while women have fared much better. Women are graduating from college in larger numbers, moving up the occupational ladder at a faster pace than men, and with few exceptions, their earnings have continued to rise while men's have tended to fall.[30]

These trends have led both village builders and traditionalists to conclude that if we could only make men more employable, marriage would revive as well.[31] The solution, they argue, is to provide more education and training, more job opportunities, and more wage subsidies to less-educated men. These are all good ideas, in principle, and should be supported, in my view, because of their effects on the well-being of men and their families. But will they work to bring back marriage? About that I am somewhat more skeptical.

First, the evidence suggests that improvements in men's economic prospects would have very small effects on marriage.[32] For example, one study finds that even a very large improvement in male earnings would increase the proportion of unmarried couples who would marry within one year of their child's birth from 9 to only 10.6 percent.[33] Second, the track record of programs designed to improve the employment or earnings of men is mixed.[34] While training programs for disadvantaged adult women have had positive effects, the results for adult men have been less encouraging, and those for youth so unimpressive that the government reduced its funding of these efforts in the 1990s.

Although most past programs to boost the skills and employability of disadvantaged men have had disappointing effects, some recent efforts are more encouraging. Community colleges and some high schools are experimenting with new models of career and technical training, which, when linked to the skills that employers need, appear to be our best shot at improving the job prospects of men. A good example is the Career Academies program, which is now operating in hundreds of public high schools. The Career Academies combine regular high school courses with a sequence of more career-oriented or technical courses. They expose students through internships or other forms of work-based learning to real-world applications of what they are learning in school. The program has increased the earnings of male graduates relative to a control group, as well as the likelihood that these male graduates will be married with children by the age of 26.[35] By expanding such efforts, while maintaining the qualities that have made them successful, future graduates should be better prepared for college or a career, and also better prepared for marriage and parenthood. My guess is that Career Academies have had such positive effects on marriage because they boosted the earnings of participants and helped them to learn a specific skill, find a secure or stable niche in the job market, and garner the respect that such a skill, along with a more stable employment history, confers on its holder.

While they successfully boosted the earnings of young men, Career Academies had no impact on the earnings of young women. This brings me to my third concern about an agenda devoted to making men more marriageable. Why focus just on men? Although women have done some catching up, they still earn less than men. If women had more education and better job prospects, they would be less likely to settle for early motherhood. And should they end up as single mothers, they would be better able to support their children.

Improving Education

We need to improve the education and thus the employment prospects of *both* men and women. With more education, both men and women will not only be more employable but will be better motivated to defer childbearing, more likely to form stable relationships (including perhaps marriage), and more likely to be better parents.[36]

A full discussion of what is needed to transform the education system into a more effective vehicle for accomplishing these objectives is beyond the scope of this book, but reform could include more resources coupled with more accountability for results, more effective teachers in the classroom, and more innovation via online learning and charter schools.[37]

Those efforts need to involve not just teaching academic skills but also a variety of noncognitive skills such as persistence and self-discipline, which are increasingly recognized as critical to success in life.[38]

In the meantime, there are effective programs that are already helping the less-advantaged to succeed in school. In our work with the Social Genome Model we have shown that if a number of proven programs were expanded to all low-income families, their lifetime income prospects would improve. We estimate that the extra income they received would greatly exceed the up-front costs of the programs.[39]

Strengthening the Safety Net

If, as many village builders contend, the problem is not the breakdown of the family but rather the poverty that produces it, then the solution is to end poverty—or at least to lend a helping hand to those who are its casualties.

Single-parent families are already quite dependent on public benefits, relying on cash and noncash assistance for 28 percent of their total income. Despite this assistance, large proportions are still living in poverty.[40] These families, village builders argue, are here to stay, and their high rates of poverty can only be alleviated if public benefits are expanded, along with efforts to help them become more self-sufficient. The federal government spent about $762 billion on means-tested payments in 2011.[41] These benefits make a huge difference in the lives of the lowest-income mothers. The average income of a single mother in the bottom income fifth of single-parent families is $4,000 to $5,000 per year. When all government taxes and benefits are taken into consideration, that average jumps to about $9,000.[42]

Additional help could come in the form of increases in cash assistance or noncash benefits such as Medicaid, food assistance (SNAP), housing subsidies, and child care subsidies. In *Creating an Opportunity Society*, Ron Haskins and I argued for making some of these supports more generous while also linking them more closely to work or other evidence of personal responsibility. The EITC, for example, is only available to those who are employed and has encouraged a big increase in employment among single mothers.[43] However, the likelihood of an increase in such supports happening in today's political and fiscal environment is extremely low. Programs such as SNAP, housing subsidies, and Head Start have already been casualties of the partisan divide in budget negotiations during the 112th and 113th sessions of Congress. Some state governments opposed to the Affordable Care Act have refused funds to expand Medicaid, leaving many low-income Americans without insurance coverage.

My own view is that America's safety net is badly frayed and needs strengthening. But I do not think that doing so will slow the growth of single-parent families. The demographic tide is strong, and for every child removed from poverty by a social program another one is likely to enter as families continue to fragment.

Child Care and Family-Friendly Workplaces

One way to help single-parent families is to supplement their incomes. Another way is to make it easier for them to be both good parents and good workers. Village builders want to do both. Traditionalists worry that this means expanding the role of government into areas where it does not belong.

Just about everyone agrees that balancing work and parenting is difficult. The number of women who are either the sole support or the main breadwinner for their families has shot up and now encompasses almost 40 percent of all mothers. Another quarter are co-breadwinners.[44] What role should government play in alleviating the time crunch that comes with trying to work and raise children at the same time?

Currently, the United States does very little to help parents cope with their dual responsibilities. In 1993, President Bill Clinton signed the Family and Medical Leave Act (FMLA), which requires employers to let their workers take up to twelve weeks of job-protected unpaid leave. Workers can use this leave to care for a new child (newborn or adopted), to recover from a grave illness, or to care for a gravely ill family member. Because smaller employers are exempted, only about 60 percent of all workers in the country are eligible.[45] In addition, because the leave is unpaid, many workers cannot afford to take it even if they qualify.[46] Mothers who cannot afford to give up the income may return to the workforce sooner than is best for both themselves and their children.[47]

The United States also has no federal policy requiring employers to provide paid sick leave in the case of personal or family illness.[48] Too often, parents are forced to send their children to school sick because they cannot afford a day off from work to care for them. Workers without paid sick leave are 1.5 times more likely to go to work while contagious than those with paid leave, resulting not just in lower on-the-job productivity due to illness but also increased health risks for those around them.[49] Ninety percent of food-service workers do not get any paid sick leave, and 70 percent of restaurant workers report cooking, preparing, or serving food while sick. Lack of access to paid leave contributed to the higher incidence of the H1N1 flu virus during the pandemic in 2009.[50]

Even when workers and their children are healthy, child care expenses still loom large in family budgets. Low-income families with children under the age of 5 spend over half of their monthly income on child care.[51] The federal government assists needy parents through the Child Care and Development Block Grant Fund, which provides matching grants to the states with which to subsidize child-care expenses for low-income families. However, there has never been sufficient funding to cover more than a small proportion of the need, and only one in six eligible children received child care assistance in 2009, the most recent year for which data are available.[52] In addition, the Child and Dependent Care tax credit allows parents to claim up to a $6,000 credit on taxes to offset the costs of paid child care, but this benefit is only available to families with sufficient income tax liability to take advantage of the deduction. One way to overcome this disadvantage is to make the credit refundable.[53] Early education programs, such as Head Start, enroll low-income children in comprehensive programs that have the dual purpose of improving children's school readiness and enabling their parents to work. (In *Creating an Opportunity Society,* we argued for more support for both early childhood education and child care, financed in part by phasing out the child care tax subsidies that currently go to high-income families.)[54]

The United States is far behind most other developed countries in establishing family-friendly government policies. Most other developed countries require paid leave for new mothers, and many also mandate paid leave for fathers, breaks for new mothers to breastfeed, and paid leave to care for children's health, developmental, and educational needs.[55] The United States also has lower public provision of child care: in the year 2000, only 54 percent of U.S. children ages 3 to 6 were in publicly supported care, whereas the percentages in continental European countries ranged from 78 to 99 percent.[56]

Those opposed to such policies argue that they are too expensive, both for companies and for the government. The business community strongly opposes paid leave programs, believing that they are not affordable or would discourage employment.[57] Child care and early education programs are indeed expensive,[58] and because the benefits of these policies, such as less employee turnover or higher employee productivity, are difficult to measure, they are a hard sell to politicians concerned about government spending and businesses concerned about the bottom line.[59]

Another point of controversy around family-friendly policies, particularly paid parental leave, is the effect these policies might have on equal opportunity for women in the workforce. On the one hand, there is no evidence that the employment or wages of women are adversely affected in countries with paid family-leave policies.[60] On the other hand, companies may avoid hiring employees that they anticipate will take advantage of paid leave opportunities—and as noted previously, there is already some hiring discrimination against mothers. If mothers take more time out of the workplace than fathers, they may be less likely to rise in the ranks as the result of their shorter tenure in the workforce.[61]

In the end, my own view is that making it more feasible for people to be both good parents and good workers should be a higher priority than it is now. But it is not likely to revive the two-parent family.

Contraception

In the debate between traditionalists and village builders, the focus is almost always on families that already exist. Neither group has given much attention to the circumstances of a child's birth, and in particular to whether a child is born to two mature adults who are ready for parenthood.

It was only fifty years ago, in 1965, that the Supreme Court ruled that prohibiting the sale or use of contraception to married couples was unconstitutional. This ruling was soon expanded to cover the unmarried as well. These rulings, along with FDA approval of the pill in 1960, ushered in an era in which controlling one's fertility was not only legally permitted and medically possible, but socially acceptable.

Today, birth control is almost universally supported by the general public. Nine out of ten Americans think that birth control is morally acceptable,[62] and practically all sexually active women have used contraception at some point in their lives.[63] Given such widespread support, you might think that birth control would no longer be controversial. But you would be wrong.

In the Affordable Care Act that was signed into law in 2010 by President Obama, there is a provision requiring insurance providers to cover preventive care, including birth control, without a co-payment by the insured person. Although there is an exemption for churches and some parochial schools, other religiously affiliated organizations, such as hospitals, universities, and charities, took umbrage at the requirement that their employer-provided insurance cover birth control. Although the Obama administration offered an accommodation that allowed churches and nonprofits not to offer contraception directly, many for-profit corporations with religious owners sought redress in the courts, arguing that this requirement violated their religious rights under the First Amendment. One such case, *Burwell* v. *Hobby Lobby Stores, Inc.*, went to the Supreme Court in spring 2014. In June, the court concluded that "closely held" for-profit corporations with religious objections to certain types of contraception do not have to cover all FDA-approved contraceptives in their employee insurance plans.[64] Hobby Lobby Stores, Inc., specifically targeted IUDs and emergency contraception (such as Plan B) as being in conflict with the owners' religious beliefs.[65] It is too early to tell what the broad effects of this ruling will be, but any attempt to limit women's reproductive freedom is troubling and potentially harmful to women's ability to control their own destinies. The *New England Journal of Medicine* editorialized in 2014 that the denial of a basic package of health services, including contraception, to an individual woman because of the religious objections of her employer would be the equivalent of denying her a blood transfusion, vaccination, or chemotherapy on the grounds that these were inconsistent with an employer's religious beliefs.[66]

The conservative opposition to birth control and abortion has extended to family planning clinics, particularly those run by Planned Parenthood.

Politicians at both the state and federal levels have sought to cut all funding for Planned Parenthood and other family planning services.[67] Critics of Planned Parenthood cite its involvement in providing abortion as the reason for their opposition. They ignore the many women's health services provided by Planned Parenthood, including cancer screenings, and the fact that any federal funds given to family planning clinics cannot legally be used for abortion services. Critics respond that money is fungible and that federal funds free up private funds for abortion. Political debates aside, advances in contraceptive methods have the potential to dramatically change the landscape for children and families, as I discuss in the next chapter.

Abortion

If birth control is still politically fraught, abortion is positively toxic. In 2013, roughly half (49 percent) of American adults believed abortion was morally wrong,[68] although a large majority (63 percent) wanted to preserve the right to an abortion either in all or in certain circumstances.[69] As President Clinton said in a speech before the Democratic National Convention in 1996, abortion should be safe, legal, and rare. Hillary Clinton appears to agree.[70] My personal view on this issue is similar to the Clintons', but I understand the profound moral issue that abortion raises for many.

Forty years have passed since abortion became legal with the Supreme Court's *Roe* v. *Wade* decision, but debates continue to rage at both the state and federal levels. Pro-life forces have had considerable success in their efforts to restrict abortion. In particular, the Hyde Amendment and the 1992 Supreme Court ruling in *Planned Parenthood* v. *Casey* have had far-reaching effects in limiting access to abortion. The Hyde Amendment, initially enacted in 1976, bars the use of federal Medicaid funds to provide abortions to low-income women except when the life of the mother would be endangered by continuing the pregnancy. It was amended in 1993 to include exceptions for rape, incest, and the mother's physical health. While seventeen states now provide public funding for abortions from their own budgets, the majority of states do not.

In *Planned Parenthood* v. *Casey,* the court ruled that the state had no right to restrict abortion services before fetal viability as early as 22 to

23 weeks, but that states could restrict abortion in ways that did not put "undue burden" on women seeking abortions. In subsequent decades, many states have followed the precedent set in this case by implementing a range of provisions, such as prohibitions on government funding of abortion under Medicaid, waiting periods, required ultrasounds, and burdensome regulations on opening or operating clinics. The latest strategy adopted by the pro-life movement has been to equate a fertilized egg with a person. Such "personhood amendments" on the ballot in many states could potentially criminalize abortion as well as some forms of birth control.[71]

The abortion rate has declined in recent decades. Both pro-choice and pro-life groups are taking credit. Those in favor of choice point to improvements in contraception; the pro-lifers point to their own efforts to change state laws and the way the public views an unborn child. The evidence suggests both can take some credit.[72]

What is mystifying to me and many others is the conflating of abortion and birth control among many on the political right. If there is one fact that is firmly established, it is that contraception dramatically reduces the need for abortion. Publicly funded contraceptive services avert an estimated 2.2 million unintended pregnancies a year and prevent about 760,000 abortions.[73] In the eyes of those who equate a fetus with a person, most forms of contraception should be viewed as life-saving measures. As President Obama stated during his 2008 presidential campaign, "We may not agree on abortion, but surely we can agree on reducing the number of unwanted pregnancies."[74] Or as one Republican strategist says, "Abortion opponents should be pro-contraception, since making contraception as affordable and available as possible reduces the number of unwanted pregnancies and abortions."[75]

Conclusions

Traditionalists want to bring back marriage, believing that it is a historically tested and successful institution for raising children. Village builders believe that single parents are here to stay and that the most appropriate response is to provide them with greater assistance in the difficult job of raising children on their own. Village builders would give priority to reducing poverty and count on improved economic circumstances to stabilize families.

The traditionalists have argued that one way to revive a culture of marriage is to adopt more marriage-friendly policies. Those include making government welfare benefits for single parents less generous, making sure that "deadbeat" dads pay child support, reducing marriage penalties in taxes and benefit programs, funding marriage education programs, and making men more marriageable. My review of each of these approaches does not give me much hope that they are capable of reversing current trends, but they may be desirable for other reasons. In some cases they have had positive effects. Child support enforcement, in particular, has reduced the incidence of unwed births, and some programs aimed at making men better providers, such as Career Academies, have had positive effects on marriage. Whatever their effects on marriage, efforts to improve the employment and earnings of less-skilled men are important for reducing poverty, crime, and other social problems, and for simply making these men better off. That said, I see no reason to give preference to men over women in such efforts just because they have been the traditional breadwinners. Today almost as many women as men are the sole or primary breadwinners for their families.

The village builders have a somewhat different view of what needs to be done. They argue for more government support for the poor, including single parents, and for more family-friendly work places. I am sympathetic with this view up to a point. I think it is particularly unfortunate that the United States has done so little to make it possible for people to combine child rearing with work.

But I think we should limit how far society moves toward socializing the support of children for two reasons. First, it could get very expensive if various benefits are enhanced and the number of single parents continues to grow. Second, and more controversially, I think it is only fair to expect parents to limit the number of children they have to something they can afford. Providing extra benefits or privileges for those with bigger families is a questionable approach. If an adult wants a large family, that should be a decision he or she is permitted to make, but not at public expense. Many people would respond that this entails visiting the proverbial sins of a parent on their children, by depriving the third or fourth child born to a poor family of assistance just because the parents are not able to support the child. On the other hand, should a struggling middle-class taxpayer be asked to support lower-income families with larger-than-average families? It is a conundrum. President Clinton believed that if you worked, you should not be poor. I would add that if you have a modestly sized family—say, no more than the current average of two children—you should not be poor. If you decide to have more children, perhaps you should be on your own financially. Your children would still be entitled to health care and a good education but not to additional income assistance.

At the same time, it would be wrong to curtail the current array of social programs just because they do not have all of the behavioral effects we want. They are a compassionate response to high levels of poverty and inequality and need no further justification. But I am not sure that a more progressive agenda, whatever its desirability on moral grounds, would have more than a modest impact on behavior. For every child kept out of poverty by the earned income tax credit or some other program, another child is about to be born into poverty because of the wholesale breakdown of the American family. Too many village builders are avoiding this unpleasant fact, and they are asking voters to support an agenda that is more expensive and less consistent with the American value of self-sufficiency than these voters will accept.

Although I do not disagree entirely with either the traditionalists or the village builders, the evidence does not make me optimistic that either approach will restabilize families in ways that improve children's prospects. In the next chapter, I discuss a third solution: changing the default from childbearing by chance to childbearing by design.

SIX

Childbearing by Design, Not by Default

By failing to prepare, you are preparing to fail.

—Benjamin Franklin

Teen pregnancy and birth rates have declined. That progress has been dramatic, as noted earlier. But over the past decade or so we have discovered a new problem: high rates of pregnancy and births to unmarried women in their twenties (see figure 6 in the appendix). We also saw that even when these women are living with the father of the child at the time of the child's birth, these relationships typically break up, creating a lot of instability in the child's life. The consequences of single parenthood and of the increasingly common practice of serial cohabitation are not benign.

Drifting into Parenthood

The key fact to understand about pregnancies and births to unmarried women in their twenties is that a large portion of them are not intended. Roughly half of all pregnancies in the United States are unintended. That is surprising enough; but among single women under 30, seven out of ten pregnancies are unintended. Many of these pregnancies are aborted, but just under half are carried to term.[1] The result is that 60 percent of all births to young, single women are unplanned.

How do we know so much about people's intentions in such a sensitive area? The government conducts a survey called the National Survey of Family Growth. The most recent data cover the period from 2006 to 2010. The survey covers over 20,000 men and women between the ages of 15 and 44 and asks women to characterize the intentionality of their pregnancies and births at the time they first learned of their pregnancy. If they say the pregnancy was unintended, they are also asked whether it was "unwanted" or "mistimed." An unwanted pregnancy is one the woman did not want ever, whereas a mistimed pregnancy is one that simply came earlier than she wanted—in some cases by only a year, but in other cases by many years. Of those who report that their pregnancy was mistimed, 70 percent say that it was mistimed by more than two years.[2]

While every effort is made to collect the data in a way that protects a woman's privacy, inevitably there is some subjectivity and some bias in the answers. Many women are not sure how they feel about a pregnancy, and this ambivalence can color their answer one way or the other. It is probably sensible to think of intentionality as a continuum. Some people have a strong desire to have a child and others an equally strong desire to *not* have a child; and a great many people probably fall somewhere in between these two extremes. Unfortunately, the data we have are not that granular. Nor do we have data on the male partners of these women.[3]

Whatever a woman's personal view, social norms may influence her response. How many parents are willing to say that a baby that has already been born and that they may have already bonded with is "unwanted?" The remarkable thing to me is how many do. Of all the unintended births to single women in their twenties, 40 percent were characterized by the woman as unwanted rather than simply mistimed.[4] Many of these unintended births are causing young adults to drift into the kind of serial cohabitations described in chapter 4 and are putting a large number of children at risk.

More-advantaged women have much greater success planning their pregnancies than their less-advantaged counterparts.[5] Among single women in their twenties, whites have lower unintended pregnancy rates than blacks or Hispanics; more affluent women have lower rates than poorer women; and well-educated women have lower rates than the less-educated (see figure 7 in the appendix).[6] Reducing unplanned births is the first step to reducing out-of-wedlock births. If all women in America were able to reduce their unintended pregnancies to the rate experienced by college-educated women, the proportion of children born outside of marriage would drop by 25 percent (see figure 8 in the appendix).

The reason these data on differences by race and income are so important is that there is a suspicion in some circles that family planning advocates are simply trying to reduce childbearing among the poor and minorities. The facts suggest otherwise. Most women in these groups say that they do not want to become pregnant as frequently as they now do.

Why Don't More People Use Contraception or Resort to Abortion?

Why, if so many unmarried women do not want to get pregnant or have a baby, do they then fail to achieve their own intentions? After all, some forms of birth control, such as condoms, are widely available. And when contraception fails, abortion is still available as a last resort.

The reasons for a high level of unwanted births are varied. As discussed in the previous chapter, new questions about access to contraception have flared up in debates about the Affordable Care Act. In addition, more than forty years after the Supreme Court's 1973 decision upholding a woman's right to have an abortion in the case of *Roe v. Wade,* the abortion debate rages on. Not only are abortions expensive, but they often require that a woman travel several hundred miles to the nearest clinic.[7] These factors may contribute to why poorer women are less likely to seek or obtain an abortion than their more affluent counterparts and thus more likely to end up raising children they didn't want to have.[8]

But difficult access to abortion is not the only barrier. Many women, particularly women in poor communities, consider abortion morally wrong. In their discussions with low-income women in the Philadelphia area, Kathryn Edin and Maria Kefalas discovered that the women they interviewed did not think it was acceptable to have an abortion except in extreme cases such as rape or incest, addiction, or homelessness. Most of the time "doing the right thing" meant carrying the pregnancy to term. The idea, for example, that one might seek an abortion in order to get more education was viewed as totally inappropriate.[9] These views contrast with those held by many middle-class women, who are more likely to terminate an unwanted pregnancy for a wider variety of reasons.

Despite the importance of access to and attitudes toward contraception and abortion, I do not want to leave the impression that these are the only reasons that so many people are experiencing unwanted births. Another factor is a lack of knowledge about different forms of birth control and their effectiveness. And still another is ambivalence about having a child, especially among those whose life prospects are limited to begin with. Most important, in my view, is the difficulty that many people have in translating their intention not to have a child into appropriate behaviors, such as consistent use of contraception. According to the Guttmacher Institute, 52 percent of unintended pregnancies are due to nonuse of contraception, 43 percent to inconsistent or incorrect use, and only 5 percent to method failure (see figure 9 in the appendix).[10]

In an in-depth study of seventy-six of the unmarried couples in the Fragile Families study described earlier, Kathryn Edin and her coauthors found that the couples had had 202 pregnancies (some with their current partner and some with another partner). Of those, only 12 percent were planned. Another 18 percent occurred between couples who felt some ambivalence about having a child. The remaining 70 percent occurred between couples who were sure they did not want a child. Some of them were using birth control but inconsistently (22 percent), some experienced contraceptive failures or thought they were infertile (23 percent), and a sizable group (25 percent) was using no contraception at all. Most of these pregnancies were carried to term; only 10 percent resulted in an abortion and another 10 percent in a miscarriage.[11]

Clearly there are a lot of unmarried couples who do not want a child but are getting pregnant and having children anyway. Why is this? Is birth control too expensive or too hard to get? Is it too hard to use, or seen as having unacceptable side effects or as a barrier to good sex? Is it because unwed births are no longer stigmatized, or because the couple expects to stay together and marry? Is it because the women themselves see little reason to postpone childbearing and value motherhood even if they are not quite ready for it? Or is it because using contraception consistently and correctly is hard, making it highly likely that mistakes will occur? All of these factors appear to play a role.

Although most young Americans do not cite cost as their reason for not using contraception, it may affect the *type* of contraception they use.[12] The most effective contraceptive methods, such as IUDs and the implant, have very high up-front costs, though they are cheaper in the long run than, say, the pill.[13] (An IUD is inserted into the uterus and an implant is placed under the skin, typically on the arm. Both procedures need to be performed by a trained health care provider, usually a physician.) With limited government funding for contraceptive services, clinics do not always offer these more expensive but more effective methods of birth control. Other providers, especially in the large network of community health centers that serve low-income communities, do not have enough doctors trained to provide the most effective methods.[14] And in states such as Texas, where some Planned Parenthood clinics have closed, people may need to drive a long distance to get effective birth control.

Some people at risk of an unintended pregnancy do not use contraception at all. The most commonly cited reason for nonuse given by women in a government survey was, "I didn't think I could get pregnant."[15] This is a puzzling answer but one that suggests that sex education classes are not doing a good job of explaining the risks associated with having sex. Evidence suggests that many young people who have had sex and not gotten pregnant infer (incorrectly) that they cannot or will not get pregnant from subsequent sexual encounters.[16] More generally, many young men and women display confusion or ignorance over how birth control works.[17]

The most commonly used forms of contraception, condoms and the pill, require some up-front planning and consistent use. The pill must be taken every day; prescriptions must be refilled; and condoms must be used properly every time one has sex. For these reasons, the proportion of women who get pregnant unintentionally over the course of a year when using a particular type of contraception varies from 18 percent among condom users to 9 percent among pill users to much less than 1 percent among users of long-acting reversible methods such as the IUD or an implant.[18] The reason for these high failure rates has nothing to do with the efficacy of the methods when they are used as intended; instead, it reflects the fact that most of us are far from perfect users. We forget to take a pill or cannot be bothered with a condom in the midst of a passionate encounter.

The above-cited failure rates are for a single year. In a society in which couples delay marriage until their mid- to late twenties, on average, most single women are at risk of an unwanted pregnancy for many years before marrying. A woman's cumulative risk of getting pregnant, relying on condoms alone, is almost 63 percent over five years.[19] In other words, the majority of women who are sexually active for five years with a partner (or partners) using condoms will become pregnant.

Even well-educated couples who are determined to avoid pregnancy may not know these odds. Among those who are more ambivalent or less determined, the chances of a pregnancy occurring are much higher. They may say they do not want a pregnancy but fail to do very much to prevent one from happening. For example, in one survey, 44 percent of young women agreed or strongly agreed with the statement, "It doesn't matter whether you use birth control or not; when it is your time to get pregnant it will happen."[20] This kind of fatalism is just the opposite of childbearing by design. To call such couples "drifters" may sound harsh, but their behavior is inconsistent with their intentions and inconsistent with what they say they want for their children.

When they analyzed their interviews with couples who were part of the Fragile Families study, Paula England, Kathryn Edin, and their coauthors categorized these couples along two dimensions. The first was how strongly the couple wanted or didn't want children (intentionality). The second was their ability to align their behavior with their intentions (efficacy).[21] What they found is eye-opening. A large fraction of these couples simply had difficulty matching their behavior to their intentions. Virtually none of the couples who had an unintended pregnancy said that birth control was too difficult to get or too expensive, or that they had changed their mind about having a child. Instead they said things like, "I simply wasn't thinking."[22] Their inability to plan was evident in other areas of their lives as well. The whole idea of not doing something now because it might make life tougher later on did not seem to be part of their behavioral repertoire.[23] In interviews with another sample of 103 women in their twenties attending both community colleges and elite schools such as Berkeley and Stanford, England and her coauthors found once again that both intentionality and efficacy matter. Efficacy, they report, has strong effects on the consistency of contraceptive use, even after adjusting for many other variables, including the strength of the desire to have (or not have) a child. The chance that a woman with high efficacy will use contraception consistently is seven times higher than for those with low efficacy. High and low efficacy are measured by the ability to self-regulate in areas other than contraception. In their interviews, these researchers discovered that many of these women admitted that despite not wanting a baby, they had difficulty following through both in this area and in other areas of their lives (for example, avoiding drugs or alcohol, or completing their school assignments on time).[24]

Many progressives believe that early childbearing reflects a lack of good alternatives for those with poor life prospects. They argue that the decision to have a child in such circumstances may be quite rational and has no serious adverse consequences for the mother.[25] They also fear that assigning responsibility to individuals for having unintended births is a form of "blaming the victim" or disrespecting those whose lives are troubled. But we should keep in mind that it is often the children who are the "victims." Also, the couples who were part of England's sample and of the Fragile Families study were not the very disadvantaged. England's sample included only women in college, including several elite public and private schools. The Fragile Families couples were somewhat less privileged but representative of a large group of young adults in American cities. The Fragile Family couples did not view the birth of a child with equanimity. Whatever their prospects in life, they clearly articulated the challenges of having a baby before one is in a good position to do so—the cost, the resulting limitations on their ability to travel or have fun, and the impact it would have on their educational or career goals. They valued children, to be sure, but they were also aware of the challenges that would await them if they had a baby before they were ready.

My conclusion from reading this and other research is that we need a much better understanding of why people do things that are not in their own self-interest. So, in the next section I take a detour into what we are learning about efficacy and the ability to make good decisions—decisions that are consistent with our own goals—and behaviors that are aligned with our own intentions. The problem does not just affect sex and pregnancy; it also affects our ability to stay on a diet, exercise regularly, complete a disagreeable task, or control anger. This topic is important because if we have not diagnosed the problem correctly, we will not focus on the right solutions.

The Difficulty of Controlling Our Own Behavior

Daniel Kahneman is a Princeton University psychologist who won the Nobel Memorial Prize in economic science for his work showing that individuals do not necessarily make rational choices based on comparing different options and choosing the one that maximizes their well-being.[26]

In his book *Thinking, Fast and Slow,* Kahneman addresses the fact that we rely on two types of thinking in our daily lives. The first type, which he calls System 1 or "fast thinking," is intuitive, effortless, quasi-automatic, and often impulsive. The second type, which he calls System 2 or "slow thinking," is more cognitive and more reflective, and it requires more effort. To illustrate these thinking styles, Kahneman describes the following problem. Imagine that you have a bat and a ball that together cost $1.10. The bat costs $1.00 more than the ball. How much does the ball cost? Most people—including more than half the students at such selective universities as Harvard, MIT, and Princeton—give the intuitive but wrong answer. To see if you're one of the people tripped up by thinking quickly, turn to the endnotes for the answer.[27]

This puzzle demonstrates one way in which our cognitive powers can fail us. It turns out that when it comes to making decisions, people are often lazy. The bat-and-ball question does not require huge mental effort. It is not that most college students are unable to get to the right answer, but rather that overconfidence in one's own intuition means that they do not even engage System 2 before giving an answer.

What does this kind of puzzle solving have to do with self-control? Economist Shane Frederick has studied the characteristics of students who perform poorly on questions similar to the bat-and-ball problem and found that they are more likely to be impulsive, impatient, and present-biased. For example, this type of person was more likely to prefer a small sum of money today than a larger sum of money in a month's time.[28] Many social scientists now believe that the ability to control one's impulses, to delay gratification, is at least as important as IQ in determining a child's later success.[29]

In a famous experiment conducted by Stanford University psychologist Walter Mischel, a group of 4-year-old children were each offered a marshmallow.[30] They were free to eat the marshmallow immediately, but if they waited fifteen minutes, they were told, they would get a second marshmallow. Some of the children were good at resisting the temptation to eat the marshmallow, and some were not. Those who could resist the temptation often employed self-control techniques such as looking away from the marshmallow or distracting themselves. Ten or fifteen years later, those who at age 4 had been most successful at resisting temptation were found to have higher levels of intelligence, were less likely to take drugs, and showed more ability to control their behavior in general.[31]

More recent research has found that self-control may be related to how certain an individual is that a reward is actually coming and how long it will take to arrive.[32] If the person giving the reward is unreliable (for example, a researcher who did not follow through on an earlier promise of a snack or toy), a child is much more likely to give up waiting and give in to temptation.[33] One interpretation of the class divide discussed in chapter 4 is that it stems in part from the uncertain or chaotic environments experienced by children growing up in lower-income households. A sense of self-efficacy may be undermined by early experiences with adults who are distracted or unreliable caretakers.

These self-control problems are not limited to preschoolers or to the poor. When presented with a box of chocolate truffles, how many of us have sufficient willpower to resist eating them? It may be better to rely on strategies that force one to think and plan before one acts. If the box of chocolates is on the top shelf and requires getting out a step ladder to reach it, temptation is reduced.

It is not a coincidence that many experiments with self-control deal with food. Hunger is an example of what George Loewenstein calls a visceral factor, something that changes behavior by influencing emotional and/or mental focus. Other examples of visceral factors include fatigue, fear, thirst, sexual desire, pain, depression, and addiction. A person who is under the influence of a visceral factor makes decisions in what Loewenstein calls a "hot" state. Attention is focused almost entirely on satisfying a need or avoiding pain. This phenomenon will be familiar to anyone who has gone grocery shopping on an empty stomach. Hungry shoppers buy more high-calorie foods than those who have a snack before they shop.[34] The problem is not just the hot state behavior itself; it is the fact that most people misjudge what they will do in a hot state. Loewenstein calls this phenomenon the "hot-cold empathy gap." People are overconfident about their own willpower and underestimate how easily they will give in to temptation.

In an experiment testing the empathy gap, researchers constructed a scenario in which they described to their subjects three people who had taken a hike in Colorado in August, gotten lost, and run out of water. They then asked their subjects to rate the importance of packing water for a hike. They found that only people who were thirsty themselves realized the importance of such precautionary measures. When they were still in a "cold" state, only 52 percent thought the hikers should have taken more water. But when they were in a "hot" state" themselves (in this case, literally, because they had just been to the gym), the proportion rose to 92 percent.[35]

Sex is, of course, the quintessential example of a "hot" state in which behavior is impulsive and difficult to control. No one is thinking about changing diapers or paying college tuition when they are in love and in bed. The passion of the moment totally eclipses possible worries about an unintended pregnancy. Psychologists Dan Ariely and George Loewenstein have examined how sexual arousal affects men's willingness to participate in various questionable sexual behaviors, including unsafe sex. Male participants were asked to rate their willingness to engage in these behaviors while watching pornography and masturbating and also during a different session in their "normal" state.[36] Overall, the men were significantly more likely to engage in risky behavior in the pursuit of sex while aroused than while not. For example, they were asked, "Would you use a condom even if you were afraid that a woman might change her mind while you went to get it?" The men were much more likely to say no while aroused.[37] This speaks to a key problem with condoms. They require individuals to use them while in the heat of the moment.

Kahneman's ideas about the problems that occur when "slow thinking" fails to control our more intuitive and impulsive selves is similar to what others would call a failure of "executive function" or the part of our brain (the prefrontal cortex) that is more deliberate and rational than the portion that governs such basic instincts as hunger and sex. This executive ability is undoubtedly the result of genetic inheritance, environmental influences, and training. While individuals vary greatly in the strength of their executive function and thus their ability to control their impulses, no one is impervious to weaknesses in self-control that cause them to eat too much, exercise too little, or have unprotected sex. Moreover, executive function can be improved by training people to "think before they act." For example, a program at the Rikers Island jail in New York City is trying to reduce recidivism among juvenile offenders by using cognitive behavioral therapy to help them understand how impulsive behavior got them into trouble in the past and how to avoid it in the future.[38]

Once people have gained some sense of self-control or efficacy in one area, it may spread to others. Psychologist Roy Baumeister and colleagues compare willpower to a muscle.[39] Using self-control regularly strengthens your willpower in the same way that lifting weights strengthens your biceps. But just as lifting weights tires you out if you overdo it, practicing self-control for too long drains cognitive resources. Avoiding a cheeseburger at lunch makes it that much harder to resist ice cream at dinner. In addition, it is much harder to exert willpower when you are mentally or emotionally drained. For example, someone who gets too little sleep is more likely to use the kind of fast thinking that leads to the stereotyping of other people.[40]

Economists Sendhil Mullainathan and Eldar Shafir have written about how environmental factors, including the stresses associated with poverty, can affect one's decisionmaking.[41] For example, in a study with two other coauthors, they looked at how financial worries can affect cognitive skills.[42] A subgroup of American shoppers were asked to solve some cognitive problems after they had been told to assume that their car had broken down and would need some costly repairs. One group was told that the repairs would be relatively cheap ($150). In this case, both high-income and low-income Americans performed similarly on the cognitive test. Another group was told that the repairs would be much more expensive ($1,500). In this scenario, low-income Americans did significantly worse on the test than those with higher incomes, suggesting that priming them to worry about a big expense distracted them from doing well. These authors also looked at a nonhypothetical example of this same problem: the cognitive skills of Indian sugar cane farmers across the span of their growing season. Just before the harvest, farmers have less money than afterward, giving the researchers an opportunity to examine how an individual's cognitive ability changes as his income changes. Similar to the American shoppers, farmers showed diminished cognitive performance during the period when they were poorest.

Struggling with poverty makes life harder not only because you have fewer material resources, but also because you have less cognitive bandwidth for dealing with everything from parenting to remembering to take your medications. Mullainathan and Shafir's research points to one possible explanation for why low-income individuals seem to have a harder time matching their actions to their intentions. Their findings might shed some light on the growing class divide in family formation behaviors described earlier, and why low-income individuals are more likely to drift in and out of relationships and to have children both out of wedlock and with multiple partners.

The Role of Culture in Behavior

Whatever the effects of individual poverty on the ability to avoid self-destructive behaviors, there is inevitably a cultural component to these behaviors as well. Once having unprotected sex, drifting into relationships, and having children outside of marriage become commonplace in a community, the behaviors take on a life of their own. If one's friends and neighbors are having children at a young age and managing to raise them, typically without the benefit of a committed partner, then following in their footsteps is the path of least resistance—the natural outcome of thinking fast and not slow. As David Brooks puts it, "an individual mind couldn't handle the vast variety of fleeting stimuli that are thrust before it. We can function in the world only because we are embedded in the scaffold of culture. We absorb ethnic cultures, institutional cultures, regional cultures, which do most of our thinking for us."[43]

Sometimes culture is a positive influence on people's lives. The strong familial culture among Hispanics is usually applauded. But sometimes culture's influence is less benign: Russians drinking too much vodka comes to mind. And what may be positive in one environment can turn negative in another. Respect for male breadwinners was important in an era when women had no other source of support. Now it is creating a "male mystique," making it hard for men to fill other roles. It is acceptable for girls to act like boys but usually not for boys to act like girls.

The problem is that culture is sticky.[44] Even were we to improve the material prospects of the poor, it is not clear that their behaviors would quickly change without a complementary effort to change the cultural default to not having children early. Because of the high value accorded to children in poor communities, one way to change the default might be to appeal to the natural instinct of low-income parents to do right by their children.

Culture embeds a particular set of norms into people's behavioral repertoire. Those with little education or sense of self-efficacy and few material resources may be less skilled at slow thinking than their more-educated or resource-rich peers, and thus more dependent on the culture to provide them with guidelines on how to live.[45] Once a culture goes sour, for whatever reasons, it becomes extremely difficult to turn it around. By the same token, if one can find a way to jump-start the process in the opposite direction, it can quickly produce a positive cascade.[46] Liberals tend to believe that if you improve people's economic circumstances, more constructive behavior patterns will follow. Conservatives tend to think that without new cultural understandings in which to embed such change, money alone will be insufficient to overcome existing patterns. In my view, both matter. For example, imagine a charter school that insists on the orderly behavior and discipline that the learning process requires and guarantees a college scholarship for those who make the academic grade. Such schools exist, and their achievements have been remarkable.[47] They combine norms and expectations with concrete opportunities to improve their students' prospects.

New Ways to Change the Default

If some people are not very good at controlling their behavior and often engage in behavior that is not consistent with their own well-being, what can be done to change that? Can we have any hope of persuading people to behave in more rational and more self-regarding ways? Will it ever be possible to convince people that it makes sense to always use contraception, and to use it carefully and consistently, except when they want to have a child? What exactly can be done to reduce unplanned births?

Until very recently, the answer might have been "not much." The stork will always arrive at inconvenient moments. But the kind of new thinking by behavioral psychologists and economists reported above has created room for more optimism. Their key insight is to recognize that our behavior is not always well aligned with our preferences. In a pathbreaking book, Richard Thaler and Cass Sunstein argue that we can be encouraged to make better decisions by the way in which choices are structured.[48] We especially need nudges when decisions are very consequential but rare (for example, choosing whom to marry or to have a baby with), where the costs are immediate (the hassle of using birth control) but the benefits are delayed (avoiding an unwanted birth), and where issues of self-control loom large (as with having sex).

There are three ways that policymakers and private sector leaders can nudge individuals toward making better decisions about marriage and childbearing: (1) change the message about contraception; (2) motivate commitment to a partner by linking it to the well-being of children; and above all, (3) change the default through greater use of long-acting contraceptives.

Changing the message

Sunstein and Thaler's book is full of examples of how changing the social dialogue has changed behavior. For example, for years, Texas had a big problem with littering. The biggest offenders were young men between the ages of 18 and 24. To address this group, the state launched a campaign called "Don't Mess with Texas." By using a tough-talking slogan and sports figures as spokesmen, the campaign played to people's identities both as men and as Texans. It was wildly successful: there was a 72 percent reduction in highway littering over the six-year period following the start of the campaign.[49]

Another example is social marketing campaigns aimed at improving public health. One such campaign, to reduce smoking among teens, has been credited not only with reducing the number of teens who smoke by 22 percent over three years but also with increasing the number of people who hold anti-tobacco views.[50] Similarly, campaigns about HIV awareness and condom use have affected the behavior of up to 6 percent of the targeted population.[51] While 6 percent may sound small, given the broad reach of such campaigns, their cost-effectiveness is quite high.

How can we apply these principles to the problem of unplanned pregnancies? A message that says "Not everyone is having sex" encourages teenagers to delay sex, since teenagers are hugely responsive to what they think their peers are doing.[52] The widespread belief among young people that you can't get pregnant the first time you have sex or that you can't get pregnant standing up can be countered by good public information delivered by youth-savvy social media instead of in a pamphlet handed out in ninth-grade health class.[53] A website that tells women the location of the nearest clinic dispensing birth control or sends a message to her cell phone reminding her to get her prescription refilled helps her to avoid an unplanned pregnancy. A message to parents that they need to talk to their adolescent sons and not just to their daughters counters the ingrained but counterproductive belief that "boys will be boys."[54] The National Campaign to Prevent Teen and Unplanned Pregnancy has pioneered these and other methods of helping young men and women to align their behaviors with their intentions.[55]

Messages matter for other reasons as well: people are bad at estimating risks but are influenced by the way in which risks are presented to them. For example, it is difficult for people to keep track of how likely pregnancy is when they are not using contraception, never mind what it means when someone says that a condom has an 18 percent failure rate. (Ask a young adult you know what they think the answer is to the first half of this question; and see the endnotes if, like most people, you do not know the answer yourself.)[56] Often, a person's interpretation of a statistic depends on how that statistic is framed. For example, when patients are given the positive message that 90 percent of people will survive a particular operation rather than the negative message that 10 percent will die, they are more likely to elect to have surgery. This behavior is not rational—a 10 percent risk of dying is the same as a 90 percent survival rate—but people consistently let small changes in messaging influence how they act. Analogously, telling someone that condoms, the pill, and long-acting reversible contraception have, respectively, 18 percent,

9 percent, and 0.2 percent failure rates will be interpreted differently than telling people that the birth control pill is twice as effective as a condom and that IUDs are forty times again as effective as the pill. The second frame emphasizes the relative effectiveness of the methods rather than their absolute failure rates, potentially encouraging more people to make the switch to these more user-friendly and less failure-prone methods. Similarly, it may help to express the risks in terms of the likelihood of getting pregnant over multiple years, rather than just over one year while using a particular method, to drive home the importance of cumulative risks and having a long-term plan. Finally, rebranding long-acting contraceptives, such as IUDs, and calling them safe but low-maintenance methods (which they are) has the further benefit of highlighting their primary advantages to a user.[57]

Commitment devices in a post-marriage landscape

We can resist temptation if we recognize its power and take actions to restrain ourselves before encountering it. When Ulysses tied himself to the mast of his ship in order to avoid responding to the cries of the sirens, he was protecting himself against what he knew to be his own worst instincts. Ulysses tying himself to a mast is similar to my putting a box of chocolate truffles out of reach on the top shelf of a cabinet. The key idea here is that you must decide when you're still in a cold state to take actions that will prevent making mistakes later when you're in a hot state.[58]

One example of a commitment device is the website stickk.com. This website allows people to set goals, such as losing weight or quitting smoking, and then create a financial commitment to reach that goal by a certain date. If they do not reach their goal, they will have to donate a sum of money to a charity. Sometimes, people pick what is known as an "anti-charity," a charity that supports a cause they are opposed to (for example, NARAL for someone who is pro-life, or Americans United for Life for someone who is pro-choice). Having to contribute to a cause that they find repugnant if they fail to meet their goal gives them an even greater incentive to succeed. This website commits people to their goals in two ways: it makes their commitment public and holds them accountable to at least one other person (known as the referee); and it makes the cost of breaking the commitment immediate rather than distant. For most people, the prospect of losing $200 now is much more salient than the long-term costs of obesity.

I personally use commitment devices to achieve my objectives. For example, I try to exercise every day on a machine that is in front of a TV. I watch movies rented from Netflix, but only when I am exercising. Thus, if I want to see the rest of an exciting movie, I must climb onto the machine and start pedaling again. I used another commitment device in writing this book. When I am in the office, I am distracted by colleagues, meetings, a variety of unrelated writing assignments, and a flood of addictive e-mail. To resist such distractions I committed myself to staying home one or two days a week and established a rule for myself that those days had to be devoted to the book.

In the world of relationships, marriage is, of course, the ultimate commitment device. A marriage creates both social and legal barriers to ending a relationship. It is much harder to end a relationship after two people have stood in front of their friends and families (and sometimes their religious congregation) and promised to stay together for the rest of their lives. In addition, people who marry are more likely to combine assets in joint bank accounts or through shared property ownership than couples who are merely cohabiting. This comingling of assets along with the legal process associated with ending a marriage means that couples who are married are more likely than unmarried couples to stay together through times of trouble. These external supports also motivate both partners to make the marriage work, making its durability and its satisfactions, to some extent, a self-fulfilling prophecy.

As earlier chapters have discussed, marriage is no longer the norm among young couples without a college degree. Some hope it will be rejuvenated as the example set by the well-educated trickles down to the rest of society. I am skeptical that this will happen unless we first help the less-educated to defer childbearing. Given a choice between earlier marriage and later childbearing, we know that the latter is more consistent with what extended education and a modern economy require. It is also more consistent with good parenting. Delayed childbearing might also help to restore marriage, since young women are more marriageable when they do not yet have children, and later marriages or relationships are more durable than earlier ones.

Changing the Default

As we have seen, unintended pregnancies and births are all too common among young single women and men. One possible way to prevent unintended pregnancies is to encourage more abstinence from sex outside of committed relationships. One does not have to be a prude, or unaware of today's liberated attitudes, to caution young people to be more discriminating and disciplined about when and with whom to have sex. The 1996 welfare reform law included a provision requiring states to teach abstinence to teens. The literature evaluating what this has accomplished is not encouraging.[59] However, a majority of teens say they wish they had waited longer before having sex, and it is likely that young adults often regret some of their sexual encounters as well.[60]

Sexually active young adults are going to get pregnant unless they use contraception carefully and consistently. Consider for a moment a woman who is having unprotected sex. (I do not mean to blame this solely on women rather than their male partners. Obviously, it takes two to create a baby, but we do not have sufficient data on men, and the most effective forms of birth control are for use by women.) The chances that she will get pregnant are high—about 85 percent over the course of a year and virtually certain over multiple years.[61] So the current default—what happens if the woman does nothing—is a pregnancy. As noted earlier, even if she and her partner are using condoms, the risk of pregnancy over one year is 18 percent and over five years is 63 percent.[62] What if, instead, the default outcome were that a woman was always protected even if she or her partner did nothing? This could make a huge difference in the incidence of unwanted pregnancy.

As Thaler and Sunstein argue, "defaults are ubiquitous and powerful."[63] Consider the example of 401(k) plans. Most employers have replaced defined benefit plans, which guarantee an employee a fixed-dollar pension, with 401(k) plans in which money is invested on behalf of an employee, but the employee shares in the financing and bears the risk of his or her investments not doing well. Although these retirement plans are tax-favored and often highly subsidized, not enough people take advantage of them. About 30 percent of those eligible for 401(k) plans fail to enroll.[64] The problem with these low enrollment rates is that people are not saving enough for their retirement. The difficulty will become more acute as people live longer and Social Security and old-fashioned defined-benefit pension plans become rarer and less generous. But what happens when, instead of having to opt in to a 401(k) plan, the default is automatic enrollment? Making this change in the default has proven highly effective.[65] If enrollment in a 401(k) plan is automatic (albeit with an option to decline such coverage), the proportion of enrolled employees skyrockets. In one study, enrollment jumped from 65 percent (after thirty-six months) to 98 percent.[66] Moreover, people did not later drop out, suggesting that once enrolled in a plan, employees recognized its benefits.

Another example of a default cited by Thaler and Sunstein is organ donation. The demand for transplantable organs far exceeds the supply from deceased donors, with the result that there are long waiting lists and many deaths among those waiting for, say, a kidney. The major obstacle is the need to get the consent of the donor (before death) or surviving family members (after death). Most states require explicit consent, and most people say they are willing to donate their organs in the event of their unexpected death. Still, most citizens have not taken the trouble to indicate their willingness to be an organ donor on either their driver's license or an organ donor card. The solution is to change the default from one of explicit consent to presumed consent. In one experiment, when participants had to opt in to being an organ donor, only 42 percent did. But when they had to opt out, 82 percent agreed to be donors.[67] Nearly all U.S. states require explicit consent; in Europe presumed consent is much more common. When researchers compared the policies across countries, specifically between Austria, which uses presumed consent, and Germany, which has an opt-in system, they found dramatic differences. In Germany only 12 percent gave consent. In Austria virtually everyone gave consent.[68] Granted, organ donation is a very sensitive issue about which it is risky to presume anything. So another approach involves mandating choice. Such a policy does not presume that people want to donate, but would require them to indicate their preference when they get a driver's license. The state of Illinois is using mandated choice to good effect, with 60 percent of drivers registered as donors.

Why are defaults so powerful? First, because of inertia. The status quo always wins in any contest that requires effort. Second, because the chosen default often contains normative information. When Austria presumes organ donation, making it the default, it is signaling that this is what most people should choose. When an employer makes automatic enrollment in a 401(k) plan the norm, it sends a signal that this is something that the human resources department recommends and that other employees are doing. We are social animals. What others are doing and what the experts recommend both matter.

This new research on defaults is highly applicable to the problem of too many unplanned pregnancies and births. The reason many people don't use contraception, or don't use it consistently or correctly, is because it's hard. It requires sophisticated knowledge, planning, and self-discipline. As discussed above, much more could be done to reduce misconceptions (pun intended) and to change the way birth control is perceived. We should not give up on traditional approaches. Publicly funded contraceptive services currently in place are averting over 2 million unwanted pregnancies a year and saving taxpayers approximately $7.6 billion in the process.[69] If we did more to eliminate all unwanted and mistimed pregnancies, we could save an additional $6 billion.[70]

But we should not stop there. In the world of family planning, LARCs (long-acting reversible contraceptives) are the most exciting new development. LARCs include intrauterine devices (IUDs) and implants. Both last up to three years, and some brands of IUDs can last up to twelve years. Though IUDs require semi-regular checkups to ensure that they are still in place, both of these methods are very low maintenance and therefore good choices for someone who does not want to worry about remembering to use birth control every day or in the heat of the moment.

LARCs are safe, cost-effective, and well liked by users. They have much lower failure rates than other forms of contraception, such as the condom, the pill, the patch, and the ring. In a careful test with over 7,000 women in the St. Louis region, the risk that a contraceptive-using woman would get pregnant was twenty times higher if that contraceptive was the pill, transdermal ring, or hormonal patch rather than a LARC.[71] The reason for the much lower failure rate of LARCs has almost nothing to do with the effectiveness of the other methods when used consistently and correctly. It has everything to do with the fact that LARCs are user-friendly. Once in place, they can be ignored until one is ready to have a child. In short, they change the default. They are forgiving of human frailty. No longer does a woman or her partner have to take active steps to prevent an unwanted pregnancy. Quite the contrary, she has to take action only if she wants to become pregnant. At that point she must see a doctor to have the device removed. LARCs are especially effective among groups that have high rates of unintended pregnancy because of poor compliance with other methods. These include younger and more disadvantaged women, who are the most at risk for unintended pregnancy.[72]

The family planning community is optimistic about the potential of LARCs to change the pregnancy landscape. An editorial in the journal *Contraception*, based on many citations to the literature, notes that they "have a proven record of very high effectiveness, many years of effectiveness, convenience, cost effectiveness, suitability for a wide variety of women and, in general, high user satisfaction."[73] It goes on to note that LARCs represent a much smaller fraction of contraceptive use in the United States than in other countries. Between 2006 and 2008, in the United States, only 5 percent of women between the age of 15 and 44 used IUDs. In contrast, in the same time frame 10 percent of British women, 22 percent of French women, and 40 percent of Chinese women used IUDs.[74] IUD use in the United States is increasing but still remains much lower than in other countries (see figure 10 in the appendix).[75]

What accounts for the low utilization of LARCs in the United States? First, many people have never heard of them and are not told about their availability when they seek care.[76] Myths about them are widespread. For example, 40 percent of young adults incorrectly believe that surgery is required to implant an IUD, and nearly half (46 percent) think that IUDs can move around in a woman's body.[77] Second, health care providers themselves are often reluctant to suggest them because they lack training or familiarity with the latest research. Many older providers remember the problems with the Dalkon Shield, which in the 1950s and 1960s caused bacterial infections of the uterus resulting in fulminating pelvic inflammatory disease, spontaneous or septic abortion, ectopic pregnancy, or infertility. The poor design of this particular IUD produced one of the largest tort liability cases in history and scared generations of women away from IUDs. Over half (54 percent) of surveyed women state that they are less likely to use IUDs because they fear contracting an infection from an IUD.[78] Although there is still a very small risk of pelvic inflammatory disease or premature expulsion, the latest research suggests that LARCs are safe for women of all ages, including adolescents, and safe whether they have ever had a baby or not.

One potential barrier to the widespread use of LARCs is their cost. The up-front cost ranges from $200 to $436 at public sector prices and is even higher in the private sector.[79] That price only covers the initial insertion of the device. With clinical services and follow-up doctor visits included, the total price tag can be $500 to $1,000 or even higher.[80] However, spread over the useful life of the device, it is cheaper than the birth control pill, so subsidies that reduce the up-front cost could be a good investment. A case can also be made for not just subsidizing the cost but also rewarding those who choose it.[81] The St. Louis demonstration program mentioned earlier offered LARCs at no cost, which greatly enhanced the willingness of women to choose them over other forms of contraception. Two-thirds of them chose a LARC over the pill or another hormonal method.[82] These choices are driven by cost as well as by the messages delivered by doctors and other providers. It has been traditional in family planning clinics to offer women a menu of choices. But in other areas, most doctors are willing to recommend the treatment that they think will be most effective. Why shouldn't providers do the same in the family planning world? LARCs are the most effective way of avoiding pregnancy. Yet many providers do not even offer them as an option, much less as the most effective and thus most highly recommended way of avoiding pregnancy.[83]

Conclusions

Widespread alarm about the growing number of children being born outside of marriage, bolstered by evidence that this does not augur well for their life prospects, has produced two quite different reactions. On the one hand are the traditionalists who want to restore a culture of marriage in the United States. They want to use the tax and benefit system along with marriage education and other programs to encourage more marriage. Although well-intended, such efforts do not seem to me to be up to the task. The traditionalists are swimming upstream against a powerful tide of demographic and cultural change. But because we know that marriage is good for children and for adults as well, in most cases, we should continue to sing its praises as an ideal environment in which to raise children, and a very satisfying arrangement for many adults as well.

While the traditionalists are focused on marriage, the village builders are more accepting of the idea that single parents or "fragile families" are here to stay. What these families most need is a variety of social supports to make their jobs as both breadwinners and parents more feasible. The goals and the ideas of the village builders, like those of the traditionalists, have considerable merit. I favor programs like the earned income tax credit and child care subsidies that make it a little easier for a low-wage mother to support her family. I also strongly believe that until we improve the education of people at the bottom of the skills distribution, their economic prospects will be poor and their motivation to avoid an unplanned pregnancy limited. But I am less convinced that education reform or an expansion of social programs will change family formation patterns anytime soon.

For the above reasons, I have argued for a third way that could supplement these efforts and, in concert with them, make a big difference in the lives of children and their families. My central idea involves changing the default from having children to not having children. I am not arguing that people with limited resources should not have children. I am arguing that when they do have a child, it should be a conscious choice.

Behavioral economics has taught us that controlling our behavior is incredibly difficult, especially where sex is concerned, but it has also taught us strategies to wrest back control. Given that marriage is less of a commitment device than it used to be, we need to create new social policies and norms that encourage adults to raise children in good environments. Specifically, we need to encourage the use of methods, such as LARCs, that change the default from opting out of pregnancy to opting in.

The benefits of changing the default will accrue not just to women but also to children and to society at large. Too often in the past this issue has been framed as a matter of respecting women's reproductive rights. But it is not just women who benefit when they and their partners are able to take greater control over their reproductive lives. A wanted child, born to committed and mature parents, begins life with all kinds of advantages.

The advantages of being wanted may even outstrip the advantages of being born to a married couple. A single woman who really wants to be a parent and is prepared to take on that responsibility will almost surely be a better mother than a married woman who is unhappy in that role. The ideal arrangement for a child, of course, is to be both wanted and raised within a stable two-parent family. But that may not always be possible.

If we are concerned about the great crossover, the solution is not to hurry up marriage; the solution is to slow down the decision to have a child. The delay will make it more likely that parents are mature enough, established enough in their jobs, and sufficiently committed to each other to be good parents. With the adults in better control of their lives, children will be greatly helped in the process. Well-raised children, in turn, set the stage for a virtuous circle. They will grow up to be better parents themselves. Indeed, it is the prospect of a virtuous circle that should make this agenda most appealing.

My hope is that we are on the brink of a new era in which all children are wanted and are born to parents ready to raise them to be successful adults.

SEVEN

The Future:
Less Marriage, Fewer Children?

It is always wise to look ahead, but difficult to look further than you can see.

—Winston Churchill

We already have a great diversity of families and household types in the United States. One might wonder, then, what families will look like as we move forward. What is in store for the future of marriage and children? Will we one day become a society in which more and more people simply live alone and women who bear children raise them on their own? Will fertility continue to decline to the point where we cannot replace our current population and it begins to shrink? Will greater affluence and better education cause more people to adopt the married lifestyles and helicopter parenting of today's college-educated adults? Will same-sex marriage become widely accepted and become a new model for what a truly committed relationship can look like?

Another set of questions is about how people will balance work and family life. Will governments and employers adopt policies that allow parents to spend less time at work and more time caring for their families? Will more men take responsibility for raising children, thereby relieving women of the burden they have disproportionately borne? Will marriages involve a more equal sharing of these burdens?

129

The right answer to each question, of course, is that no one knows. But just asking the questions allows us to think about what we might like the future to look like, as well as what we think will actually happen.

The Future of Marriage

I do not think marriage is a dying institution as much as it is an evolving one. A world in which everyone lived alone or formed a series of short-term relationships would likely leave most adults unsatisfied. Marriage is about commitment. It brings with it many benefits: shared aspirations and experiences, built-in companionship, physical and psychological intimacy, an extended family, and the knowledge and security that comes with knowing that someone cares about you and puts your welfare above that of all others. That said, committed relationships do not have to be called marriage or be sanctified in a church or involve separate roles for men and women. Other advanced countries have gone further than the United States in ratifying the evolution of committed relationships. Cohabitation, which is still primarily a short-term relationship in the United States, has evolved into a longer-term and more stable type of relationship in some other countries, such as Sweden. And the marriages of the future do not have to involve children. (Some couples are as devoted to their pets as others are to their children. Speaking for myself, in addition to a fine grandson, I have two wonderful grand-dogs.)

Today's well-educated young adults, who are delaying both marriage and childbearing until they are established in their careers and ready to become parents, are role models for the future. Later marriage leads to much less divorce, and later parenting leads to much better parenting. In short, maturity and experience matter. We accept that they matter for success in the labor market. But they also help in matters of the heart. The large numbers of less-educated young adults who have put the baby carriage before the ring, for the most part did not intend to do so. They need help in aligning their behaviors with their intentions.

If one assumes that same-sex couples will eventually be fully accepted by the rest of society, they may show the way to a better future. Some of these couples will marry and then have children, but their children will, by definition, not be the result of an unplanned pregnancy. And whatever division of labor occurs between them will be freely chosen, not based on a gendered definition of who brings home the bacon and who makes the scrambled eggs.

Finally, I suspect there will also be more single women, and perhaps men, who want to be parents and decide to have or raise a child on their own. The operative words in the last sentence are "want" and "decide." There is no reason that these families cannot flourish. We can worry about the lack of a male (or female) role model in the household and the stresses of lone parenting. We can also worry about whether they are making a wise choice—are they fully functioning, mature adults with a plan to support themselves—but in my view, these questions are largely eclipsed by the fact that such individuals say they want to be, and are prepared to be, good parents.

In her book *Marriage Confidential,* Pamela Haag suggests other ways in which marriage could evolve over time. She writes about the millions of husbands and wives who are secretly troubled about their marriages, not because they are miserable or conflict-ridden, but because they feel that something is missing and yearn for something better. She writes convincingly about the Scylla of unrealistic expectations on the one hand and the Charybdis of settling for an empty-shell marriage on the other. Her idea is not to throw out marriage as an institution but to consider new models that might work better in the future: something more than just a reallocation of domestic duties but something less than polygamy. These could include marriage as a partnership for parenting, commuter marriages for two-earner couples whose careers keep them apart for long periods, nonresidential marriages in which each spouse retains a separate house or apartment, child-free marriages with an emphasis on travel and adventure, open marriages that are not sexually exclusive, term-limited marriages that come with an expiration date and an option to recontract for a longer period, and other alternatives that represent outside-the-box arrangements. She does not advocate for any of these alternatives—clearly they have both benefits and costs—but rather argues that an institution that does not bend with the times may be doomed to extinction.[1] Having participated in a commuter marriage for five years of my life, I would extoll its virtues for rekindling romance and refreshing the foundations of a relationship. Absence doesn't just make the heart grow fonder; it can foster a greater appreciation of what each partner brings to a relationship and the dangers of taking that for granted.

Whether marriage is reinvented or not, it is likely that decisions to have children will almost surely change. Fertility rates have been declining for a long time, and the proportion of women who are having only one child or remaining childless by choice has risen sharply. Fertility has fallen in all advanced countries and will almost surely continue to fall in the future. In the United States, the fertility rate is now 1.9 children per woman, a little below the replacement level of 2.1. It waxes and wanes with the state of the economy and other factors, but the long-term trend is pretty clear: women have fewer children as their own opportunities, along with their ability to control their reproductive destinies, expand.

In the past a woman (and to a lesser extent a man) who chose not to have children, or had fewer children than was dictated by current norms, was viewed with sympathy or suspicion. Over time, those pressures have abated. No one today would strongly chastise an American middle-class woman for not having enough children, as President Theodore Roosevelt did in his state of the union address in 1903.[2]

Bear in mind that right now 60 percent of all childbearing among young single adults in the United States is unintended. As women's education and employment opportunities continue to grow, and as the promise of newer and more effective forms of contraception is realized, women will almost surely have even fewer children than they do today, with more women and men opting out of childbearing altogether.

In addition to new opportunities for women, better birth control, and fewer social pressures to have children, another reason that childbearing is likely to decline is the rising cost of children. People are likely to have fewer children but invest more in each one.

Finally, much has been written about changes in the economy that have increased the demand for skilled workers and the fact that the supply of such workers has not kept pace with the need.[3] In a similar vein, family formation patterns have not kept pace with what a modern economy requires: delayed marriage and childbearing. Such lags between what technology demands and what social norms encourage are inevitable, but one role that policy can play is to hasten the adjustment process.

All in all, there are many reasons to think that we are still in the midst of what might be called a third demographic transition. Before the eighteenth century, both birth and death rates were very high. Then, after the Industrial Revolution and the improvements in standards of living that revolution made possible, mortality rates declined sharply. After a lag, birth rates fell too. With fewer people dying, especially infants, and greater access to contraception, parents were able to have fewer children and still have enough people to run the family farm and support them in their old age. David Willetts summed up this first demographic transition as follows: "First, we stop dying like flies, and then we stop breeding like rabbits."[4]

A second demographic transition occurred when growing affluence enabled more people to free themselves from traditional family commitments to pursue more individual goals, leading to the great diversity described in this book. But there has been a giant hiccup in the process. Although fertility has declined and choices have expanded, the proportion of children born outside of marriage, many as the result of unplanned pregnancy, has risen sharply.

I am cautiously predicting a third demographic transition. There will be further declines in fertility as adults are better able to prevent unintended or unwanted births in and out of marriage and invest more in any children they choose to have. Children who are planned for and wanted will increasingly be born to couples who have made a long-term commitment to each other and to their children. It is an optimistic prediction, but one supported by the facts enumerated above. But this is a long-term view; we are not there yet—far from it. In the meantime, because of a new kind of lag—between when people have children (early and often inadvertently) and when they marry (late and less often than in the past)—families are in trouble.

Addressing Some Likely Objections to My Arguments

I wrote this book in the hopes of catalyzing a broader debate on the issues it raises. Although I cannot anticipate where that debate might end up, I can already imagine some of the objections to the arguments I have made, and I would like to address several of them.

Objection 1: Marriage is still alive and well among the educated classes, and they can show the way to a better future.

This argument is made by Charles Murray in his book *Coming Apart*. He emphasizes the huge differences in marriage rates between professional couples in "Belmont" and working-class couples in "Fishtown." He believes that if the well-educated and those in leadership positions were to sing the praises of marriage, they could revive its importance across all segments of society. Like Murray, I believe that cultural norms are important and that marriage is beneficial. But when marriage has virtually collapsed among so many members of the youngest generation, the fact that it is still alive and well for the elites does not leave much room for optimism. Moreover, there is little evidence that marriage education programs, changes in tax laws, or other efforts to restore marriage have had much success. Finally, unless the men in Fishtown change their attitudes and their willingness to share more equally in the burdens of caring for home and children, women are not going to respond well to entreaties to tie the knot. Yes, it would help if the men had an easier time making a living, but that will take a long-term effort to improve education and skills. One way to do that is to improve the quality of parenting and the circumstances of a child's birth *now*, since family background has a large effect on later success and especially, it seems, on the success of boys.

Of course, we should want *both* men and women to do better in the labor market. I favor more resources devoted to career and technical education. I also favor a higher minimum wage and a more generous earned income tax credit.[5] But more prosperity by itself is not likely to create a marriage culture. It will, instead, almost surely lead to more household fragmentation. Living alone, including raising a child on one's own, is a luxury that was unaffordable in the past. Conversely, from a strictly economic perspective, marriage is a powerful tool for boosting household income. If a man and a woman have any earnings at all, they will be better off pooling their resources under one roof. As an economist, I am naturally biased toward economic explanations for what has been happening to marriage, but in this case, the economic argument about the declining economic prospects of men being the problem is flawed. The arithmetic doesn't work. Two incomes are always better than one. The problem is cultural; it is the failure of men to adjust as well as women have—both to the new economy and to new gender roles. Men have not kept pace with women educationally; they may be less willing to work in the kind of low-wage jobs that many women hold; and they continue to insist on certain male perquisites in their social and domestic lives. This is all understandable. Culture and sources of identity are very sticky if not biologically ordained; one can empathize with the circumstances of today's less-skilled young men who are trying to survive in an economy and a culture that bears no resemblance to what their fathers experienced. But solutions need to involve aligning behavior with where the economy and the culture are headed, not with where they have been.

Objection 2: If fewer children are born, we will have a smaller and grayer population, which will lead to less economic growth, less military power, and less ability to pay for retirement.

Should we be concerned about those things? Most definitely, says Jonathan Last, in his interesting book *What to Expect When No One's Expecting.* In his words, we can "forget the debt ceiling. Forget the fiscal cliff, the sequestration cliff and the entitlement cliff. Those are all just symptoms. What America really faces is a demographic cliff: The root cause of most of our problems is our declining fertility rate." These problems, according to Last, include not just an aging population but also less innovation, lower productivity, slower growth, and less ability to project our military power around the world. Just look at Japan, he says, where consumers bought more adult diapers than baby diapers last year! While America still has a fertility rate that is higher than Japan's or most of Europe's, Last believes it will likely decline (and I agree). Already, he notes, pets outnumber children in the United States by a ratio of more than four to one.[6]

But is Last right? It is certainly true that the aging of the population is a big fiscal problem in Japan, and to some extent in the United States. Spending on pensions and health care is rising sharply as the number of working-age adults per elderly person shrinks. But more babies are not the only solution. We can solve the problem by allowing more immigrants to enter the country—legally. What we need is a new immigration system that both creates a path to citizenship for the 11.7 million now here illegally and puts greater emphasis on skills, not just family ties.

The fact is that immigration, done the right way, is good economic policy. The key point from an economic perspective is that the 7 billion people in the world are a potential pool of talent that any advanced country should want to attract. Ignoring that pool is the equivalent of General Motors recruiting all its workers from Michigan while ignoring the other forty-nine states.

Fears that immigrants will replace or undermine the wages of American workers are, for the most part, unfounded. They may have hurt the job prospects of some of our least-skilled workers, such as high school dropouts, but they have become the backbone of many sectors of the economy, from construction to agriculture, thereby producing jobs for Americans in businesses that would otherwise be less likely to flourish. If we move to a more employment-based immigration system in which the needs of the economy are given greater weight and family reunification a smaller role, immigration can become a dynamic force for growth and a partial solution to our fiscal problems. Countries such as Canada and Australia, in which skills-based immigration is the norm, have benefited from such a system.

Immigration is often feared because immigrants are "different," because they place a burden on local social services, and because they fail to assimilate by learning English and the other hallmarks of our culture. Yet we have been a nation of immigrants from the beginning with each new wave raising such fears and later becoming almost fully assimilated into society. With a more rational and controlled immigration system, one based more on employer needs, any short-run problems of adjustment would be far easier to deal with, and the resulting longer-term diversity would be a potential source of strength for the nation as a whole. In the meantime, if fertility does decline, and there are fewer American children to support, whatever resources parents and governments have to invest in the education and health care of the next generation will go much further.

Expecting women to rededicate themselves to producing children is not in the cards, even with the kind of pro-natalist policies that have been tried in other countries. Jonathan Last does a nice job of reviewing these policies, and despite his concerns about falling fertility, he concludes they have been a failure. Take Singapore, for example. In 2000, the government offered parents a "baby bonus" of $9,000 for a second child and $18,000 for a third child. It then established "child development accounts"—analogous to 401(k) plans, but for children, and with the added benefit that the government matches parents' own savings dollar-for-dollar up to a limit. Combined with paid maternity leave and child-oriented housing policies, Singapore is, in Last's words, "a natalist utopia" but a country that has "met with total and unremitting failure" in achieving its fertility goals.[7] Europe, with the possible exception of France and some of the Nordic countries, has not fared much better. At 1.6 children per woman, the fertility rate in Europe is well below U.S. levels.

Objection 3. Women and men are not the same. Women are programmed to be mothers and to take primary responsibility for the raising of children. Evolutionary biology favored men who sired lots of offspring and women who did a good job of raising their children to maturity so that these children could then reproduce the species.

I have thought and read a fair amount about this question and have concluded that there probably are some gender-based differences, *on average,* but that both social context and individual variation around the average matter far more than biology. This debate will not be resolved any time soon. Some people believe culture trumps biology. Feminists, in particular, have questioned whether there is such a thing as a "maternal instinct." They reject the biological basis for such an instinct, pointing to the data on widespread abandonment, infanticide, and indifferent and neglectful mothers as evidence that such an instinct must be lacking. Other experts disagree. The noted primatologist Sarah Hrdy, while acknowledging the tremendous influence of culture and of economic and social conditions, argues that there may be some biological basis for "mother love."[8] That special maternal feeling for a child appears to be most clearly rooted in the hormonal changes associated with pregnancy and breastfeeding an infant.[9] In the end, probably all we can reasonably conclude is that both biology and social factors play a role and that their relative importance is likely to vary not only from one culture to another but also from one individual to another. Related to the debate about the influence of gender is research on how same-sex married couples behave in comparison with straight couples and how lesbian couples differ from gay couples. What is under way here is a kind of natural experiment in which marriage or a committed relationship is the fixed element in the story but gender roles within that relationship are ill-defined and up for grabs. Are these same-sex relationships more egalitarian than traditional ones? Liza Mundy has reviewed the available research and concluded that they are. It is not that same-sex couples share everything equally and that money doesn't matter. The higher-earning spouse typically has more authority in the household and less responsibility for domestic tasks. But "because there was no default assignment based on gender, such patterns evolved organically, based on preferences and talents." Interestingly, not everyone works when there are children to be cared for. Gay fathers are just as likely to be stay-at-home parents as are women in straight marriages. Lesbian couples are particularly egalitarian but more likely to split up than their male counterparts. Mundy attributes this to the fact that women may be more demanding of relationships than men, concluding that "maybe even women don't know what women want."[10]

Objection 4. All of the arguments about the need to reduce unplanned pregnancies are just another attempt to limit the rights of poor and minority parents. We have a history of using compulsory sterilization in the United States and do not want to repeat that history.

That history is, indeed, shameful. The good news is that our awareness of it should cause us never to go down that road again.[11] Nothing in this book is meant to be compulsory; this is all about choice. But as research documents, sometimes we don't do the things that are in our own self-interest and a gentle nudge is needed. Just as more people than ever are signing up for employer-provided retirement benefits in response to a more creative framing of this choice, something similar needs to happen in the family planning arena. To be sure, there are some serious questions about what it means to be ready for parenthood. If a teenager or a drug-abusing woman or a homeless and unemployed man wants to have a baby, should we simply say "That's their choice," or should we be a bit more paternalistic? For some, these questions will suggest their own answers, but I believe that there is plenty of gray between the black and white in this sensitive area. In the end, however, the biggest dagger in the heart of the argument about discrimination against poor or minority women is that they themselves do not want to have as many children as they are currently having. Unintended pregnancy rates are much higher among the poor, minority groups, and the less-educated than among more-advantaged women. We need to make the most effective forms of birth control free and widely available. In that way we can help poorer and less-educated women align their behavior with their intentions.

Objection 5. There is no reason an affluent society cannot afford to support its children, including those born to low-income or single-parent families. If there is a new class divide in American society, the solution is not finger-wagging about high rates of unwed childbearing but more resources and opportunities for those in the lower ranks.

I believe we should be spending a lot more on children and on the poor. We can afford it. The problem is not a lack of resources as much as it is a lack of political will. Many single parents are not single parents by choice, and many are doing an exemplary job of raising their children. I hope that the arguments in this book are not used as a reason to cut back on efforts to fund child care, parental leave, supports for working single parents, or other measures that might make raising children a more reasonable task in today's world. That said, more money just can't be the whole answer. There is not enough money to create adequate supports for the growing number of "fragile families." For every child saved from a life of poverty by more spending on the social safety net, a new child is born into poverty as the result of current demographic trends.

In 1996, we reformed the welfare system in a way that tied taxpayer-supported assistance to work. A time may come when we want to tie such assistance to responsible childbearing. We already do that in the sense that some benefit programs, such as the EITC, do not provide additional benefits to those who have bigger-than-average families. Why should a middle-class family that is struggling to make ends meet, and as part of that struggle is limiting the number of children it has, be required to pay higher taxes to support those with larger families? In the meantime, a first step should be to encourage women who want to avoid pregnancy to use the most effective forms of contraception available. Such contraception should be free, and it should be coupled with counseling and other benefits that encourage its use. But no amount of subsidies and counseling in this area will do much good for women whose opportunities are extremely limited as the result of poor education and related factors. We need to improve their opportunities by providing high-quality early education by recruiting better teachers, improving career and technical education, and the like, to give them the motivation as well as the means to become deliberate parents.

Objection 6. How will someone know when he or she is "ready to be a parent"? Is anyone ever really ready? And aren't you condemning those with limited resources to a life without children?

Many people, liberals in particular, are wary of seeming judgmental about who is fit to be a parent and who is not. In most cases, however, individuals *themselves* know intuitively what this means. We do not need a new manual or checklist that spells this out. We can rely on people's good judgment, reinforced by a new social norm: childbearing should not be about what adults want; it should be about what children need. Young adults from privileged backgrounds probably obsess about this more than they need to. Those from less-privileged backgrounds may wonder if they will ever be ready. However, combined with a reasonable level of social supports, such as paid parental leave, wage supplements, and subsidized child care, there is no reason that a dual-earner couple cannot make ends meet and raise one or two children. Even with no additional supports beyond those that exist now, a two-parent family in which one parent works full-time and the other half-time will have an income above the poverty line. Yes, life might be tough; trade-offs will probably be required; and more supports for those playing by the rules are needed. But it is not a scenario that precludes parenthood for those at the bottom of the income scale. What it does preclude, as a matter of principle, is having children or additional children too casually, or with the wrong person, without thinking about the consequences. Being a parent requires more planning and less drifting.

Views on all of these issues will differ. My goal with this book is to encourage a broader debate over where we are, and where we should be headed. There is no one script for everyone. But changing the default is necessary. New choices imply new responsibilities.

What We Need to Do

I have argued that the families of the future will likely be smaller, more diverse, and more egalitarian. Smaller because women have new roles and identities in addition to being mothers, and more ability to control their fertility. More diverse because of greater affluence and tolerance for different family forms. And more egalitarian because women now have the bargaining power to insist on a more equal division of labor in both the market and the home.

These expanded options are confronting the youngest generation with a wealth of new choices in the areas of sex, parenthood, and marriage. Some of them ("the planners") are getting a college degree, launching a career, marrying in their late twenties or early thirties, and jointly committing to making big investments in one or two children. Others ("the drifters"), typically those without a college degree, are having children early and outside of marriage, often in a series of cohabiting relationships with different partners. As a result, a large proportion of all children in the United States (between one-third and one-half) are experiencing a huge amount of household churning or family instability early in life, with adverse consequences for their health and education. These changes in family formation patterns, along with rising gaps in income and education, are a threat to intergenerational mobility and the American ideal of a classless society.

Some observers of these trends have suggested a role for government in restoring the traditional family by funding marriage education programs, creating a more family-friendly tax and welfare system, or improving the economic prospects of less-skilled men. Others favor supporting the growing number of single parents with a more adequate safety net and work-related benefits such as child care and paid leave. My own view is that both approaches have some merit. But much more critical than anything else are improvements in education. Until the United States gets serious about the need to link spending on education to improvements in teaching, to innovative models such as those used by the best charter schools and by the Career Academies now found in many high schools, and to more effective postsecondary education and training opportunities, we will continue to have a large contingent of young adults who, because they are effectively excluded from participating fully in the modern economy, will also continue to drift into too-early childbearing. That said, these education reforms take time, may require significant new resources, and are best thought of as a longer-term solution to the problems addressed in this book. Moreover, improving the education and skills of the future workforce cannot be a task left only to the schools. Without the active participation of parents and students themselves, no amount of classroom reform will change current trajectories very much. Education begins in the home, and the ability to take advantage of what schools have to offer comes from good parenting and motivated students, not just from good schools.

While I have spent much of my career arguing for better social policies, what motivated me to write this book is my sense that although these policies have received plenty of attention, the issue of preventing unplanned and too-early childbearing has been either ignored or sidelined in a separate policy silo, despite the fact that it has the potential to change the life trajectories of both the current and the next generation. Policies to reduce unplanned births can complement sensible social policies like those outlined above in a way that is not only affordable but will actually save money, and over time lead to change in the demographic destinies of a whole generation. Without such change, the effectiveness of the rest of the social policy agenda will be limited and its political acceptability and affordability strained by a demographic tide of family breakdown that puts more children at risk of growing up without the firm foundation that only families can provide.

So, what exactly can be done to turn the tide? How do we change the default from couples having children by accident to couples not having children until they are quite sure they want to be parents and are ready to take on the task?

First, we should monitor the implementation of the Affordable Care Act to make sure that private health plans are providing all forms of birth control, including those with higher up-front costs (such as an IUD or an implant) without a co-pay. Insurers may not like these high initial costs, but all of the evidence suggests IUDs and implants are a cheaper form of birth control over the long run, and that the savings from less prenatal and postnatal care and delivery of a baby far exceed these costs. When one adjusts for the fact that most of the women who postpone giving birth will still have children—just later in life—the savings are not as large but are still very significant.[12] More important, whatever the costs, delaying parenthood is better for children.[13]

Second, we should encourage more states to expand Medicaid coverage of family planning services to a broader group of low-income individuals, as allowed by the Affordable Care Act. Past family planning expansions have reduced unintended births in a very cost-effective manner.[14] Limiting such eligibility, as some states have done, to only the very poor is shortsighted and costly. In 2010, the average cost for one Medicaid-covered birth was $12,770, whereas the annual cost of providing publicly funded contraception for a woman was $239.[15]

Third, we should use the power of the media, including social media, to educate the young and change social norms. Sex education in the schools is fine, but young people report that their "health class" was often too little, too late, or too boring. They are almost always online and prefer to get their information in small and relevant bites when they most need it. In an attempt to improve young adults' knowledge of the many different ways of preventing an unwanted birth, The National Campaign to Prevent Teen and Unplanned Pregnancy's website, Bedsider.org, is reaching a large number of young adults in an effective way. Just as sites like WebMD are changing the way people get health care information, so too can more specialized sites like Bedsider change the way they get specific information on contraception. Television shows and movies can also play a role in simultaneously educating and entertaining one of their favorite demographics: young adults. One study by Melissa Kearney and Phil Levine suggests that MTV's show *Sixteen and Pregnant* accounted for about one-third of the reduction in the teen birth rate between June 2009 and December 2010.[16] Given the power of the media, one specific option is to develop and implement a serious social marketing campaign on the relative effectiveness of different forms of contraception, modeled after Iowa's "Avoid the Stork" campaign.[17] This campaign targeted women ages 18 to 30 through television ads, billboards, print and Web ads, college events, and giveaway promotions. The campaign used humor and created a "brand" with a mascot in the form of a large awkward stork who interrupts a person's life plans. By the end of the campaign, over 70 percent of women surveyed reported having seen or heard of the campaign, and Iowa has seen impressive declines in unintended pregnancy (8 percent in the period 2006–2011).[18] Building on this example, in addition to the successes of some other national campaigns such as the Truth campaign (to reduce smoking) and VERB (to combat obesity), such an effort would likely be very cost-effective.[19]

Fourth, we should encourage more educational institutions, including both high schools and colleges, to offer a free health screening to every entering student. As part of the screening, students should be provided information and counseling about how to prevent an unintended pregnancy, a full spectrum of birth control and abstinence options, and help with securing family planning services, if needed. Where this is not feasible, entering students should at least be provided with better information about the risks of pregnancy and how to prevent it.

Fifth, many physicians are simply not up to date or trained in how to provide long-acting reversible contraceptives (LARCs) to their patients.[20] Training paraprofessionals to do the job is feasible and would greatly expand the supply of providers.[21] The Department of Health and Human Services should provide funding to professional organizations or medical schools for this purpose.

Finally, the larger society needs to engage in a dialogue about the role that birth control can play in reducing the abortion rate, in preventing child poverty, and in improving social mobility. Until more people in leadership positions are willing to take a stand on these important issues, progress will get mired in the culture wars that a small minority wants to keep alive for political or religious reasons. Involving the leaders of various faiths in this dialogue could not be more important, but taking religious scruples about sex or contraception out of the public square has to be one of the goals. About three-fourths of Americans agree that religion should be kept out of public debates on social issues.[22]

Concluding Thoughts

I have been an advocate of marriage for most of my life. I consider myself very lucky to have enjoyed a forty-year marriage with a man who was fully committed to our partnership.

Moving from the personal to the professional, my research and that of many others has suggested that marriage is the best environment for raising children. I wrote an article for the *Washington Post* in 2012 summarizing my view that marriage is the best environment for children.[23] The article marked the twentieth anniversary of a speech by former vice president Dan Quayle in which he criticized Murphy Brown, a popular TV character, for giving birth to a child outside of marriage. He was roundly criticized at the time for his old-fashioned, intolerant views. I defended him in my article and would defend him still. Twenty years ago it might have been possible to change the attitudes of the younger generation, and he was right to try.

The process of writing this book has forced me to revisit these issues and come to a slightly different set of conclusions. I no longer think it is possible to put the marriage genie back in the bottle. Marriage as an institution is disappearing in most advanced countries, including the United States. What will replace it is uncertain, but current trends and the experience of some other countries suggest we are headed for both more diverse living arrangements and a lot more cohabitation—a kind of "marriage light" that may look very much like a stable marriage without the piece of paper. That is not what we have now. To be sure, one group, the well-educated elite, appears to be forming stable relationships. But for the majority of Americans the amount of relationship churning and complexity in the early environments of today's children is troubling. Children simply arrive and parents make do. There is seldom the kind of commitment that marriage and childrearing should entail. This has created a parenting gap that is opening up a new class divide in American society and threatening the life chances and social mobility of these children.

This new class divide must be addressed on a variety of fronts, from a better education system to more child-care subsidies for working parents. But no amount of outside resources can substitute for the kind of good decisionmaking and personal responsibility that raising a child should entail. Even were our current politics a lot more progressive, I doubt that the picture would change very significantly. To quote my favorite line used by both Bill and Hillary Clinton, "Governments don't raise children; parents do."

On the normative front, women need to be freed from the expectation that they will be parents. Parenthood is as much a social as a biological imperative. Some women yearn to be mothers; others do not. Many more are simply ambivalent and caught in a web of social expectations and practices. Anyone who thinks that all women are programmed to be good mothers has not seen the data on child abuse and neglect or the extent of inadequate parenting that exists in America. Michael Wald, a well-respected expert on child abuse and neglect, believes that about 20 percent of all parents in America are doing an unacceptable job.[24] Progressives will chalk this up to a lack of resources in such families. That lack can exacerbate a bad situation and is worth correcting for all kinds of reasons, but it should not be used as an excuse for poor parenting. By all means, those who yearn to be parents should follow their dreams; those who don't should be free to follow theirs as well. That freedom will come, in part, from providing all women, including the poorest, with more education and greater opportunities, but it will also come from a new social ethic about what it takes to be a good parent—and a belief that it is O.K. *not* to be a parent.

Second, even if women felt freer to eschew motherhood or embraced an ethic of responsible parenthood, there is the inconvenient little problem that they might still like sex, and sex leads to pregnancy. Pregnancies can be aborted, but getting an abortion, especially if one is poor and less-educated, is difficult and expensive. In addition, for many, it is morally unacceptable. The solution is to make sex safe, to decouple sex and pregnancy, and to find more effective ways to do this. We now understand that we are weak-willed creatures, especially where sex is concerned. But if we are responsible adults, we will understand, as Ulysses did, that we need to bind ourselves to a mast in advance in order to prevent the siren song of sexual pleasure from derailing our plans. Long-acting contraceptives that protect against pregnancy until such time as one wants to get pregnant totally change the default. They tie a woman and her partner to the mast until they make a deliberate and active decision to cut themselves loose. Policies that both subsidize and encourage the use of such long-acting contraceptives are an inexpensive and highly effective way to reduce unplanned or unwanted pregnancies. They would also greatly reduce the number of abortions.

Imagine a world in which every child is wanted and planned for, in which every child's parents make a commitment to each other to raise the child together, and in which they make this a priority. Utopia? Perhaps, but even were we to get halfway there, it would be a huge improvement over what we have now, a nation in which at least half of all pregnancies are unintended at the time of conception. I believe this is an attainable vision because women are already moving in this direction. As having children becomes more a matter of choice, the quality of parenting should improve. The process of choosing will screen out those who don't like the job very much or don't feel up to the task and, for one or both reasons, are less likely to succeed at it. Finally, it is a lot easier to accelerate an existing trend than it is to reverse one that is going in the wrong direction. Even if we believe that more marriage would be helpful to children (as I do), turning the tide here, given the steep drop in marriage rates, is likely to be difficult. Reducing fertility, on the other hand, is going with the tide, and has even more potential to improve child well-being. It means fewer children to be raised, more resources to devote per child, and higher-quality parenting all at the same time. It means focusing on the quality of parenting, not just on the structure of the family. They are related but are not the same thing. Marriage advocates tend to ignore this fact.

We need a new set of norms and a new set of government policies directed more clearly at changing the default from having children to not having them until and unless you are ready to make the kind of commitment that good parenting entails. I firmly believe that moving toward a world in which most pregnancies and births are planned would be a huge benefit to everyone involved—women, men, children, and the American taxpayer. There would be far fewer abortions and births to young women outside of marriage. Children would be healthier, do better in school, be less likely to commit crimes, and grow up to be more successful parents and employees.

Appendix

FIGURE 1. The Number of Single-Parent Households Has Grown, 1950–2012

Percent of all families with children under 18

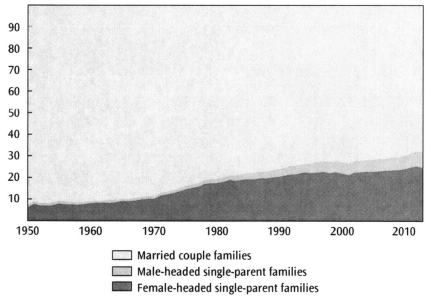

Married couple families
Male-headed single-parent families
Female-headed single-parent families

Source: U.S. Census Bureau, *America's Families and Living Arrangements* (Washington, 2012), table FG10.

FIGURE 2.   The Divorce Rate Has Declined since 1980

Number of divorces per 1,000 married women

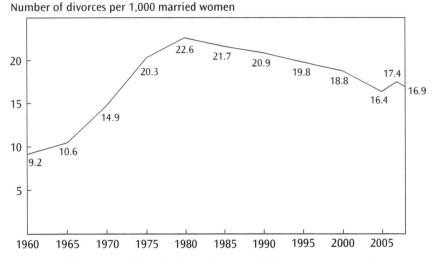

Source: William Bradford Wilcox, *The State of Our Unions 2012, Marriage in America: The President's Marriage Agenda* (Charlottesville, Va.: National Marriage Project, University of Virginia, 2012) (www.state ofourunions.org/2012/SOOU2012.pdf).

FIGURE 3.   Two Parents Have More Income than One Parent

Median family income (2012 dollars)

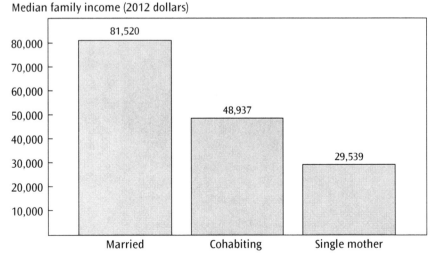

Source: U.S. Bureau of Labor Statistics, *Current Population Survey 2012: Annual Social and Economic Supplement* (2012), table HINC-04.

FIGURE 4. Marriage Is Good for Social Mobility

Percent who reach each income quintile by age 40

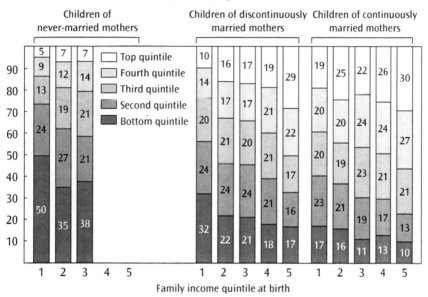

Source: Author calculations using the Social Genome Model.

FIGURE 5. Single-Parent Families' Need for Government Assistance

Average income (2010 dollars)

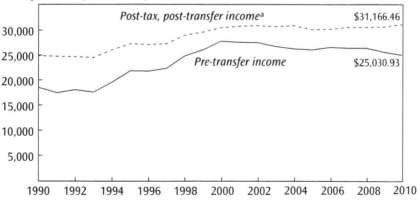

Source: U.S. Bureau of Labor Statistics, *Current Population Survey 2012: Annual Social and Economic Supplement* (2012), table HINC-04.

a. Includes earned income, child support, social insurance, means-tested cash benefits, food stamps, housing benefits, earned income tax credit (EITC), and other tax or stimulus payments.

FIGURE 6. Unmarried Births Have Shifted up the Age Range: Births to Unmarried Women Aged 15 to 29, 1980–2012

Births per 1,000 unmarried women in specified age group

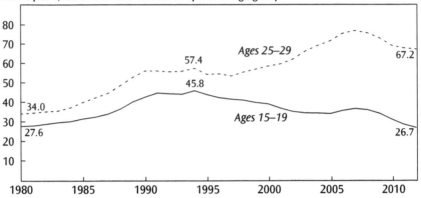

Sources: B. E. Hamilton, J. A. Martin, and S. J. Ventura, "Births: Preliminary Data for 2011," *National Vital Statistics Reports* 61, no. 5 (Hyattsville, Md.: National Center for Health Statistics, 2012); J. A. Martin, B. E. Hamilton, S. J. Ventura, M. J. K. Osterman, E. C. Wilson, and T. J. Mathews, "Births: Final Data for 2010," *National Vital Statistics Reports* 61, no. 1 (Hyattsville, Md.: National Center for Health Statistics, 2012); B. E. Hamilton, P. D. Sutton, and S. J. Ventura, "Revised Birth and Fertility Rates for the 1990s: United States, and New Rates for Hispanic Populations, 2000 and 2001," *National Vital Statistics Reports* 51, no. 12 (Hyattsville, Md.: National Center for Health Statistics, 2003); S. J. Ventura and C. A. Bachrach, "Nonmarital Childbearing in the United States, 1940–99," *National Vital Statistics Reports* 48, no. 16 (Hyattsville, Md.: National Center for Health Statistics, 2000).

FIGURE 7. Disadvantaged Women Are More Likely to Have Unintended Pregnancies

Births per 1,000 unmarried women in their 20s

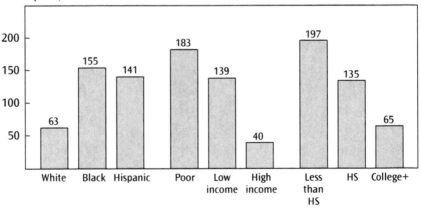

Source: Quentin Karpilow, Jennifer Manlove, Isabel Sawhill, and Adam Thomas, "The Role of Contraception in Preventing Abortion, Nonmarital Childbearing, and Child Poverty," paper presented at Association for Public Policy Analysis and Management, November 2013.

FIGURE 8.   Decreases in Unintended Births Reduces Unwed Births: Births to Unmarried Women Aged 20 to 44, 2006–10

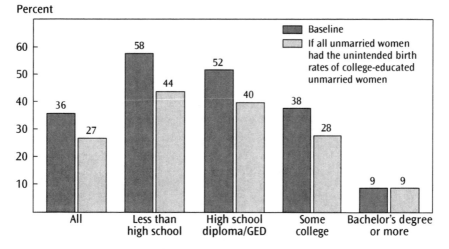

Percent

Source: Calculations from the National Vital Statistics System (NVSS), the Current Population Survey (CPS), and the National Survey of Family Growth (NSFG). Note that 2010 birth data from NVSS were combined with March CPS population estimates of numbers of unmarried women in 2010 in order to derive unmarried birth rates for women 20–44. Tabulations of NSFG 2006–10 data on birth intentionality were then applied in order to construct unintended birth rates.

FIGURE 9.   Unintended Pregnancies Result Mostly from Non-Use or Misuse of Contraception

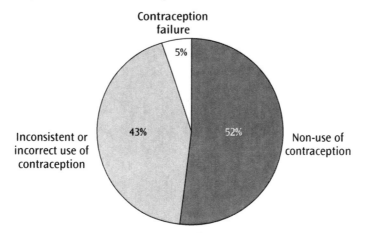

Source: Rache Benson Gold, Adam Sonfield, Cory L. Richards, and Jennifer J. Frost, "Next Steps for America's Family Planning Program: Leveraging the Potential of Medicaid and Title X in an Evolving Health Care System" (New York: Guttmacher Institute, 2009) (www.guttmacher.org/pubs/NextSteps.pdf).

FIGURE 10. Women in the United States Use IUDs Less than Those in Other Developed Countries

Percent of women using IUDs

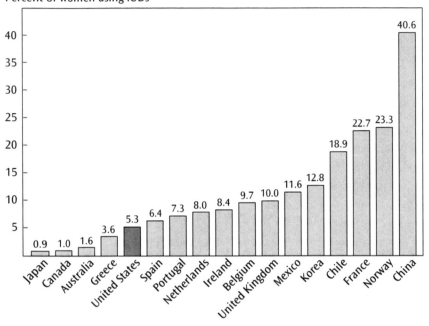

Source: United Nations, Department of Economic and Social Affairs, Population Division, *World Contraceptive Use 2012* (POP/DB/CP/Rev2012).

Notes

Chapter 1

Oprah Winfrey is quoted in "What Oprah Knows for Sure about Freedom," *O Magazine*, February 2002.

1. Charles Murray, *Coming Apart: The State of White America, 1960–2010* (Random House Digital, 2013).

2. William J. Clinton, "Address Accepting the Presidential Nomination" (speech, Democratic National Convention, New York, July 16, 1992).

3. Harry J. Holzer and Isabel Sawhill, "Payments to Elders Are Harming Our Future," *Washington Post*, March 8, 2013, sec. Opinions, www.washingtonpost.com/opinions/payments-to-elders-are-harming-our-future/2013/03/08/08c9030c-82bd-11e2-b99e-6baf4ebe42df_story.html.

4. Sarah Brown, personal communication with author, April 8, 2014.

5. Kathryn Edin and Timothy J. Nelson, *Doing the Best I Can: Fatherhood in the Inner City* (University of California Press, 2013); Kathryn Edin and Maria Kefalas, *Promises I Can Keep: Why Poor Women Put Motherhood before Marriage* (University of California Press, 2005), pp. 212–13.

6. Hanna Rosin, *The End of Men: And the Rise of Women* (New York: Riverhead Books, 2012), p. 7.

7. Ron Haskins and Isabel V. Sawhill, *Creating an Opportunity Society* (Brookings Institution Press, 2009), pp. 70–71.

Chapter 2

Opening quotation is taken from Paula McLain's *The Paris Wife* (New York: Ballantine Books, 2012).

1. Richard A. Settersten and Barbara Ray, *Not Quite Adults: Why 20-Somethings Are Choosing a Slower Path to Adulthood, and Why It's Good for Everyone* (New York: Bantam Books Trade Paperbacks, 2010), p. ix.

2. Ibid., p. 19.

3. Fifty-three percent of births to women under the age of 30 were out of wedlock in 2011. Jennifer Manlove and Elizabeth Wildsmith, "Trends in Marriage and Fertility," Child Trends blog, childtrends.org/2011/12/16/trends-in-marriage-and-fertility/.

4. When asked if they think they will someday get married, 78 percent of those who have never been married say that they plan to someday. "In U.S., Importance of Marriage Varies by Age, but Most Singles Want to Marry," Gallup, August 2, 2013, www.gallup.com/video/163652/importance-marriage-varies-age-singles-marry.aspx.

5. According to a Pew Research Center analysis of the Decennial Survey and the American Community Survey, much of the blame for the decline in marriage rates falls on younger Americans: among those age 18 to 29 the percentage married fell from 59 percent in 1960 to only 20 percent in 2010. D'Vera Cohn, Jeffrey S. Passel, Wendy Wang, and Gretchen Livingston, "Barely Half of U.S. Adults Are Married—A Record Low," Social & Demographic Trends (Washington: Pew Research Center, 2011), www.pewsocialtrends.org/2011/12/14/barely-half-of-u-s-adults-are-married-a-record-low.

6. The mean age of mothers at first birth was 25.6 years in 2011. Joyce A. Martin, Brady E. Hamilton, Stephanie J. Ventura, Michelle Osterman, and T. J. Matthews, "Births: Final Data for 2011," *National Vital Statistics Report* 62, no. 1 (2013): 1–90.

7. In 1989, the average age of both first marriage and first birth for women was about 24. The average age at first birth has not risen as quickly as the age at first marriage has. Kay Hymowitz, Jason S. Carroll, W. Bradford Wilcox, and Kelleen Kaye, "Knot Yet: The Benefits and Costs of Delayed Marriage in America" (Washington: National Campaign to Prevent Teen and Unplanned Pregnancy; Provo, Utah: Relate Institute, and Charlottesville, Va.: National Marriage Project, 2013).

8. In addition to the nineteen states that have officially approved same-sex marriage, courts in eight states (Indiana, Kentucky, Michigan, Arkansas, Idaho, Texas, Oklahoma, Utah, and Virginia) have found the states' ban on same-sex marriage unconstitutional. These decisions have not gone into effect, however, pending court hearings in the higher court.

9. Brady E. Hamilton, Joyce A. Martin, and Stephanie J. Ventura, "Births: Preliminary Data," *National Vital Statistics Report* 62, no. 3 (2013): 1–32.

10. Daniel T. Lichter and Deborah R. Graefe, "Finding a Mate? The Post-Birth Marital and Cohabitation Histories of Unwed Mothers," in *Out of Wedlock:*

Trends, Causes, and Consequences of Nonmarital Fertility, edited by L. L. Wu, R. Haveman, and B. Wolfe (New York: Russell Sage Foundation, 2001).

11. During the first half of the 1990s, over 90 percent of Swedish women in their twenties were currently cohabiting or had at some point cohabited. For other European countries, around 80 percent of 20-somethings had at some point cohabited. The European countries surveyed with similar proportions of women cohabiting included Sweden, Finland, Austria, Switzerland, Germany, and France. For exact percentages, see Kathleen Kiernan, "Unmarried Cohabitation and Parenthood: Here to Stay? European Perspectives," *The Future of the Family* 66 (2004): fig. 3.1.

12. For a discussion of ways in which American and European unions differ, see Andrew J. Cherlin, *The Marriage-Go-Round: The State of Marriage and the Family in America Today* (Random House Digital, 2010), pp. 16–19.

13. For example, he notes that in the mid-1990s the proportion of women married at least once by age 40 is 84 percent in the United States, but only 59 percent in Germany, 68 percent in France, and 70 percent in Sweden. It should be noted that although Cherlin is working from older data from the 1990s, the gaps in U.S. and European marriage and cohabitation rates are still comparable to or larger than his estimates. Ibid., pp. 16–17.

14. Forty-seven percent of children will experience the dissolution of their parents' relationship by their 15th birthday. Cohabiting couples in the United States are much less stable than married couples; about three-quarters of them break up before the child is age 15. The proportion of marriages ending in divorce or separation within five years is 23 percent in the United States and half that in most European countries. Ibid., pp. 206–7.

15. The median age at first marriage is 28 in the United States, 34 in Sweden, 31 in France, and 32 in Germany. United Nations Economic Commission for Europe, "Mean Age at First Marriage," http://w3.unece.org/pxweb/Dialog/varval.asp?ma=052_GEFHAge1stMarige_r&ti=Mean+Age+at+First+Marriage+by+Sex%2C+Country+and+Year&path=../DATABASE/Stat/30-GE/02-Families_households/&lang=1.

16. In 1982, 3 percent of women were currently cohabiting with an opposite-sex partner, whereas in 2006–2010, 11 percent were. Men's rates of cohabitation have also increased, though the National Survey of Family Growth did not collect data on men's rates until 2002. Kimberly Daniels, Jonathan Vespa, and William D. Mosher, *First Marriages in the United States: Data from the 2006–2010 National Survey of Family Growth* (Washington: U.S. Department of Health and Human Services, Centers for Disease Control and Prevention, National Center for Health Statistics, 2012).

Moreover, the changes are even more striking when people are asked if they have ever cohabited. Forty-eight percent of women interviewed between 2006 and 2010 reported that their first union was a cohabiting partner; only 34 percent reported this in 1995. Casey E. Copen, Kimberly Daniels, and William D. Mosher, "First Premarital Cohabitation in the United States: 2006–2010 National Survey of Family Growth," *National Health Statistics Reports* 64 (April 4), www.cdc.gov/nchs/data/nhsr/nhsr064.pdf.

17. Of survey respondents who were cohabiting at the time of the interview, 44 percent said they definitely or probably would marry their current partner. Based on Brookings tabulations of data from the National Survey of Families and Households, 2001–2003.

18. Copen, Daniels, and Mosher, "First Premarital Cohabitation in the United States."

19. Specifically, they found that the relationship between cohabitation and later divorce could be explained by already known risk factors, including premarital fertility, family structure, educational attainment, and number of premarital sex partners. Wendy D. Manning and Jessica A. Cohen, "Premarital Cohabitation and Marital Dissolution: An Examination of Recent Marriages," *Journal of Marriage and Family* 74, no. 2 (2012): 377–87.

20. This study assesses intimacy through responses to a series of questions in the National Longitudinal Study of Adolescent Health, on issues such as how much the respondent loved his or her partner (and vice versa), satisfaction with the relationship, and the number of meals eaten together per week (demonstrating shared time). It included a visualization using overlapping circles to represent how close participants felt to their partners. Michael Pollard and Katherine Mullan Harris, "Cohabitation and Marriage Intensity: Consolidation, Intimacy, and Commitment," RAND Working Paper Series (June 2013), p. 18, www.ssrn.com/abstract=2284457.

21. Ibid.

22. In the Fragile Families study, 52 percent of mothers who were cohabiting with their child's father at birth were still living with the father (26 percent were married and 26 percent were still cohabiting). In contrast, 80 percent of mothers married at the child's birth were still with the same partner. "Parents' Relationship Status Five Years after a Non-Marital Birth," Fragile Families Research Brief 39 (Princeton University, June 2007), www.fragilefamilies.princeton.edu/)/briefs/ResearchBrief39.pdf; Sara McLanahan, "Fragile Families and Children's Opportunity," Research Briefing (Washington: Annual Meeting of the National Academy of Sciences, 2012), crcw.princeton.edu/workingpapers/WP12-21-FF.pdf.

23. Eighty-two percent of those born in the 1940s had had premarital sex before they turned 30. Lawrence B. Finer, "Trends in Premarital Sex in the United States, 1954–2003," *Public Health Reports* 122, no. 1 (2007): 73.

24. Kate Taylor, "Sex on Campus: She Can Play That Game, Too," *New York Times*, July 12, 2013, sec. Fashion & Style. This piece is only one of many articles and books released in the past five years on the hookup culture. They include: Hanna Rosin, "Boys on the Side," *The Atlantic*, August 22, 2012; Caitlin Flanagan, "Love, Actually," *The Atlantic*, May 11, 2010; Kathleen A. Bogle, *Hooking Up: Sex, Dating, and Relationships on Campus* (NYU Press, 2008); Donna Freitas, *The End of Sex: How Hookup Culture Is Leaving a Generation Unhappy, Sexually Unfulfilled, and Confused about Intimacy* (New York: Basic Books, 2013); Hanna Rosin, *The End of Men: And the Rise of Women* (New York: Riverhead Books, 2012), p. 7.

25. Elizabeth A. Armstrong, Laura Hamilton, and Paula England, "Is Hooking Up Bad for Young Women?," *Contexts* 9, no. 3 (2010): 22–27.

26. Laura Sessions Stepp, *Unhooked: How Young Women Pursue Sex, Delay Love and Lose at Both* (New York: Riverhead Books, 2007).

27. Rosin, *The End of Men*, p. 39.

28. England's findings are cited in Taylor, "Sex on Campus."

29. Among the 1988–1996 cohort, 65 percent reported having sex weekly or more often in the past year, in comparison with 59 percent of college students from the 2002–2010 cohort; 31.9 percent of the earlier cohort reported having more than one sexual partner in the past year, in comparison with 31.6 percent of the later cohort. Martin A. Monto and Anna Carey, "A New Standard of Sexual Behavior? Are Claims Associated with the "Hookup Culture" Supported by Nationally Representative Data?," forthcoming in *Journal of Sex Research*.

30. Laura Hamilton and Elizabeth A. Armstrong, "Gendered Sexuality in Young Adulthood: Double Binds and Flawed Options," *Gender & Society* 23, no. 5 (2009): 589–616.

31. Paul Taylor and Scott Keeter, "Millennials: Confident. Connected. Open to Change" (Washington: Pew Research Center, 2010), p. 6, www.pewsocialtrends. org/files/2010/10/millennials-confident-connected-open-to-change.pdf.

32. Pamela Haag, *Marriage Confidential: The Post-Romantic Age of Workhorse Wives, Royal Children, Undersexed Spouses, & Rebel Couples Who Are Rewriting the Rules* (New York: HarperCollins, 2011), p. 11.

33. Daniel Ariely, *The Upside of Irrationality: The Unexpected Benefits of Defying Logic* (New York: HarperPerennial, 2011), p. 214.

34. Ibid., p. 219.

35. Cherlin, *The Marriage-Go-Round*.

36. Twenty-three percent of births between 2006 and 2010 to women aged 15–44 years were to unmarried women who were cohabiting, which is 58 percent of all births to unwed mothers between 15 and 44. Gladys Martinez, Kimberly Daniels, and Anjani Chandra, "Fertility of Men and Women Aged 15–44 Years in the United States: National Survey of Family Growth, 2006–2010," *National Health Statistics Reports* 51 (April 2012): table 12.

37. These numbers do not include single mothers living in other people's households (for example, a single mother living with her parents), but do include those who are cohabiting. To calculate this statistic, add the number of mothers and fathers in families with a child under the age of 18 and divide by the sum of couples, single parents, and grandparents living with a child under the age of 18. Lynne M. Casper and Suzanne M. Bianchi, *Continuity and Change in the American Family* (Thousand Oaks, Calif.: Sage Publications, 2001); U.S. Census Bureau, *America's Families and Living Arrangements* (Washington, 2012), table FG10.

38. U.S. Census Bureau, *America's Families*.

39. W. Bradford Wilcox, *The State of Our Unions 2012, Marriage in America: The President's Marriage Agenda* (Charlottesville, Va.: National Marriage Project, University of Virginia, 2012), www.stateofourunions.org/2012/SOOU2012.pdf.

40. Andrew J. Cherlin, "American Marriage in the Early Twenty-first Century," *The Future of Children* 15, no. 2 (2005): 36; Betsey Stevenson and Justin Wolfers, "Marriage and Divorce: Changes and Their Driving Forces," *Journal of Economic Perspectives* 21, no. 2 (2007): 30.

41. Betsey Stevenson and Justin Wolfers, "Trends in Marital Stability," in *Research Handbook on the Economics of Family Law*, edited by Lloyd R. Cohen and Joshua D. Wright (Northampton, Mass.: Edward Elgar, 2011), p. 104.

42. David T. Ellwood and Christopher Jencks, "The Spread of Single-Parent Families in the United States since 1960," *SSRN Electronic Journal* (2004), www.ssrn.com/abstract=517662.

43. Heather L. Ross and Isabel V. Sawhill, *Time of Transition: The Growth of Families Headed by Women* (Washington: Urban Institute, 1975).

44. For a similar view, see Stevenson and Wolfers, "Trends in Marital Stability," p. 107. They write: "While the causes of the dramatic rise in the divorce rate between 1965 and 1975 are still being debated, it is likely that part of the explanation lies in the transition in family life and gender roles occurring through the 1960s and 1970s."

45. In a review of this literature covering thirteen nationally representative studies, Liana Sayer and Suzanne Bianchi found that about half of the studies

supported the thesis that women's economic opportunities affect marital stability and about half did not. They found that, once one accounts for marital quality and other relevant factors, the effect of women's relative income on divorce is no longer significant. This suggests that earlier studies that found that a woman's income affected her ability to divorce were tapping into a woman's being more able to leave a bad marriage once she was able to support herself. See Liana C. Sayer and Suzanne M. Bianchi. "Women's Economic Independence and the Probability of Divorce: A Review and Reexamination," *Journal of Family Issues* 21, no. 7 (2000): 906–43; Hiromi Ono, "Husbands' and Wives' Resources and Marital Dissolution," *Journal of Marriage and Family* 60, no. 3 (1998): 674–89; Valerie Kincade Oppenheimer, "Women's Rising Employment and the Future of the Family in Industrial Societies," *Population and Development Review* 20, no. 2 (1994): 293–342.

46. Sayer and Bianchi, "Women's Economic Independence and the Probability of Divorce"; Marianne Bertrand, Jessica Pan, and Emir Kamenica, "Gender Identity and Relative Income within Households," Working Paper 19023 (Cambridge, Mass.: National Bureau of Economic Research, 2013).

47. A 1998 study found that wives who made 50–75 percent of the family's income had a significantly higher chance of divorce than wives who made less than their husbands. More recently, Marianne Bertrand and colleagues found that a man is less likely to get married if the average income of women in his "marriage market" is higher than his income. A marriage market is defined as the set of possible romantic partners given geography, age, and educational background. In addition, they found that women who earn more than their husbands are more likely to report that they are unhappy with the marriage, to think their marriage is troubled, and to say that they have discussed separation recently. Neither of these studies indicate whether these trends are due to the husband's making "too little" money or to the wife's making "too much" money, but they do control for the absolute income levels of both spouses, meaning that the negative effects of a woman making relatively more money holds whether her husband is a CEO or a minimum-wage worker. Bertrand, Pan, and Kamenica, "Gender Identity and Relative Income within Households"; D. Alex Heckert, Thomas C. Nowak, and Kay A. Snyder, "The Impact of Husbands' and Wives' Relative Earnings on Marital Disruption," *Journal of Marriage and Family* 60, no. 3 (1998): 690–703.

48. This newer view of marriage has been well articulated by several scholars of the family, including Robert Pollack and Shelly Lundberg, who see marriage as a commitment device for raising children; and Betsey Stevenson and Justin Wolfers, who see it more as a way of enjoying the good things of life with someone

who shares your interests. Shelly Lundberg and Robert A. Pollak, "Cohabitation and the Uneven Retreat from Marriage in the U.S., 1950–2010," Working Paper 19413 (Cambridge, Mass.: National Bureau of Economic Research, 2013), pp. 1–38; Stevenson and Wolfers, "Marriage and Divorce."

49. For all single-parent families, including male-headed one-parent families, 39 percent live in poverty. U.S. Census Bureau, *Annual Social and Economic Supplement*, 2012, table POV11: People in Families with Related Children under 18 by Number of Working Family Members and Family Structure.

50. William Julius Wilson, *The Truly Disadvantaged: The Inner City, the Underclass, and Public Policy* (University of Chicago Press, 2012).

51. Between 1940 and 1990, demand for workers in the bottom wage decile fell 30 to 50 percent, whereas demand for high-wage workers increased 50 to 70 percent. Kevin M. Murphy and Finis Welch, "Occupational Change and the Demand for Skill, 1940–1990," *American Economic Review* 83, no. 2 (1993): 122–26.

For the least-skilled workers, joblessness increased by around four weeks between the 1960s and the 1980s. Increases for mid-skilled workers was one-seventh as large, and high-skill workers had no change in levels of joblessness. Chinhui Juhnand others, "Why Has the Natural Rate of Unemployment Increased over Time?," *BPEA*, no. 2 (1991): 75–142; David H. Autor and Melanie Wasserman, *Wayward Sons: The Emerging Gender Gap in Labor Markets and Education* (Cambridge, Mass.: Third Way, 2013).

52. The United States' share of worldwide manufacturing fell from nearly 30 percent in 1980 to under 20 percent in 2010. See Marc Levinson, "U.S. Manufacturing in International Perspective" (Washington: Congressional Research Service, 2013), www.fas.org/sgp/crs/misc/R42135.pdf.

53. National Center for Education Statistics, "Income of Young Adults," http://nces.ed.gov/fastfacts/display.asp?id=77. Ron Haskins, Julia Isaacs, and Isabel Sawhill, "Getting Ahead or Losing Ground: Economic Mobility in America" (Washington: Brookings Institution Press, 2008), p. 62.

54. Between 1973 and 2007, college completion rates for women age 25 to 34 more than doubled, from 16 to 36 percent; the rates for men in the same age range increased from 24 to 29 percent. Sheldon Danziger and David Ratner, "Labor Market Outcomes and the Transition to Adulthood," *The Future of Children* 20, no. 1 (2010): 141.

55. The United States has seen large growth in the service industry since the 1980s; the share of U.S. labor hours in the service industry grew by 30 percent between 1980 and 2005. The increase was even larger among workers without

a college degree (53 percent). David H. Autor and David Dorn, "The Growth of Low Skill Service Jobs and the Polarization of the U.S. Labor Market," Working Paper 15150 (Cambridge, Mass.: National Bureau of Economic Research, 2009), p. 3.

56. The Belmont and Fishtown stories are based on real neighborhoods, but Murray's data analysis is based on national representative data sets. Murray created criteria based on the characteristics of these towns (for example, well-educated professionals versus blue-collar high school graduates) and then used representative survey data to assign people to be "citizens" of Belmont or Fishtown according to those criteria. Charles Murray, *Coming Apart: The State of White America, 1960–2010* (Random House Digital, 2013), pp. 148–52.

57. In 1978, 94 and 84 percent of those in Belmont and Fishtown, respectively, were married. In contrast, by 2010, 83 percent of the people in Belmont were married but only 48 percent of those in Fishtown. Ibid., pp. 158–59.

58. Data from the National Longitudinal Survey of Youth (1988–2000) show that the likelihood that a single young man will transition into marriage is higher for men with better wages and employment prospects. Similarly, data from the 1990 census show that areas with better male labor market prospects and more favorable sex ratios had higher marriage rates. Valerie Kincade Oppenheimer, "Women's Employment and the Gain to Marriage: The Specialization and Trading Model," *Annual Review of Sociology* 23 (1997): 431–53; Francine D. Blau, Lawrence M. Kahn, and Jane Waldfogel, "Understanding Young Women's Marriage Decisions: The Role of Labor and Marriage Market Conditions," Working Paper 7510 (Cambridge, Mass.: National Bureau of Economic Research, 2000).

For a larger bibliography in support of the theory that men with higher earnings have a better chance of marriage and a lower chance of divorce, see the literature review in Casper and Bianchi, *Continuity and Change in the American Family*, pp. 272–73.

59. David T. Ellwood and Christopher Jencks, "The Uneven Spread of Single-Parent Families: What Do We Know? Where Do We Look for Answers?," in *Social Inequality*, edited by Kathryn M. Neckerman (New York: Russell Sage Foundation, 2004), pp. 3–78.

60. For more information on the evolving legal status of abortion, see chapter 5.

61. Claudia Goldin and Lawrence F. Katz, "The Power of the Pill: Oral Contraceptives and Women's Career and Marriage Decisions," *Journal of Political Economy* 110, no. 4 (2002): 730–70; Martha J. Bailey, Brad Hershbein, and Amalia R. Miller, "The Opt-In Revolution? Contraception and the Gender Gap

in Wages," Working Paper 17922 (Cambridge, Mass.: National Bureau of Economic Research, 2012), www.nber.org/papers/w17922.

62. Mark Mather, "Fact Sheet: The Decline in U.S. Fertility," *World Population Data Sheets*, Population Reference Bureau, 2012, www.prb.org/Publications/Datasheets/2012/world-population-data-sheet/fact-sheet-us-population.aspx.

63. The proportion of childless women increased from 10 percent of women between the ages of 40 and 44 in 1976 to 18 percent in 2010. Gretchen Livingston and D'Vera Cohn, "Childlessness Up among All Women; Down among Women with Advanced Degrees," *Social & Demographic Trends Report* (Washington: Pew Research Center, 2010), www.pewsocialtrends.org/2010/06/25/childlessness-up-among-all-women-down-among-women-with-advanced-degrees.

64. Jonathan V. Last, *What to Expect When No One's Expecting: America's Coming Demographic Disaster* (New York: Encounter Books, 2013).

65. There are no societies with high fertility and low gender inequality, but countries with low fertility rates have varying levels of gender inequality. Philip Cohen, "Let's Not Panic over Women with More Education Having Fewer Kids," *The Atlantic*, February 12, 2013, www.theatlantic.com/sexes/archive/2013/02/lets-not-panic-over-women-with-more-education-having-fewer-kids/273070.

66. George A. Akerlof, Janet L. Yellen, and Michael L. Katz, "An Analysis of Out-of-Wedlock Childbearing in the United States," *Quarterly Journal of Economics* 111, no. 2 (1996): 277–317.

67. Cherlin, *The Marriage-Go-Round*, pp. 24–32.

68. Ibid., p. 29.

69. The proportion of the population living in families, as opposed to what the Census Bureau calls households made up of unrelated individuals, was 84.5 percent in 1962 and then declined to 66.5 percent by 2012. U.S. Census Data, 2012, table HH-1: Families and Living Arrangements, Households, by Type: 1940 to Present.

70. As quoted in Michael W. Macy, "Rational Choice," in *Contemporary Social Psychological Theories*, edited by Peter J. Burke (Stanford University Press, 2006), p. 70.

71. Malcolm, Gladwell. *The Tipping Point: How Little Things Can Make a Big Difference* (New York: Little, Brown, 2000).

72. Based on Brookings tabulations of General Social Survey data.

73. Fifty-three percent of adults in a 1957 survey expressed negative views of people who chose not to get married. In 1962, 85 percent of adult respondents believed that "all married couples who can, ought to have children." Arland

Thornton, "Changing Attitudes toward Family Issues in the United States," *Journal of Marriage and Family* 51, no. 4 (1989): 875; Arland Thornton and Linda Young-DeMarco, "Four Decades of Trends in Attitudes toward Family Issues in the United States: The 1960s through the 1990s," *Journal of Marriage and Family* 63, no. 4 (2001): 1028.

74. Thirty-four percent of Americans disapproved of those who did not marry, and the number of people who believed all married couples ought to have children dropped to 43 percent. Numbers for these "late 1970s and 1980s" figures come from the same surveys referenced in the previous two notes. Thornton, "Changing Attitudes toward Family Issues in the United States."

75. Though premarital sex was widely condemned among Americans in the early 1960s, by 1972 only one-fifth of Americans thought that premarital sex was immoral, and it has remained widely accepted by society in subsequent decades. Thornton, "Changing Attitudes toward Family Issues in the United States."

76. Fifty-two percent of millennials say that being a good parent is "one of the most important things" in life. Only 30 percent say that having a successful marriage is equally important. For Generation Xers in 1997, there was a much smaller gap between the number who valued children and the number who valued marriage. Wendy Wang and Paul Taylor, *For Millennials, Parenthood Trumps Marriage* (Washington: Pew Social and Demographic Trends, Pew Research Center, 2011).

77. Frank Newport and Igor Himelfarb, "In U.S., Record-High Say Gay, Lesbian Relations Morally OK," *Gallup Politics*, May 20, 2013, www.gallup.com/poll/162689/record-high-say-gay-lesbian-relations-morally.aspx.

78. Christina M. Gibson-Davis, Kathryn Edin, and Sara McLanahan, "High Hopes but Even Higher Expectations: The Retreat from Marriage among Low-Income Couples," *Journal of Marriage and Family* 67, no. 5 (2005): 1301–12.

79. Paul Taylor and Cary Funk, *As Marriage and Parenthood Drift Apart, Public Is Concerned about Social Impact* (Washington: Pew Research Center, 2007).

80. "World Values Survey 1981–2008 Official Aggregate, 2009," World Values Survey Association, www.worldvaluessurvey.org.

81. In 1976, around one-third of female and one-half of male high school seniors thought that living together before marriage was a good idea. By 1997 around two-thirds of both female and male seniors thought that cohabitation before marriage was a good idea. In the first decade of the twenty-first century, only a small minority (27 percent) of Americans disapproved of men and women living together before marriage. Thornton and Young-DeMarco, "Four Decades

of Trends in Attitudes toward Family Issues in the United States"; *Gallup*, September 7–8, 2007, www.gallup.com/poll/117328/marriage.aspx.

82. Scott M. Stanley, Galena Kline Rhoades, and Howard J. Markman, "Sliding versus Deciding: Inertia and the Premarital Cohabitation Effect," *Family Relations* 55, no. 4 (2006): 499–509.

83. Twenty-one percent of single women who were not cohabiting when they became pregnant were cohabiting at the time of the birth of their child. These shotgun cohabitations far exceeded the percentage of shotgun marriages (7 percent). Andrew J. Cherlin, "Demographic Trends in the United States: A Review of Research in the 2000s," *Journal of Marriage and Family* 72, no. 3 (2010): 403–19; Daniel T. Lichter, "Childbearing among Cohabiting Women: Race, Pregnancy, and Union Transitions," in *Early Adulthood in a Family Context* (New York: Springer, 2012), pp. 209–19.

84. Settersten and Ray, *Not Quite Adults*, p. 80.

85. Barry Schwartz, *The Paradox of Choice: Why More Is Less* (New York: Ecco, 2004).

86. Betsey Stevenson and Justin Wolfers, "The Paradox of Declining Female Happiness," *American Economic Journal: Economic Policy* 1, no. 2 (2009): 190–225.

87. Jennifer Silva, *Coming Up Short: Working Class Adulthood in an Age of Uncertainty* (Oxford University Press, 2013), p. 59.

88. Barry Schwartz cites a well-known study by Sheena Iyengar and colleagues in which shoppers in a mall were given the chance to sample jams and then buy the jam if they liked one of them. Some shoppers had six jams to choose from and some had twenty-four. Those with fewer options rated the jam higher and were more likely to buy a jar than those with many options. More choices meant the shoppers were less happy with their samples. Schwartz, *Paradox of Choice*, pp. 19–20.

89. For example, Schwartz notes that the fear of missing out on a lost opportunity often leads people to avoid making decisions—essentially, "choosing not to choose." He describes doctors faced with a patient suffering from osteoarthritis and asked if they would recommend a medication or a referral to a specialist. When they are only given one choice of medicine to recommend, about three-quarters recommend medication. But when they are given two options for the medication to recommend, only half recommend medication. Rather than make a choice and risk being wrong, half of the doctors would prefer to avoid the decision by referring the patient to another doctor. Schwartz, *Paradox of Choice*, p. 128.

Chapter 3

Opening quotation is taken from John Stuart Mill's *On Liberty* (London: Longman, Roberts & Green, 1869).

1. Public resistance to paying the needed taxes may seem heartless to some, but it is well known that our empathy for others depends in large measure on family or other ties that enable us to relate to those we help. Ron Haskins and Isabel V. Sawhill, *Creating an Opportunity Society* (Brookings Institution Press, 2009), pp. 19–31.

2. Stephanie Coontz, *Marriage, a History: From Obedience to Intimacy, or How Love Conquered Marriage* (New York: Penguin, 2006), p. 7.

3. Richard Reeves, "How to Save Marriage in America," *The Atlantic*, February 13, 2014, www.theatlantic.com/business/archive/2014/02/how-to-save-marriage-in-america/283732/.

4. See discussion of Betsey Stevenson and Justin Wolfers's work on this topic in chap. 2.

5. Linda J. Waite and Maggie Gallagher, *The Case for Marriage: Why Married People Are Happier, Healthier, and Better Off Financially* (New York: Doubleday, 2000).

6. Lee A. Lillard and Linda J. Waite, "'Til Death Do Us Part': Marital Disruption and Mortality," *American Journal of Sociology* 100, no. 5 (1995): 1131–56.

7. Robert Lerman has written a good review of the literature comparing unmarried fathers to married fathers. Robert I. Lerman, "Capabilities and Contributions of Unwed Fathers," *The Future of Children* 20 , no. 2 (2010): 63–85. On average, married men make significantly more ($33,572) than unmarried men ($15,465). Some of this difference can be attributed to selection bias, but only half of the gap in earnings between married and unmarried fathers is explained by differences in education, work experience, and race and ethnicity. In addition, fathers of children born outside of wedlock who later marry do better than unwed fathers who never marry. Entering marriage between the birth of the child and one year later is associated with an earnings gain of 29 percent at the one-year point, 44 percent after three years, and 66 percent after five years.

8. James Wilson, *The Marriage Problem* (London: HarperCollins World, 2003), p. 16; George A. Akerlof, "Men without Children," *Economic Journal* 108, no. 447 (1998): 287–309.

9. Quoted in Waite and Gallagher, *The Case for Marriage*, p. 16.

10. Using the fact that different states introduced unilateral divorce laws at different times to estimate these effects, they find that no-fault laws led to an average

decline of 5 to 10 percent in female suicide over twenty years, roughly a 30 percent decline in domestic violence against both men and women, and a 13 percent decline in the number of women murdered by their partners. Betsey Stevenson and Justin Wolfers, "Bargaining in the Shadow of the Law: Divorce Laws and Family Distress," *Quarterly Journal of Economics* 121, no. 2 (2006): 267–88.

11. Evelyn Lehrer and Yu Chen, "Delayed Entry into First Marriage and Marital Stability: Further Evidence on the Becker-Landes-Michael Hypothesis," *Demographic Research* 29 (September 20, 2013): 521–42; Dana Rotz, "Why Have Divorce Rates Fallen? The Role of Women's Age at Marriage," *SSRN Electronic Journal* (2011), http://papers.ssrn.com/sol3/papers.cfm?abstract_id=1960017.

12. Earlier research by Gary Becker and several colleagues suggested that as women aged and ran up against their biological clock, they would be forced to make compromises that led to mismatches between partners and a U-shaped relationship between age at marriage and divorce. More recent empirical research cited in the previous note does not support the U-shaped pattern, however. There may be some mismatching, but it is counterbalanced by more education, resources, and maturity that older adults bring to a marriage. Gary S. Becker, "A Theory of Marriage: Part I," *Journal of Political Economy* (1973): 813–46.

13. Jennifer Senior, *All Joy and No Fun: The Paradox of Modern Parenthood* (New York: Ecco, 2014).

14. Mark Lino, *Expenditures on Children by Families, 2012* (U.S. Department of Agriculture, Center for Nutrition Policy and Promotion, 2013), www.cnpp.usda.gov/Publications/CRC/crc2012.pdf.

15. This estimate is from *What to Expect When No One's Expecting*, by Jonathan Last. The author assumes that the mother takes off work until the child is 5 and then works half-time until the child is 17. Her salary before giving birth was $45,000, and the author assumes she gets the same hourly wage upon returning to work, meaning that her yearly half-time salary is $22,500. The author assumes that if she had not taken time off from work and decided to work part-time, the mother would have received a 4 percent annual raise, but given her labor choices will only get a 2 percent raise. Jonathan V. Last, *What to Expect When No One's Expecting: America's Coming Demographic Disaster* (New York: Encounter Books, 2013), pp. 42–43.

16. Today's mothers tend to return to work within the first six months after a birth, and over half of mothers with children under 18 work full-time. Kim Parker and Wendy Wang, "Modern Parenthood: Roles of Moms and Dads Converge as They Balance Work and Family" (Washington: Pew Research Center, 2013), www.pewsocialtrends.org/2013/03/14/

modern-parenthood-roles-of-moms-and-dads-converge-as-they-balance-work-and-family/. Therefore, to get this statistic, I assume that the mother takes off six months post-birth and then works part-time until her child starts school. Rather than try to estimate how her raises might vary with pregnancy, I use Budig and England's calculation of the wage penalty for motherhood; they found that having a child, on average, reduces a woman's yearly income by 7 percent. In this scenario, the woman loses $204,852 in income; over $80,000 of that loss comes from having lower wages due to motherhood, and the remainder is simply lost income from hours that she chose not to work. See Michelle J. Budig and Paula England, "The Wage Penalty for Motherhood," *American Sociological Review* 66, no. 2 (2001): 204–25.

17. Linda Laughlin, "Who's Minding the Kids? Child Care Arrangements: Spring 2011," Household Economic Studies (U.S. Census Bureau, 2013), p. 14, www.census.gov/prod/2013pubs/p70-135.pdf.

18. Ibid., table 6: "Average Weekly Child Care Expenditures of Families with Employed Mothers that Make Payments, by Age Groups and Selected Characteristics: Spring 2011."

19. College Board, "Average Published Undergraduate Charges by Sector, 2013–14," 2013, www.trends.collegeboard.org/college-pricing/figures-tables/average-published-undergraduate-charges-sector-2013-14.

20. These findings are discussed in brief by Nattavudh Powdthavee in "Think Having Children Will Make You Happy?," *The Psychologist* 22, no. 4 (2009): 308–11. For the full articles and methodologies, see A. Alesina, R. Di Tella, and R. MacCulloch, "Inequality and Happiness: Are Europeans and Americans Different?," *Journal of Public Economics* 88 (2004): 2009–42; R. Di Tella, R. MacCulloch, and A. J. Oswald, "The Macroeconomics of Happiness," *Review of Economics and Statistics* 85, no. 4 (2003): 809–27; A. E. Clark and A. J. Oswald, "Wellbeing in Panels," Department of Economics, University of Warwick, 2002; Ranae J. Evenson and Robin W. Simon, "Clarifying the Relationship between Parenthood and Depression," *Journal of Health and Social Behavior* 46, no. 4 (2005): 341–58.

21. Jean Twenge and colleagues, in a meta-analysis of the relationship between parenthood and marital satisfaction, found that having more children is associated with less happiness within a marriage and that this relationship is most pronounced among the mothers of infants and for the youngest generation of parents. Jean M. Twenge, W. Keith Campbell, and Craig A. Foster, "Parenthood and Marital Satisfaction: A Meta-Analytic Review," *Journal of Marriage and Family* 65, no. 3 (2003): 574–83.

22. Carolyn Pape Cowan and Philip A. Cowan, *News You Can Use: Are Babies Bad for Marriage?*, Brief Reports (Washington: Council on Contemporary Families, 2009), www.contemporaryfamilies.org/news-can-use-babies-bad-marriage.

23. Students of happiness and well-being make a distinction between different dimensions of this elusive concept. Well-being is increased by activities that are pleasurable or provide contentment. But well-being is also increased by leading a purposeful or fulfilling life, especially among those who have a strong sense of agency that enables them to achieve their longer-term goals. See Carol Graham's discussion of Aristotelian versus Benthamite definitions of happiness. Carol Graham, *The Pursuit of Happiness: An Economy of Well-being* (Brookings Institution Press, 2012), p. 33.

24. Mathew P. White and Paul Dolan, "Accounting for the Richness of Daily Activities," *Psychological Science* 20, no. 8 (2009): 1000–08.

25. Jennifer Senior, "All Joy and No Fun: Why Parents Hate Parenting," *New York Magazine*, July 4, 2010, www.nymag.com/news/features/67024/.

26. For a fuller account of how an evolutionary biologist sees this issue, see Sarah Blaffer Hrdy, *Mother Nature: Maternal Instincts and How They Shape the Human Species* (New York: Ballantine Books, 2003). For a different take, see Elisabeth Badinter and Adriana Hunter, *The Conflict: How Modern Motherhood Undermines the Status of Women* (New York: Metropolitan Books/Henry Holt, 2011).

27. Sheryl Sandberg, *Lean In: Women, Work, and the Will to Lead* (New York: Knopf, 2013); Anne-Marie Slaughter, "Why Women Still Can't Have It All," *The Atlantic*, June 2012, www.theatlantic.com/magazine/archive/2012/07/why-women-still-cant-have-it-all/309020/.

28. Budig and England, "The Wage Penalty for Motherhood," p. 204; Jane Waldfogel, "The Effect of Children on Women's Wages," *American Sociological Review* 62, no. 2 (1997): 209.

29. Shelley J. Correll, Stephen Benard, and In Paik, "Getting a Job: Is There a Motherhood Penalty?," *American Journal of Sociology* 112, no. 5 (2007): 1297–1339.

30. Budig and England, "The Wage Penalty for Motherhood," p. 220.

31. Waldfogel, "The Effect of Children on Women's Wages," p. 209.

32. Sylvia Ann Hewlett, "Executive Women and the Myth of Having It All," *Harvard Business Review* 80, no. 4 (2002): 3.

33. Ibid., p. 2.

34. Ibid., pp. 8–9.

35. George A. Akerlof and Rachel E. Kranton, "Economics and Identity," *Quarterly Journal of Economics* 115, no. 3 (2000): 715–53.

36. Marianne Bertrand, Emir Kamenica, and Jessica Pan, "Gender Identity and Relative Income within Households," Working Paper 19023 (Cambridge, Mass.: National Bureau of Economic Research, February 2013), www.faculty.chicago booth.edu/emir.kamenica/documents/identity.pdf.

37. R. Kelly Raley and Megan M. Sweeney, "Explaining Race and Ethnic Variation in Marriage: Directions for Future Research," *Race and Social Problems* 1, no. 3 (2009): 132–42; Philip Cohen, "Especially if They're Black: A Shortage of Men for Poor Women to Marry," *Family Inequality* (February 5, 2014), www. familyinequality.wordpress.com/2014/02/05/marriage-shortage.

38. Couples in which the wife earns more than the husband are also more likely to divorce. As an interesting specific example, there have been more divorces among those receiving the Academy Award for best actress than among those receiving the award for best actor. Cited in Bertrand, Kamenica, and Pan, "Gender Identity and Relative Income."

39. The second study is Akerlof and Kranton, "Economics and Identity."

40. Brookings tabulations of General Social Survey data.

41. Reeves, "How to Save Marriage in America," pp. 4, 10.

42. Gerson interviewed a representative group of 120 young men and women between the ages of 18 and 32 in the New York metropolitan area who had grown up in many different parts of the country and experienced a broad range of family living arrangements and parental roles. They represented a broad range of racial, ethnic, and class backgrounds. Most important, they represent what Gerson calls the "children of the gender revolution," a generation that saw their mothers enter the work force, their parents divorce in large numbers, and the economy evolve into one in which it became increasingly difficult to achieve a middle-class lifestyle without a second paycheck. Kathleen Gerson, *The Unfinished Revolution: How a New Generation Is Reshaping Family, Work, and Gender in America* (Oxford University Press, 2010), p. 3.

43. Ibid., pp. 11, 122.

44. Parker and Wang, "Modern Parenthood," p. 1.

45. Ibid., p. 2.

46. Ibid.

47. Ibid., p. 4.

48. Lauren Sandler, "The Childfree Life: Having It All without Having Children," *Time Magazine*, August 2013, www.time.com/241/having-it-all-without-having-children.

49. Gretchen Livingston and D'Vera Cohn, "Childlessness Up among All Women; Down among Women with Advanced Degrees," *Social & Demographic*

Trends Report (Washington: Pew Research Center, 2010), www.pewsocialtrends. org/2010/06/25/childlessness-up-among-all-women-down-among-women-with-advanced-degrees.

50. Badinter and Hunter, *The Conflict*.

51. This percentage is the sum of mother-only- and father-only-headed families with children under 18 divided by all families with children under the age of 18. U.S. Census Bureau (2012), FM-1: "Families, by Presence of Own Children under 18: 1950 to Present," www.census.gov/hhes/families/data/families.html.

52. Adam Thomas and Isabel Sawhill, "For Richer or for Poorer: Marriage as an Antipoverty Strategy," *Journal of Policy Analysis and Management* 21, no. 4 (2002): 587–99.

53. U.S. Bureau of Labor Statistics, *Current Population Survey 2012: Annual Social and Economic Supplement* (2013), table HINC-04.

54. U.S. Census Bureau, "POV21: Related Children under 18 by Householders Work Experience and Family Structure: 2012," www.census.gov/hhes/; www/cpstables/032013/pov/pov21_100.htm.

55. Calculations done using data from ibid.: Shift-share poverty rate = (2012 poverty rate for children in single parent families) x (1970 proportion of children in single parent families) + (2012 poverty rate for children in married families) x (1970 proportion of children in married-parent families).

As explained in the text, this estimate of the effects of the growing number of single parents on childhood poverty is somewhat exaggerated because married and unmarried parents are not drawn from the same universe. Thomas and Sawhill, "For Richer or for Poorer."

56. Ibid. The data are for 1998, but the conclusions are not likely to be much different using more recent data.

57. Ron Haskins and Isabel Sawhill, "Work and Marriage: The Way to End Poverty and Welfare," in *Welfare Reform and Beyond*, edited by Isabel V. Sawhill and others (Brookings Institution Press, 2003).

58. A 2013 study by a group of researchers at Columbia University has shown that the increase in cash assistance between 1967 and 2012 reduced the official child poverty rate by 3.2 percentage points and a broader measure that accounts for in-kind benefits and taxes by 11 percentage points. This suggests that virtually all of the growth in cash assistance was needed just to hold families harmless against the demographic shifts that have occurred, but that noncash benefits and the earned income tax credit (EITC) have gone much further than this in keeping a broader measure of child poverty rates lower than they would be in the absence of these measures. Christopher Wimer, Liana Fox, Irv Garfinkel, Neeraj Kaushal, and Jane Waldfogel, "Trends in Poverty with an Anchored Supplemental Poverty

Measure," Working Paper, Columbia University Population Research Center, December 5, 2013.

59. This section draws on a number of excellent review papers, especially Paul R. Amato, "The Impact of Family Formation Change on the Cognitive, Social, and Emotional Well-being of the Next Generation," *The Future of Children* 15, no. 2 (2005): 75–96; Wendy Sigle-Rushton and Sara McLanahan, "The Living Arrangements of New Unmarried Mothers," *Demography* 39, no. 3 (2002): 415–33; E. Mavis Hetherington and Margaret Stanley-Hagan, "The Adjustment of Children with Divorced Parents: A Risk and Resiliency Perspective," *Journal of Child Psychology and Psychiatry* 40, no. 1 (1999): 129–40; Sara McLanahan, "Fragile Families and the Reproduction of Poverty," *Annals of the American Academy of Political and Social Science* 621, no. 1 (2009): 111–31; also see Haskins and Sawhill, *Creating an Opportunity Society*; Sara McLanahan and Gary Sandefur, *Growing Up with a Single Parent: What Hurts, What Helps* (Harvard University Press, 1994).

60. Amato, "The Impact of Family Formation Change."

61. McLanahan and Sandefur, *Growing Up with a Single Parent*; Jane Waldfogel, Terry-Ann Craigie, and Jeanne Brooks-Gunn, "Fragile Families and Child Wellbeing," *The Future of Children* 20, no. 2 (2010): 87.

62. David H. Autor and Melanie Wasserman, *Wayward Sons: The Emerging Gender Gap in Labor Markets and Education* (Cambridge, Mass.: Third Way, 2013).

63. Marianne Bertrand and Jessica Pan, "The Trouble with Boys: Social Influences and the Gender Gap in Disruptive Behavior," *American Economic Journal: Applied Economics* 5, no. 1 (2013): 32–64; Autor and Wasserman, *Wayward Sons*; Kay S. Hymowitz, "Boy Trouble," *City Journal*, Manhattan Institute (Autumn 2013), www.city-journal.org/2013/23_4_boy-trouble.html.

64. Jeanne Brooks-Gunn, Wen-Jui Han, and Jane Waldfogel, "Maternal Employment and Child Cognitive Outcomes in the First Three Years of Life: The NICHD Study of Early Child Care," *Child Development* 73 (2002): 1052–72.

65. A careful review of the most rigorous research on the role of selection concludes that "studies using more rigorous designs continue to find negative effects of father absence on offspring well-being, although the magnitude of these effects is smaller than what is found in traditional cross-sectional designs." Sara McLanahan, Laura Tach, and Daniel Schneider, "The Causal Effects of Father Absence," *Annual Review of Sociology* 39, no. 1 (2013): 399.

66. McLanahan, "Fragile Families and the Reproduction of Poverty."

67. Amato, "The Impact of Family Formation Change."

68. For further review of the evidence and the emerging consensus, see Haskins and Sawhill, *Creating an Opportunity Society*, p. 204.

69. Estimates from the 2010 Census suggest that there are nearly 650,000 same-sex couples living in the United States. An estimated 19 percent of households with same-sex couples include children under age 18. There are around 500,000 children being raised by a gay or lesbian parent or parents. About half of these children are being raised by a couple; the rest are being raised by a single parent. Seventy-three percent of same-sex households with children are households with biological children. Corbin Miller and Joseph Price, "The Number of Children Being Raised by Gay or Lesbian Parents," Working Paper, Population Association of America 2013 Annual Meeting Program (Princeton University, 2013), www.paa2013.princeton. edu/papers/132066); Daphne Lofquist, "Same-Sex Couple Households" (U.S. Census Bureau, 2011), www.census.gov/prod/2011pubs/acsbr10-03.pdf.

70. The Regnerus study defines children of an LGBT parent as children who have at least one parent who has at some point had a same-sex partner. When compared with children who grew up in continuously intact, biological families, the children of women who reported a same-sex relationship had significantly worse outcomes on a number of measures, such as education, depression, employment status, or feelings of safety and security in their family of origin. In contrast, the Allen study only counted a person as the child of same-sex parents if he or she responded in the affirmative to the question "Are you a child of a male (female) same-sex married or common-law couple?" Allen found that children of same-sex couples were about 65 percent as likely to graduate from high school as children living in opposite-sex married families, controlling for demographics, including parents' marital status. Mark Regnerus, "How Different Are the Adult Children of Parents Who Have Same-Sex Relationships? Findings from the New Family Structures Study," *Social Science Research* 41, no. 4 (2012): 752–70; Douglas W. Allen, "High School Graduation Rates among Children of Same-Sex Households," *Review of Economics of the Household* 11, no. 4 (2013): 635–58.

71. Critics of Regnerus have pointed out a number of flaws in his study. First, his characterization of any child with one parent who has ever engaged in same-sex relations as a child being raised by same-sex parents is far too broad. In addition, among children who said their mother had a same-sex relationship, only 23 percent said they had spent at least three years living in the same household with a romantic partner of their mother's; and among those who said their father had a same-sex relationship, less than 2 percent said they had spent at least three years together in the same household. This means that a very small portion of the children in Regnerus's study were living in a stable same-sex two-parent household, unlike the comparison group, which was children in "intact biological families." Though the criticism of Regnerus's study has been harsher, Allen's study presents

similar issues regarding comparison groups. Also, methodological concerns have been raised about how Allen boosted his sample size to include enough same-sex couples. For more on these concerns, see the American Sociological Society's amicus brief filed during the 2012 Supreme Court cases on same-sex marriage, www.asanet.org/press/asa_files_amicus_brief_in_same-sex_marriage_cases.cfm.

72. Charlotte J. Patterson, "Lesbian and Gay Parenting" (Washington: American Psychological Association, 2005), www.apa.org/pi/lgbt/resources/parenting-full.pdf.

73. For example, about three-quarters of the studies referenced in the 2005 paper are based on small, nonrepresentative, convenience samples of fewer than 100 participants. Loren Marks, "Same-Sex Parenting and Children's Outcomes: A Closer Examination of the American Psychological Association's Brief on Lesbian and Gay Parenting," *Social Science Research* 41, no. 4 (2012): 735–51.

74. Research by UCLA demographer Gary Gates shows that 80 percent of the children raised in same-sex households come from prior heterosexual relationships, which may explain why such a high proportion of children of lesbian and gay parents are being raised by a single parent. LGBT individuals who were previously married are much more likely to have children than those who have never been married. Gary J. Gates, "LGBT Parenting in the United States" (Washington: Williams Institute, 2013), www.williamsinstitute.law.ucla.edu/wp-content/uploads/LGBT-Parenting.pdf.

75. In fact, research suggests that any differences in relationship stability for same-sex and opposite-sex couples come from the barriers to marriage. Relationship dissolution rates are much lower for same-sex couples in civil unions than for couples who are not, and the dissolution rates of same-sex couples in civil unions is fairly similar to rates for married opposite-sex couples. Kimberly F. Balsam, Theodore P. Beauchaine, Esther D. Rothblum, and Sondra E. Solomon, "Three-Year Follow-Up of Same-Sex Couples Who Had Civil Unions in Vermont, Same-Sex Couples Not in Civil Unions, and Heterosexual Married Couples," *Developmental Psychology* 44, no. 1 (2008): 102–16.

76. U.S. Census Bureau, *America's Families and Living Arrangements: 2013*, (Washington, 2013), table AVG3, "Average Number of People per Family Household with Own Children under 18, by Race and Hispanic Origin, Marital Status, Age, and Education of Householder."

77. Ariel Kalil and Rebecca M. Ryan, "Mothers' Economic Conditions and Sources of Support in Fragile Families," *The Future of Children* 20, no. 2 (2010): 39–61.

78. Ibid., p. 48.

79. These benefits include social insurance, means-tested cash benefits, nutritional benefits (including food stamps and school lunch benefits), housing, and the EITC. It should be noted that this estimate excludes a number of other programs, such as child care, Head Start, and child welfare services, that disproportionately serve single parents. Tabulations by Richard Bavier, based on U.S. Census Bureau March Current Population Survey (2010).

80. In 2012, the United States spent $432 billion on Medicaid. Table 3 of the 2012 Actuarial Report on the Financial Outlook for Medicaid, www.medicaid.gov/ Medicaid-CHIP-Program-Information/By-Topics/Financing-and-Reimbursement/ Downloads/medicaid-actuarial-report-2012.pdf. Since the elderly account for the bulk of Medicaid costs, I looked only at the percentage of spending on dependents and adults in families with dependents, which is 28 percent of the total cost, or $121 billion (based on the author's calculations of data in table II.4 from the Centers for Medicare and Medicaid Services, 2011 Data Compendium, www. cms.gov/Research-Statistics-Data-and-Systems/Statistics-Trends-and-Reports/Data Compendium/2011_Data_Compendium.html). In total, 42 percent of families with dependent children covered by Medicaid in 2013 were single-mother-headed families (author's calculations using data from the Current Population Survey, www. census.gov/cps/data/cpstablecreator.html), meaning that we spent about $51.9 billion on Medicaid for families headed by single mothers. Dividing that by the total number of single-parent families gives us a cost of $4,225 per single-parent family.

81. These estimates are based on data from the same sources as the 2012 estimates. I used 2002–12 data and estimated a logarithmic function that fits the changes we have seen over the past ten years. I then extrapolated out what the benefit levels would be in 2030 if they were to follow the same trend line. However, these are big assumptions. What will happen to benefit costs is very uncertain, particularly health care costs per capita.

Chapter 4

Andrew Cherlin is quoted in Jason DeParle, "Two Class, Divided by 'I Do,'" *New York Times*, July 15 2012, p A1.

1. For example, in 1960, 76 percent of adults with a college degree and 72 percent of those with a high school diploma were married—a gap of only 4 percentage points. By 2008, not only was marriage less likely, but the gap had quadrupled, to 16 percentage points, with 64 percent of adults with college degrees getting married and only 48 percent of adults with a high school diploma. Isabel Sawhill, "Are We Headed toward a Permanently Divided Society?," CCF Brief 43 (Brookings Institution, 2012).

2. Jonathan Rauch, "The Widening Marriage Gap: America's New Class Divide," *National Journal* 19 (2001): 1471.

3. Charles Murray, *Coming Apart: The State of White America, 1960–2010* (Random House Digital, 2013), p. 168.

4. W. Bradford Wilcox, *The State of Our Unions 2012, Marriage in America: The President's Marriage Agenda* (National Marriage Project, University of Virginia, 2012), p. ix, www.stateofourunions.org/2012/SOOU2012.pdf, p. ix.

5. Sawhill, "Are We Headed toward a Permanently Divided Society?"; Isabel Sawhill, "The Behavioral Aspects of Poverty," *Public Interest* (Fall 2003): 9.

6. As the University of Virginia's Eric Turkheimer put it, "No complex behaviors in free-ranging humans are caused by a linear and additive set of causes. Any important outcome, like adolescent delinquent behavior, has a myriad of interrelated causes, and each of these causes has a myriad of potential effects, inducing a squared myriad of environmental complexity even before one gets to the certainty that the environmental effects co-determine each other, or that the package interacts with the just-as-myriad effects of genes." I think this overstates the case but is a fair warning to anyone who thinks there is a simple explanation for human behavior or that we can always tease out the effects of one variable from another. Turkheimer quoted in David Brooks, *The Social Animal: The Hidden Sources of Love, Character, and Achievement* (New York: Random House Trade Paperbacks, 2013), p. 111.

7. June Carbone and Naomi Cahn, *Marriage Markets: How Inequality Is Remaking the American Family* (Oxford University Press, 2014).

8. This section draws on Isabel Sawhill, "Family Structure: The Growing Importance of Class," *Washington Monthly*, February 5, 2013, www.brookings.edu/research/articles/2013/01/family-structure-class-sawhill.

9. Daniel P. Moynihan, "The Negro Family: The Case for National Action" (Washington: Office of Policy Planning and Research, U.S. Department of Labor, 1965), p. 5.

10. Sawhill, "Family Structure."

11. Joyce A. Martin, Brady E. Hamilton, Michelle Osterman, Sally C. Curtin, and T. J. Matthews, "Births: Final Data for 2012," *National Vital Statistics Report* 62, no. 9 (2013): table 15.

12. See, for example, a cover story in *Newsweek* written by Joshua Dubois, a White House adviser to President Obama. His telling of this history and its legacy is especially moving. He notes that there are more African Americans on probation, parole, or in prison today than there were slaves in 1850. This mass incarceration is less the result of an increase in crime than of a criminal justice system that has locked up too many young men (often those lacking a father in

their life) for minor offenses and then effectively blocked them from getting jobs after their release. The president's initiative My Brother's Keeper, announced on March 6, 2014, is an attempt to deal with that legacy and its implications for men and boys of color. Joshua Dubois, "The Fight for Black Men," *Newsweek*, June 2013, http://mag.newsweek.com/2013/06/19/obama-s-former-spiritual-advisor-joshua-dubois-on-the-fight-for-black-men.html.

13. Adam Thomas and Isabel Sawhill, "For Richer or for Poorer: Marriage as an Antipoverty Strategy," *Journal of Policy Analysis and Management* 21, no. 4 (2002): 587–99.

14. Note that Kathryn Edin and Maria Kefalas found few differences across racial groups among the low-income mothers they interviewed. See Kathryn Edin and Maria Kefalas, *Promises I Can Keep: Why Poor Women Put Motherhood before Marriage* (University of California Press, 2005), pp. 212–13.

15. Kay Hymowitz, Jason S. Carroll, W. Bradford Wilcox, and Kelleen Kaye, "Knot Yet: The Benefits and Costs of Delayed Marriage in America" (Washington: National Campaign to Prevent Teen and Unplanned Pregnancy, the Relate Institute, and National Marriage Project, 2013), pp. 18–19.

16. U.S. Census Bureau (2012), table 2: "Educational Attainment in the United States: 2012"—Detailed Tables, http://www.census.gov/hhes/socdemo/education/data/cps/2013/tables.html.

17. More information about the Fragile Families and Child Wellbeing Study can be found at www.fragilefamilies.princeton.edu/index.asp. In addition to the data in the original survey, qualitative data are also available from the Time, Love, and Cash in Couples with Children Study (TLC3). The survey was conducted by Kathryn Edin and Paula England.

18. The cities had to have populations of more than 200,000. Some suburban as well as rural areas were not included. Nonetheless, an analysis of the sample done by Robert L. Wagmiller Jr. indicates that this sample is representative of the population of U.S. cities, although the sample is somewhat less well educated, lower-income, and more likely to be African American than the country as a whole. Robert L. Wagmiller Jr., "How Representative Are the Fragile Families Study Families?: A Comparison of the Early Childhood Longitudinal Study–Birth Cohort and Fragile Families Samples," Working Paper (Center for Research on Child Wellbeing, Woodrow Wilson School of Public and International Affairs, Princeton University 2010), p. 19.

19. An effort to collect data from 15-year-olds was initiated in 2014.

20. Sara McLanahan, "Fragile Families and Children's Opportunity," research briefing presented at the Annual Meeting of the National Academy of the Sciences, Washington, April 2012, www.crcw.princeton.edu/workingpapers/WP12-21-FF.pdf.

21. Some scholars call this the "family-go-round." Kathryn Edin and Timothy Nelson use this term in their book *Doing the Best I Can*, picking up on Andrew Cherlin's earlier labeling of the instability of marriage in the United States as a "marriage-go-round." See Kathryn Edin and Timothy J. Nelson, *Doing the Best I Can: Fatherhood in the Inner City* (University of California Press, 2013), p. 226; Andrew J. Cherlin, *The Marriage-Go-Round: The State of Marriage and the Family in America Today* (Random House Digital, 2010).

22. McLanahan, "Fragile Families and Children's Opportunity."

23. Isabel Sawhill, "Family Complexity: Is It a Problem, and if So, What Should We Do?," *Annals of the American Academy of Political and Social Science* (forthcoming 2014).

24. Most of the remainder were still living with their original parents, and a few were in a stable single-parent home. Laura Tach, Kathryn Edin, and Sara McLanahan, "Multiple Partners and Multiple Partner Fertility in Fragile Families," PowerPoint presentation at the Family Task Force Meeting, February 10, 2011, Brookings Institution, www.crcw.princeton.edu/workingpapers/WP11-10-FF.pdf.

25. Ariel Kalil, Rebecca Ryan, and Elise Chor, "Time Investments in Children across Family Structures," *Annals of the American Academy of Political and Social Science* (forthcoming 2014).

26. McLanahan, "Fragile Families and Children's Opportunity."

27. Sara McLanahan and Gary Sandefur, *Growing Up with a Single Parent: What Hurts, What Helps* (Harvard University Press, 1994); Jane Waldfogel, Terry-Ann Craigie, and Jeanne Brooks-Gunn, "Fragile Families and Child Wellbeing," *The Future of Children* 20, no. 2 (2010): 87.

28. David H. Autor and Melanie Wasserman, *Wayward Sons: The Emerging Gender Gap in Labor Markets and Education* (Cambridge, Mass.: Third Way, 2013).

29. Waldfogel, Craigie, and Brooks-Gunn, "Fragile Families and Child Wellbeing."

30. Edin and Nelson, *Doing the Best I Can*.

31. Edin and Kefalas note that empirical support for any of the three major hypotheses about why marriage has disappeared is "amazingly slim." The three hypotheses are the independence theory, the welfare-state hypothesis, and the marriageable-male hypothesis. Of the three, they think the last does the best job but go on to note that women are setting a higher bar than they have in the past and that many will no longer marry the men available to them "even if unskilled men's employment hadn't declined at all." Edin and Kefalas, *Promises I Can Keep*, p. 199.

32. Ibid., p. 203.

33. This is a theme in both *Promises I Can Keep* and *Doing the Best I Can*.

34. Edin and Nelson, *Doing the Best I Can*, pp. 203, 205, 213, 207.

35. Jeremy Greenwood, Nezih Guner, Georgi Kocharkov, and Cezar Santos, "Marry Your Like: Assortative Mating and Income Inequality," Working Paper 19829 (Cambridge, Mass.: National Bureau of Economic Research, 2014).

36. The Social Genome Model is now based at the Urban Institute; it is a collaborative effort between the Brookings Institution, the Urban Institute, and Child Trends.

37. Isabel Sawhill and Joanna Venator, "Three Policies to Close the Class Divide in Family Formation," *Social Mobility Memos* (Brookings Institution, 2014), http://www.brookings.edu/blogs/social-mobility-memos/posts/2014/01/21-3-policies-to-close-family-formation-class-divide-sawhill.

38. Raj Chetty, Nathan Hendren, Patrick Kline, and Emmanuel Saez, "The Economic Impacts of Tax Expenditures: Evidence from Spatial Variation across the U.S.," Working Paper (2013), www.equality-of-opportunity.org/.

In addition, the *New York Times* article and interactive mobility map may interest the less data-driven reader. Areas of low mobility were heavily concentrated in the southeastern United States and tend to be those with low levels of education, high levels of income inequality, and high concentrations of black and single-parent families. David Leonhardt, "In Climbing Income Ladder, Location Matters," *New York Times*, July 2, 2013, www.nytimes.com/2013/07/22/business/in-climbing-income-ladder-location-matters.html?hp&_r=3&.

39. Annette Lareau, *Unequal Childhoods: Class, Race, and Family Life* (University of California Press, 2011).

40. Ariel Kalil, Rebecca Ryan, and Michael Corey, "Diverging Destinies: Maternal Education and the Developmental Gradient in Time with Children," *Demography* 49, no. 4 (2012): 1361–83.

41. For a very readable account of these differences in parenting styles, see Brooks, *The Social Animal*, pp. 104–5.

42. Kalil, Ryan, and Corey, "Diverging Destinies"; Ariel Kalil, "Inequality Begins at Home: The Role of Parenting in the Diverging Destinies of Rich and Poor Children," paper presented at the 21st Annual Symposium on Family Issues, Pennsylvania State University, October 2013, www.bridgethewordgap.files.wordpress.com/2013/10/kalil-inequality-and-parenting-kalil-psu-september-12-2013.pdf; Betty Hart, *Meaningful Differences in the Everyday Experience of Young American Children* (Baltimore, Md.: P. H. Brookes, 1995); Lareau, *Unequal Childhoods*; Ellen E. Pinderhughes, Kenneth A. Dodge, John E. Bates, Gregory S. Pettit, and Arnaldo Zelli, "Discipline Responses: Influences of Married

Socioeconomic Status, Ethnicity, Beliefs about Parenting, Stress, and Cognitive-emotional Processes," *Journal of Family Psychology* 14, no. 3 (2000): 380–400; Jack P. Shonkoff and Deborah A. Phillips, *From Neurons to Neighborhoods: The Science of Early Childhood Development* (Washington: Joseph Henry Press/National Academies Press, 2000); Jane Waldfogel and Elizabeth Washbrook, "Early Years Policy," *Child Development Research* (2011): 1–12; Greg J. Duncan and Richard J. Murnane, *Whither Opportunity: Rising Inequality, Schools, and Children's Life Chances* (New York and Chicago: Russell Sage Foundation and Spencer Foundation, 2011).

43. Anne Fernald, Virginia A. Marchman, and Adriana Weisleder, "SES Differences in Language Processing Skill and Vocabulary Are Evident at 18 Months," *Developmental Science* 16, no. 2 (2013): 234–48.

44. Richard V. Reeves and Kimberly Howard, "The Parenting Gap" (Brookings Institution, 2013), p. 6, www.brookings.edu/research/papers/2013/09/09-parenting-gap-social-mobility-wellbeing-reeves.

45. Ibid., p. 8.

46. Ibid., pp. 8, 10.

47. For more on the success sequence and its importance, see Ron Haskins and Isabel V. Sawhill, *Creating an Opportunity Society* (Brookings Institution Press, 2009), pp. 70–71.

48. For more on this debate between liberals and conservatives, see ibid., pp. 85–105.

49. Brink Lindsey, *Human Capitalism: How Economic Growth Has Made Us Smarter—and More Unequal* (Princeton University Press, 2013); Brooks, *The Social Animal.*

50. Lindsey, *Human Capitalism*, p. 104.

51. Edin and Kefalas, *Promises I Can Keep.*

Chapter 5

Marco Rubio is quoted in "Reclaiming the Land of Opportunity: Conservative Reforms for Combatting Poverty," speech, Washington D.C., January 8, 2014.

1. Ron Haskins and Isabel V. Sawhill, *Creating an Opportunity Society* (Brookings Institution Press, 2009), p. 203.

2. Rick Santorum, *It Takes a Family: Conservatism and the Common Good* (Wilmington, Del.: ISI Books, 2006), p. 15.

3. Ross Douthat, "Social Liberalism as Class Warfare," *New York Times*, January 29, 2014, www.douthat.blogs.nytimes.com/2014/01/29/social-liberalism-as-class-warfare/.

4. As quoted in W. Bradford Wilcox, *Soft Patriarchs, New Men: How Christianity Shapes Fathers and Husbands* (University of Chicago Press, 2004), p. 1.

5. Ibid., p. 201.

6. Naomi R. Cahn and June Carbone, *Red Families v. Blue Families: Legal Polarization and the Creation of Culture* (Oxford University Press, 2010).

7. Disclaimer: I am a member of the advisory board of the National Marriage Project.

8. W. Bradford Wilcox, *The State of Our Unions 2012, Marriage in America: The President's Marriage Agenda* (Charlottesville, Va.: National Marriage Project, University of Virginia, 2012), p. xii, www.stateofourunions.org/2012/SOOU2012.pdf.

9. Hillary Rodham Clinton, *It Takes a Village: And Other Lessons Children Teach Us* (New York: Simon & Schuster, 2006), p. 1.

10. Nancy Folbre, *The Invisible Heart: Economics and Family Values* (New York: New Press, 2001).

11. Melissa Harris-Perry, "What Paul Ryan and Obama Have in Common," *The Nation*, March 19, 2014, www.thenation.com/article/178918/what-paul-ryan-and-obama-have-common.

12. Ann O'Leary, "Marriage, Motherhood, and Men," *The Shriver Report* (January 2014): 3.

13. Charles Murray's 1984 book, *Losing Ground: American Social Policy, 1950–1980* (New York: Basic Books), is widely regarded as helping to spur a national reversal of views on welfare and its effects. After the passage of welfare reform in 1996, the *New York Times* called it the "book that many people believe begat welfare reform." Scott Janny, "Turning Intellect into Influence: Promoting Its ideas, the Manhattan Institute has Nudged New York Rightward," *New York Times*, May 12, 1997, p. B1.

14. For more thorough discussions of welfare reforms of the 1990s and the current state of the welfare system, see Ron Haskins, *Work over Welfare: The Inside Story of the 1996 Welfare Reform Law* (Brookings Institution Press, 2006); Isabel V. Sawhill, ed., *Welfare Reform and Beyond: The Future of the Safety Net* (Brookings Institution Press, 2002); R. Kent Weaver, *Ending Welfare as We Know It* (Brookings Institution Press, 2000).

15. Lisa Gennetian and Virginia Knox of MDRC conducted an analysis of fourteen different programs to search for the effects of welfare reform on marriage and found little conclusive evidence that welfare affected people's choices to cohabitate or marry. Lisa A. Gennetian and Virginia Knox. "Staying Single: The Effects of Welfare Reform Policies on Marriage and Cohabitation" (New York: MDRC, 2003), www.mdrc.org/publications/373/org.

16. A review of studies linking welfare to marriage and fertility decisions by Robert Moffitt comes to a similar conclusion. He finds that a simple majority of studies identify a correlation between welfare generosity and marriage/fertility decisions but that the direction and strength of that correlation is very dependent on methodology and sampling, calling into question how much we can depend on that conclusion. See Robert A. Moffitt, "The Effect of Welfare on Marriage and Fertility," in *Welfare, the Family, and Reproductive Behavior: Research Perspectives* (Washington: National Academies Press, 1998), p. 50.

17. Kathryn Edin and Timothy J. Nelson, *Doing the Best I Can: Fatherhood in the Inner City* (University of California Press, 2013), p. 111.

18. Elaine Sorenson, "Child Support Reforms in PRWORA: Initial Impacts," *Assessing the New Federalism* (Washington: Urban Institute, 2001), www.urban.org/Uploadedpdf/410421_discussion02-02.pdf.

19. U.S. Department of Health and Human Services, Administration for Children and Families, "Child Support Enforcement, FY 2012, Preliminary Report," 2013, chart 2; Haskins and Sawhill, *Creating an Opportunity Society*.

20. Timothy Grall, "Custodial Mothers and Fathers and Their Child Support: 2011," *Current Population Reports* (U.S. Census Bureau, 2013), www.census.gov/people/childsupport/data/files/chldsu11.pdf.

21. Anne Case, "The Effects of Stronger Child Support Enforcement on Nonmarital Fertility," in *Fathers under Fire*, edited by Irwin Garfinkel, Sara S. McLanahan, Daniel R. Meyer, and Judith A. Seltzer (New York: Russell Sage, 1998).

22. Robert G. Wood, Sheena McConnell, Quinn Moore, Andrew Clarkwest, and JoAnn Hsueh, "The Effects of Building Strong Families: A Healthy Marriage and Relationship Skills Education Program for Unmarried Parents: Effects of Building Strong Families," *Journal of Policy Analysis and Management* 31, no. 2 (2012): 228–52.

23. JoAnn Hsueh, Desiree Principe Alderson, Erika Lundquist, Charles Michalopoulos, Daniel Gubits, David Fein, and Virginia Knox, "The Supporting Healthy Marriage Evaluation: Early Impacts on Low-Income Families," *SSRN Electronic Journal* (2012), www.ssrn.com/abstract=2030319.

24. Haskins and Sawhill, *Creating an Opportunity Society*, p. 230. We are indebted to Marlene Pearson and Barbara Defoe Whitehead for inventing the term "success sequence."

25. One question we regularly get asked is whether our analysis takes into account selection effects. The answer is that we looked at much of the more rigorous research on this question and concluded that selection is a big issue, in principle, but that its empirical impact in this context is modest. Ibid., p. 71.

26. Depending on their circumstances, individuals may also experience a marriage subsidy rather than a penalty when they marry. For example, if a high-earning man marries a woman with no earnings, the couple can split their income for tax purposes and pay a lower tax rate on each half of his income. In a graduated system in which tax rates rise with total household income, this "income-splitting" provision can produce a marriage subsidy for a high-salaried man.

27. For a review of relevant literature, see Adam Carasso and C. Eugene Steuerle, "The Hefty Penalty on Marriage Facing Many Households with Children," *The Future of Children* 15, no. 2 (2005): 161.

28. Ibid.

29. For example, in Sweden, child benefits are a flat amount paid out to whichever parent is registered with Försäkringskassan, the Swedish social insurance agency. Individuals, rather than households, are the tax-paying units, meaning that benefits, such as their earned income tax credit, do not change if a person chooses to marry or not to marry. For more on how the Swedish system works, see Karin Edmark, Eva Moerk, Che-Yuan Liang, and Hakan Selin, "Evaluation of the Swedish Earned Income Tax Credit," *SSRN Electronic Journal* (2012), www.ssrn.com/abstract=2066470.

30. The exceptions are female high school dropouts, whose earnings have fallen, and male college graduates, whose earnings have risen over this period. Most economists believe that these changes are the result of technological developments that have automated many routine production and administrative jobs, the outsourcing of work to lower-wage countries, and the decline of labor unions. It remains something of a puzzle why men have failed to respond to the rising returns to higher education in the same way that women have. David H. Autor and Melanie Wasserman, *Wayward Sons: The Emerging Gender Gap in Labor Markets and Education* (Cambridge, Mass.: Third Way, 2013).

31. William Julius Wilson, *The Truly Disadvantaged: The Inner City, the Underclass, and Public Policy* (University of Chicago Press, 2012).

32. See, for example, the literature cited in Kathryn Edin and Joanna M. Reed, "Why Don't They Just Get Married? Barriers to Marriage among the Disadvantaged," *The Future of Children* 15, no. 2 (2005): 117–37.

33. Marcia Carlson, Sara McLanahan, and Paula England, "Union Formation in Fragile Families," *Demography* 41, no. 2 (2004): 237–61.

34. For a comprehensive review, see Robert J. Lalonde, "Employment and Training Programs," in *Means-Tested Transfer Programs in the United States*, edited by Robert A. Moffitt (University of Chicago Press, 2003).

35. See MDRC's evaluations of Career Academies for descriptions and the evaluation results for these programs. James J. Kemple, "Career Academies: Impacts on Labor Market Outcomes and Educational Attainment" (New York: MDRC, 2004); James J. Kemple and Cynthia J. Willner, "Career Academies: Long-term Impacts on Labor Market Outcomes, Educational Attainment, and Transitions to Adulthood" (New York: MDRC, 2008).

36. For example, a woman's education level is directly related to both the number of children she has and her health before and after a pregnancy. Using the availability of colleges in a geographic area as an instrument for maternal education, researchers found that, in addition to more maternal education improving the health outcomes for the child, it significantly reduces the number of children a woman has. Janet Currie and Enrico Moretti, "Mother's Education and the Intergenerational Transmission of Human Capital: Evidence from College Openings," *Quarterly Journal of Economics* 118, no. 4 (2003): 1495–1532.

37. Many other works have done a more thorough job of describing the interventions needed. For example, *The Future of Children*, a joint publication of the Brookings Institution and Princeton University, has published four journals on the topics of improving educational outcomes for children (see www.futureof children.org/). For more on these topics, see Greg J. Duncan and Richard J. Murnane, *Restoring Opportunity: The Crisis of Inequality and the Challenge for American Education* (Cambridge, Mass.: Harvard Education Press, 2014); Haskins and Sawhill, *Creating an Opportunity Society*, pp. 125–66.; Eric Alan Hanushek, Paul E. Peterson, and Ludger Woessmann, *Our Schools and Our Prosperity: A Global View of the American School* (Brookings Institution Press, 2013); Isabel Sawhill and Sara Goldrick-Rab, "Should Pell Grants Target the College-Ready?," *Education Next* 14, no. 2 (2014): 58–64.

38. Angela L. Duckworth and Martin E. P. Seligman, "Self-Discipline Outdoes IQ in Predicting Academic Performance of Adolescents," *Psychological Science* 16, no. 12 (2005): 939–44; Paul Tough, *How Children Succeed: Grit, Curiosity, and the Hidden Power of Character* (New York: Mariner Books, 2013); James J. Heckman, Jora Stixrud, and Sergio Urzua, "The Effects of Cognitive and Noncognitive Abilities on Labor Market Outcomes and Social Behavior," *Journal of Labor Economics* 24, no. 3 (2006): 411–82.

39. Kerry Searle Grannis and Isabel Sawhill, "Improving Children's Life Chances: Estimates from the Social Genome Model," Social Genome Project Research 49 (Brookings Institution, 2013), www.brookings.edu/research/ papers/2013/10/11-improving-childrens-life-chances-sawhill-grannis.

40. Ariel Kalil and Rebecca M. Ryan, "Mothers' Economic Conditions and Sources of Support in Fragile Families," *The Future of Children* 20, no. 2 (2010): 39–61, p. 47.

41. Means-tested programs include the earned income tax credit, the Supplemental Nutrition Assistance Program (SNAP, formerly food stamps), and other child nutrition programs, housing programs, employment and training programs, Medicaid and other health programs, Supplemental Security Income, Temporary Assistance for Needy Families, social service programs, and education programs. For more, see Maria Cancian and Ron Haskins, "The Impacts of Changes in Family Composition on Income, Poverty, and Inequality," presented at the IRP Family Complexity, Poverty, and Public Policy Conference, Madison, Wisc., July 2013.

42. Ibid., fig. 12.

43. Isabel Sawhill and Quentin Karpilow, "A No-Cost Proposal to Reduce Poverty & Inequality," CCF Policy Brief 51 (Brookings Institution, January 2014).

44. In 2007, 39 percent of mothers were primary breadwinners and 24 percent were co-breadwinners. Primary breadwinners are defined as mothers who are either single mothers who make all of a household's income or married mothers who make more than their husbands. Co-breadwinners make between 25 and 50 percent of the household's income. Heather Boushey, "The New Breadwinners," in *The Shriver Report* (Washington: Center for American Progress, 2009), p. 37, www.americanprogress.org/wp-content/uploads/issues/2009/10/pdf/awn/chapters/economy.pdf.

45. An employee must have worked 1,250 hours in the past year, must work at a company with 50 or more employees, and must have worked at the company for at least a year, though that year does not have to be consecutive. Heather Boushey, "The Role of the Government in Work-Family Conflict," *The Future of Children* 21, no. 2 (2011): 163–90.

46. Jane Waldfogel, "Family and Medical Leave: Evidence from the 2000 Surveys," *Monthly Labor Review* (September 2001): 17–23.

47. Taking parental leave is associated with better mental health and energy in mothers. Data on parental leave policies in sixteen European countries for the period 1969–1994 show that the right to a year of paid leave is associated with a 25 percent lower chance of post-neonatal mortality and more than a 10 percent decline in child fatalities between the ages of 1 and 5. Analysis from the National Longitudinal Survey of Youth shows that a parent's early return to work (within three months of birth) results in lower cognitive development for the child. Christopher J. Ruhm, "Parental Leave and Child Health," *Journal of Health Economics* 19, no. 6 (2000): 931–60; P. McGovern, B. Dowd, D. Gjerdingen, I.

Moscovice, L. Kochevar, and W. Lohman, "Time off Work and the Postpartum Health of Employed Women," *Medical Care* 35, no. 5 (1997): 507–21; Charles L. Baum, "Does Early Maternal Employment Harm Child Development? An Analysis of the Potential Benefits of Leave Taking," *Journal of Labor Economics* 21, no. 2 (2003): 409–48.

48. One state, Connecticut, has passed legislation requiring companies to provide paid sick days to workers; and a handful of cities, including Seattle, San Francisco, Washington, Newark, and New York City, have passed similar legislation. "State and Local Action on Paid Sick Days," National Partnership on Women and Families, http://paidsickdays.nationalpartnership.org/site/DocServer/NP_PSD_Tracking_Doc.pdf?docID=1922.

49. This is most important for low-income workers whose employers often have "no-fault" absence policies, in which you can be fired for unexpected absences. Low-income workers in hourly positions also often have to have "maximum availability" in which they must be able to be put on the schedule for more hours than they actually will work. For example, full-time employees at Starbucks must be available to be scheduled for a shift for eighty hours each week. The phenomenon of workers going into the office while sick is known as "presenteeism" and costs employers an estimated $160 billion a year. Sarah Jane Glynn and Joanna Venator, "Fact Sheet: Workplace Flexibility" (Washington: Center for American Progress, 2012), www.americanprogress.org/issues/labor/news/2012/08/16/11981/fact-sheet-workplace-flexibility/; T. Smith and J. Kim, "Paid Sick Days: Attitudes and Experiences, National Opinion Research Center and the Public Welfare Foundation," *NORC Report* (June 2010); National Partnership for Women and Families, "Paid Sick Days: Good for Businesses, Good for Workers" (Washington: National Partnership for Women and Families, 2011), www.paidsickdays.nationalpartnership.org/site/DocServer/PSD_Business_FINAL.pdf?docID=7825.

50. Jane Farrell and Joanna Venator, "Fact Sheet: Paid Sick Days" (Washington: Center for American Progress, 2012), www.americanprogress.org/issues/labor/news/2012/08/16/12031/fact-sheet-paid-sick-days/; Ruhm, "Parental Leave and Child Health."

51. This refers to parents who have a monthly income of less than $1,500, or $18,000 a year. Families with yearly incomes between $18,000 and $36,000 a year spend 23 percent of their income on child care. For more information, see U.S. Census Bureau, 2013, table 6, "Average Weekly Child Care Expenditures of Families with Employed Mothers That Make Payments, by Age Groups and Selected Characteristics: Spring 2011," in *Who's Minding the Kids? Child Care*

Arrangements (Spring 2011), www.census.gov/hhes/childcare/data/sipp/2011/tables.html.

52. U.S. Department of Health and Human Services, "Estimates of Child Care Eligibility and Receipt for Fiscal Year 2009," 2012, www.aspe.hhs.gov/hsp/12/childcareeligibility/ib.pdf.

53. Leonard Burman, Elaine Maag, and Jeff Rohaly, "Tax Subsidies to Help Low-Income Families Pay for Child Care," Discussion Paper 23 (Washington: Urban Institute, 2005).

54. Haskins and Sawhill, *Creating an Opportunity Society*, pp. 176–77.

55. The norm among countries labeled "highly competitive" by the World Economic Forum is closer to six months of paid leave for one parent, and all of these countries (save the United States) provide at least fourteen weeks of paid leave. Alison Earle, Zitha Mokomane, and Jody Heymann, "International Perspectives on Work-Family Policies: Lessons from the World's Most Competitive Economies," *The Future of Children* 21, no. 2 (2011): 191–210.

56. Jane Waldfogel, "International Policies toward Parental Leave and Child Care," *The Future of Children* 11, no. 2 (2001): 98–111.

57. Even FMLA, which only requires that a company not fire a worker who takes leave, lowers productivity for companies. A Washington, D.C.–based research firm, the Employment Policy Foundation (EPF), estimated that FMLA cost employers $21 billion in 2004 in lost productivity from absenteeism, continued health benefits, and net labor replacement costs. U.S. Department of Labor, "Data: FMLA Coverage, Usage, and Economic Impact," 2007, www.dol.gov/whd/FMLA2007Report/Chapter11.pdf.

The Congressional Budget Office estimated the cost to the private sector of the Healthy Families Act, a proposed law that would require employers to provide full-time employees with seven days of paid sick leave, would total about $1.5 billion in 2009. Congressional Budget Office, "Congressional Budget Office Cost Estimate: S. 910 Healthy Families Act," 2007, www.cbo.gov/sites/default/files/cbofiles/ftpdocs/81xx/doc8133/s910.pdf.

58. In fiscal year 2013, Congress's final budget for Head Start was $7.6 billion. This adds up to a little less than $8,000 per child served.

59. According to the Department of Labor, in 2012, 85 percent of employers said that complying with the law is very easy, easy, or has had no noticeable effect. Ninety-one percent of employers said that the law has had either a positive effect or no effect on employee absenteeism, turnover, and morale, all of which offset the costs to businesses. Jacob Alex Klerman, Kelly Daley, and Alyssa Pozniak, "Family and Medical Leave in 2012: Technical Report" (Cambridge, Mass.:

Abt Associates, 2012), www.dol.gov/asp/evaluation/fmla/FMLA-2012-Technical-Report.pdf.

In addition, research consistently shows that mothers are more likely to return to their jobs after a pregnancy if they have access to parental leave, which reduces the amount a business has to spend on training new employees. Elizabeth Washbrook, Christopher J. Ruhm, Jane Waldfogel, and Wen-Jui Han, "Public Policies, Women's Employment after Childbearing, and Child Well-Being," *B. E. Journal of Economic Analysis & Policy* 11, no. 1 (2011).

60. A 2013 study by economists Francine Blau and Lawrence Kahn found that over 25 percent of the decline in U.S. female labor force participation relative to that in other OECD countries over the previous twenty years is due to the other countries' implementation of family-friendly policies. Francine D. Blau and Lawrence M. Kahn, "Female Labor Supply: Why Is the United States Falling Behind?," *American Economic Review* 103, no. 3 (2013): 251–56.

A study of British and U.S. "family gaps" (that is, the difference in wages between mothers and other women) found that women who had paid leave and returned to work after childbirth did not see the same gap in wages that mothers without leave did. Jane Waldfogel, "The Family Gap for Young Women in the United States and Britain: Can Maternity Leave Make a Difference?," *Journal of Labor Economics* 16, no. 3 (1998): 505–45.

61. In fact, the study by Blau and Kahn found that U.S. women are more likely to have full-time jobs and work in management or professional positions than women in countries with paid family-leave policies. Blau and Kahn, "Female Labor Supply."

62. Frank Newport, "Americans, Including Catholics, Say Birth Control Is Morally OK," in *Polling Data. Gallup Politics* (2012), www.gallup.com/poll/154799/americans-including-catholics-say-birth-control-morally.aspx.

63. Ninety-nine percent of sexually active women between the ages of 15 and 44 have used contraception at some point in their lives. Kimberly Daniels, William D. Mosher, and Jo Jones, "Contraceptive Methods Women Have Ever Used: United States, 1982–2010," *National Health Statistics Reports* 62 (Washington: U.S. Department of Health and Human Services, 2012).

64. *Burwell v. Hobby Lobby Stores, Inc.*, 573 U. S. ___ (2014).

65. Julie Beck, "What's So Controversial about the Contraceptives in Hobby Lobby," *The Atlantic*, June 30, 2014 (www.theatlantic.com/health/archive/2014/06/whats-so-controversial-about-the-contraceptives-in-the-hobbylobby-case/373709/).

66. The Editors, "Contraception at Risk," *New England Journal of Medicine* 370, no. 1 (2014): 77–78.

67. In May 2011, the Republican-controlled House of Representatives voted in favor of defunding Planned Parenthood, though the Democrat-controlled Senate later rejected the bill.

68. Luis Lugo, Allen Cooperman, Cary Funk, Erin O'Connell, and Sandra Sencel, "Fewer See Stem Cell Research and IVF as Moral Issues; Abortion Viewed in Moral Terms" (Washington: Pew Research Center, 2013), www.pewforum. org/2013/08/15/abortion-viewed-in-moral-terms/.

69. Michael Dimock, Luis Lugo, Carroll Doherty, and Alan Cooperman, "Roe v. Wade at 40: Most Oppose Overturning Abortion Decision" (Washington: Pew Research Center's Religion & Public Life Project, 2013), www.pewforum. org/2013/01/16/roe-v-wade-at-40/.

70. Hillary Rodham Clinton, testimony before the U.S. House of Representatives Committee on Foreign Affairs, "New Beginnings: Foreign Policy Priorities in the Obama Administration," April 22, 2009.

71. "State Funding of Abortion under Medicaid," *State Policies in Brief* (New York: Guttmacher Institute, 2014), www.guttmacher.org/statecenter/spibs/spib_SFAM.pdf.

72. William Saletan, "Why Abortions Are Down," *Slate Magazine*, February 4, 2014, www.slate.com/articles/health_and_science/human_nature/2014/02/abortion_rate_decline_guttmacher_s_study_vindicates_birth_control_and_pro.html.

73. It should be noted that this figure does not take into account births that are merely mistimed as opposed to completely unintended. Therefore, the ultimate number of births averted by publicly funded family planning services is likely lower than 2.2 million. Jennifer J. Frost, Mia R. Zolna, and Lori Frohwirth, "Contraceptive Needs and Services, 2010" (Washington: Guttmacher Institute, 2013).

74. Cited in Isabel Sawhill, Adam Thomas, and Emily Monea, "An Ounce of Prevention: Policy Prescriptions to Reduce the Prevalence of Fragile Families," *The Future of Children* 20, no. 2 (2010): 136.

75. Juleanna Glover, "Republicans Must Support Public Financing for Contraception," *New York Times*, December 27, 2012, sec. Opinion Pages, www.nytimes.com/2012/12/28/opinion/republicans-must-support-public-financing-for-contraception.html.

Chapter 6

1. The share of unintended births among unmarried women under 30 can be calculated from data published by the Guttmacher Institute. Mia R. Zolna and

Laura Lindberg, "Unintended Pregnancy: Incidence and Outcomes among Young Adult Unmarried Women in the United States, 2001 and 2008" (New York: Guttmacher Institute, 2012).

2. Ibid.; see appendix table 1.

3. The NSFG does ask the women whether their partner wanted the child, but does not interview the partners.

4. Zolna and Lindberg, "Unintended Pregnancy," appendix table 1. This statistic combines the number of births to cohabiting and non-cohabiting single mothers to get to total percent of unwanted births to single women.

5. William D. Mosher, Jo Jones, and Joyce C. Abma, "Intended and Unintended Births in the United States: 1982–2010" (U.S. Department of Health and Human Services, Centers for Disease Control and Prevention, National Center for Health Statistics, 2012).

6. Zolna and Lindberg, "Unintended Pregnancy," appendix table 1.

7. In 2009, the average cost of an abortion was $470. As of 2008, there were 1,793 abortion clinics in the United States. Eighty-seven percent of all counties in the United States had no abortion clinic in 2008. But in the subsequent five years, this number dropped even further. Mississippi, for example, has only one abortion clinic. But in the Midwest abortion clinics are even scarcer. In a belt of states from northern Texas through North Dakota, the closest abortion clinics are between 100 and 200 miles away from the average woman. Roughly 400,000 women of reproductive age (between 15 and 44) live more than 150 miles from the closest clinic in this region. Rachel K. Jones, Ushma D. Upadhyay, and Tracy A. Weitz, "At What Cost?: Payment for Abortion Care by U.S. Women," *Women's Health Issues* 23, no. 3 (2013): e173–e178; Rachel K. Jones and Kathryn Kooistra. "Abortion Incidence and Access to Services in the United States, 2008," *Perspectives on Sexual and Reproductive Health* 43, no. 1 (2011): 41–50.

8. Forty-seven percent of unintended pregnancies among low-income women (those whose income is 100 to 199 percent of the poverty level) and 48 percent of unintended pregnancies among women in poverty (< 100 percent of the poverty level) end in abortion. Among high-income women (> 200 percent of the poverty level), 62 percent of unintended pregnancies end in abortion. These figures exclude pregnancies that end in miscarriage. Zolna and Lindberg, "Unintended Pregnancy," table 2.

9. Kathryn Edin and Maria Kefalas, *Promises I Can Keep: Why Poor Women Put Motherhood before Marriage* (University of California Press, 2005), p. 44.

10. Rachel Benson Gold, Adam Sonfield, Cory L. Richards, and Jennifer J. Frost, "Next Steps for America's Family Planning Program: Leveraging the

Potential of Medicaid and Title X in an Evolving Health Care System" (New York: Guttmacher Institute, 2009), www.guttmacher.org/pubs/NextSteps.pdf.

11. For more information on these statistics, see Kathryn Edin, Paula England, Emily Fitzgibbons Shafer, and Joanna Reed, "Forming Fragile Families: Was the Baby Planned, Unplanned, or in Between?," in *Unmarried Couples with Children*, edited by Paula England and Kathryn Edin (New York: Russell Sage Foundation, 2007).

12. Ibid.

13. Quentin Karpilow, Jennifer Manlove, Isabel V. Sawhill, and Adam Thomas, "The Role of Contraception in Preventing Abortion, Nonmarital Childbearing, and Child Poverty," presented at the Association for Public Policy Analysis and Management Annual Fall Research Conference, Washington, November 2013, https://appam.confex.com)/appam/2013/webprogram/Paper7979.html.

14. Susan Wood and others, "Health Centers and Family Planning: Results of a Nationwide Study," Health Policy Faculty Publications (George Washington University, 2013), hsrc.himmelfarb.gwu.edu/sphhs_policy_facpubs/60.

15. William D. Mosher and Jo Jones, "Use of Contraception in the United States: 1982–2008," *Vital and Health Statistics* (August 2010): 10.

16. Lori Frohwirth, Ann M. Moore, and Renata Maniaci, "Perceptions of Susceptibility to Pregnancy among U.S. Women Obtaining Abortions," *Social Science & Medicine* 99 (December 2013): 18–26.

17. Kelleen Kaye, Katherine Suellentrop, and Corinna Sloup, "The Fog Zone: How Misperceptions, Magical Thinking, and Ambivalence Put Young Adults at Risk for Unplanned Pregnancy" (Washington: National Campaign to Prevent Teen and Unplanned Pregnancy, 2009), www.thenationalcampaign.org/fogzone/pdf/fogzone.pdf.

18. James Trussell, "Contraceptive Failure in the United States," *Contraception* 83, no. 5 (2011): 397–404.

19. To calculate that 62.9 percent, I used the following method: The probability that a woman gets pregnant at some point in a five-year period is equal to 1 minus the probability that she does not get pregnant in any of those years. So, given an 18 percent chance of pregnancy each year, $1 - .82^5$. This assumes that there is an equal chance of not getting pregnant in every year of condom use and that successful users and failed users (where success is not getting pregnant during a year using birth control) have the same rate. The assumption is reasonable given that 18 percent is the figure for a "typical" user of some type of contraceptive.

20. Isabel Sawhill, Adam Thomas, and Emily Monea, "An Ounce of Prevention: Policy Prescriptions to Reduce the Prevalence of Fragile Families," *The Future of Children* 20, no. 2 (2010): 136.

21. Edin, England, Fitzgibbons Shafer, and Reed, "Forming Fragile Families."

22. Ibid.

23. In addition, many of these couples were in ongoing relationships and did not want to signal any lack of trust in their partner by using a condom. Moreover, they believed that having a child with a romantic partner is a natural and acceptable thing to do. The lack of stigma associated with being an unmarried parent means that marriage, while still revered as an ideal, is no longer the default or the expected way to raise a child.

24. Paula England, Monica Caudillo, Krystale Littlejohn, Brooke Conroy Bass, and Joanna Reed, "Single Women Contracepting Inconsistently: Do They Want to Get Pregnant or Lack Efficacy?," forthcoming in *American Journal of Sociology*, 2014.

25. The literature on teenage births suggests that the benefits to mothers of avoiding an early birth are negligible because their lifetime prospects are so poor to begin with. The literature on benefits for their children is much thinner. My problem with this literature is: (a) it is often based on very small samples and there is a tendency to interpret an insignificant coefficient as indicating "no effect"; (b) very few studies have been done with the much broader population of older young adults with some college education; and (c) the micro-level research conflicts with the aggregate time-series research on the benefits of the pill in improving women's education. For a review, see Karpilow, Manlove, Sawhill, and Thomas, "The Role of Contraception in Preventing Abortion, Nonmarital Childbearing, and Child Poverty."

26. For a thorough review of how people deviate from these assumptions, see Daniel Kahneman, *Thinking, Fast and Slow*, 1st ed. (New York: Farrar, Straus and Giroux, 2011).

27. Did you guess 10 cents? If so, you were tricked into giving the intuitive answer. The correct answer is 5 cents. The bat then costs $1.05 (0.05 + 1.00), which with the ball adds up to $1.10. For other puzzles that suggest intuitive but incorrect answers, see ibid., pp. 44–45.

28. Ibid., p. 48.

29. Angela L. Duckworth and Martin E. P. Seligman, "Self-Discipline Outdoes IQ in Predicting Academic Performance of Adolescents," *Psychological Science* 16, no. 12 (2005): 939–44.

30. Sometimes children were given the choice of having a marshmallow, a cookie, or a pretzel.

31. For the original study, see Walter Mischel, Ebbe B. Ebbesen, and Antonette Raskoff Zeiss, "Cognitive and Attentional Mechanisms in Delay of Gratification," *Journal of Personality and Social Psychology* 21, no. 2 (1972): 204–18.

For the follow up study on adolescent outcomes, see Yuichi Shoda, Walter Mischel, and Philip K. Peake, "Predicting Adolescent Cognitive and Self-regulatory Competencies from Preschool Delay of Gratification: Identifying Diagnostic Conditions," *Developmental Psychology* 26, no. 6 (1990): 978–86.

32. Research finds that the longer a person has to wait for a reward (for example, a movie to start up again after a delay due to technical malfunction), the longer that person predicts it will take for them to receive a reward. Joseph T. McGuire and Joseph W. Kable, "Rational Temporal Predictions Can Underlie Apparent Failures to Delay Gratification," *Psychological Review* 120, no. 2 (2013): 395–410.

33. Celeste Kidd, Holly Palmeri, and Richard N. Aslin, "Rational Snacking: Young Children's Decision-making on the Marshmallow Task Is Moderated by Beliefs about Environmental Reliability," *Cognition* 126, no. 1 (2013): 109–14.

34. See Aner Tal and Brian Wansink, "Fattening Fasting: Hungry Grocery Shoppers Buy More Calories, Not More Food," *JAMA Internal Medicine* 173, no. 12 (2013): 1146.

35. I like this example because I do a lot of hiking in the Colorado mountains and have had this experience myself! George Loewenstein, "Hot-Cold Empathy Gaps and Medical Decision Making," *Health Psychology* 24, no. 4 (Supplement, 2005): 50.

36. It should be noted that all participants completed these tasks while alone, and all responses were anonymous, reducing the likelihood that they would answer based on social desirability alone.

37. Dan Ariely and George Loewenstein, "The Heat of the Moment: The Effect of Sexual Arousal on Sexual Decision Making," *Journal of Behavioral Decision Making* 19, no. 2 (2006): 87–98.

38. David Butler, Dan Bell, and Timothy Rudd, "Using Social Impact Bonds to Spur Innovation, Knowledge Building, and Accountability," *Community Development Investment Review* (Federal Reserve Bank of San Francisco, 2013).

39. Roy F. Baumeister, Kathleen D. Vohs, and Dianne M. Tice, "The Strength Model of Self-Control," *Current Directions in Psychological Science* 16, no. 6 (2007): 351–55.

40. When stereotyping, a person assumes that an individual's characteristics match an "average" behavior associated with a person's race, gender, religion, or other background, which is known as the representativeness heuristic and is often given as a classic example of System 1 overpowering System 2.

41. Sendhil Mullainathan and Eldar Shafir, *Scarcity: Why Having Too Little Means So Much* (New York: Times Books, 2013).

42. Anandi Mani, Sendhil Mullainathan, Eldar Shafir, and Jiaying Zhao, "Poverty Impedes Cognitive Function," *Science* 341, no. 6149 (2013): 976–80.

43. He goes on to note, citing the work of Lawrence Henderson, that some cultures are better adapted for modern development than others. I would add (and suspect he would agree) that current childbearing patterns among the bottom half of the population are not well adapted to what a modern economy and society demand. David Brooks, *The Social Animal: The Hidden Sources of Love, Character, and Achievement* (New York: Random House Trade Paperbacks, 2013), pp. 149–54.

44. Brink Lindsay describes the problem well. Brink Lindsey, *Human Capitalism: How Economic Growth Has Made Us Smarter—and More Unequal* (Princeton University Press, 2013), p. 61.

45. This point is also made by Lindsay. As he puts it, the "loss of external props to self-discipline has led to a lot of self-destructive behavior." Ibid., p. 67.

46. David Brooks, based in part on the work of Eric Turkheimer, notes that you cannot break down a culture into its constituent parts or figure out what factors are primarily responsible for poverty because they interact in complicated ways. A culture emerges from this soup of interacting stresses, deprivations, norms, and modes of coping. "The difficult thing about emergence is that it is very hard in emergent systems to find the root cause of any problem. The positive side is that if you have negative cascades producing bad outcomes, it is also possible to have positive cascades producing good ones." Brooks, *The Social Animal*, p. 112.

47. Ron Haskins and Isabel V. Sawhill, *Creating an Opportunity Society* (Brookings Institution Press, 2009), pp. 144–46.

48. Richard H. Thaler and Cass Sunstein, *Nudge: Improving Decisions about Health, Wealth, and Happiness* (New York: Penguin Books, 2009).

49. Ibid., p. 60.

50. Matthew C. Farrelly, Kevin C. Davis, M. Lyndon Haviland, Peter Messeri, and Cheryl G. Healton, "Evidence of a Dose—Response Relationship between 'Truth' Antismoking Ads and Youth Smoking Prevalence," *American Journal of Public Health* 95, no. 3 (2005): 425–31; Matthew C. Farrelly, Cheryl G. Healton, Kevin C. Davis, Peter Messeri, James C. Hersey, and M. Lyndon Haviland, "Getting to the Truth: Evaluating National Tobacco Countermarketing Campaigns," *American Journal of Public Health* 92, no. 6 (2002): 901–07.

51. Adam Thomas, Emily Monea, and I reviewed these media campaigns and social marketing efforts in our 2010 article in the Fragile Families issue of *The Future of Children*. For example, see Seth M. Noar, "Challenges in Evaluating Health Communication Campaigns: Defining the Issues," *Communication*

Methods and Measures 3, nos. 1–2 (2009): 1–11; Leslie B. Snyder, Mark A. Hamilton, Elizabeth W. Mitchell, James Kiwanuka-Tondo, Fran Fleming-Milici, and Dwayne Proctor, "A Meta-analysis of the Effect of Mediated Health Communication Campaigns on Behavior Change in the United States," *Journal of Health Communication* 9, no. 1 (Supplement, 2004): 71–96; R. S. Zimmerman, P. M. Palmgreen, S. M. Noar, M. L. A. Lustria, H.-Y. Lu, and M. Lee Horosewski, "Effects of a Televised Two-City Safer Sex Mass Media Campaign Targeting High-Sensation-Seeking and Impulsive-Decision-Making Young Adults," *Health Education & Behavior* 34, no. 5 (2007): 810–26.

52. One example is the social media campaign "Not Me, Not Now," which sent teens a clear message about delaying sex and seems to have delayed the onset of sexual intercourse among younger teens. See B. Douglas Kirby, "Understanding What Works and What Doesn't in Reducing Adolescent Sexual Risk-Taking," *Family Planning Perspectives* 33, no. 6 (2001): 276–81.

53. A wonderful example of this is the website of the National Campaign to Prevent Teen and Unplanned Pregnancy (http://bedsider.org/), which approaches the topics of sex and contraception from the perspective of young adults.

54. Melissa S. Kearney and Phillip B. Levine, "Media Influences on Social Outcomes: The Impact of MTV's 16 and Pregnant on Teen Childbearing," Working Paper w19795 (Cambridge, Mass.: National Bureau of Economic Research, 2014).

55. Disclosure: I am president of the National Campaign's board.

56. The chances of getting pregnant in a year's time in the absence of contraception is 85 percent. Trussell, "Contraceptive Failure in the United States."

57. The National Campaign to Prevent Teen and Unplanned Pregnancy is currently engaged in just such a rebranding effort, and I am indebted to Sarah Brown and the staff of the campaign for their insights on this and the other issues discussed in this section.

58. George Loewenstein, "Out of Control: Visceral Influences on Behavior," *Organizational Behavior and Human Decision Processes* 65, no. 3 (1996): 272–92.

59. One review of abstinence-only education found that some school curriculums presented scientifically inaccurate information about sex, had no effect on delaying first sexual encounters, and may have contributed to the spread of sexually transmitted infections. The authors say that the programs are "inherently coercive and may cause teenagers to use ineffective (or no) protection against pregnancy and STIs." See John Santelli, Mary A. Ott, Maureen Lyon, Jennifer Rogers, Daniel Summers, and Rebecca Schleifer, "Abstinence and

Abstinence-Only Education: A Review of U.S. Policies and Programs," *Journal of Adolescent Health* 38, no. 1 (2006): 72–81.

60. Fifty-five percent of sexually experienced young people age 15–19 (including 67 percent of teen girls 15–19) say they wish they had waited longer before having sex. "Teens Say Parents Most Influence Their Decisions about Sex: New Survey Released in Advance of the National Day to Prevent Teen Pregnancy" (National Campaign to Prevent Teen and Unplanned Pregnancy, 2012), http://thenationalcampaign.org/press-release/teens-say-parents-most-influence-their-decisions-about-sex-0?display=grid.

61. Trussell, "Contraceptive Failure in the United States."

62. See note 19 for an explanation of how to calculate the chance of pregnancy over five years.

63. Thaler and Sunstein, *Nudge*, p. 85.

64. Sarah Holden, Peter Brady, and Michael Hadley, "401(k) Plans: A 25-Year Retrospective," *Research Perspective* 12, no. 2 (2006): 1–40.

65. Brigitte C. Madrian and Dennis F. Shea, "The Power of Suggestion: Inertia in 401(k) Participation and Savings Behavior," *Quarterly Journal of Economics* 116, no. 4 (2001): 1149–87; James J. Choi, David Laibson, Brigitte C. Madrian, and Andrew Metrick, "For Better or for Worse: Default Effects and 401(k) Savings Behavior," in *Perspectives on the Economics of Aging*, edited by James Wise (University of Chicago Press, 2004), pp. 81–126; John Beshears, James J. Choi, David Laibson, and Brigitte C. Madrian, "The Importance of Default Options for Retirement Savings Outcomes: Evidence from the United States," Working Paper w12009 (Cambridge, Mass.: National Bureau of Economic Research, 2009), www.nber.org/papers/w12009.pdf; John Beshears, James J. Choi, David Laibson, and Brigitte C. Madrian, "The Impact of Employer Matching on Savings Plan Participation under Automatic Enrollment," in *Research Findings in the Economics of Aging*, edited by David A. Wise (University of Chicago Press, 2010).

66. Madrian and Shea, "The Power of Suggestion."

67. E. J. Johnson, "Medicine: Do Defaults Save Lives?," *Science* 302, no. 5649 (2003): 1338–39.

68. Ibid.

69. This number does not account for the fact that some of these unintended pregnancies are mistimed, meaning that the taxpayer savings may be slightly overstated. "Publicly Funded Contraceptive Services in the United States" (New York: Guttmacher Institute, 2013), www.guttmacher.org/pubs/fb_contraceptive_serv.pdf.

70. Adam Thomas and Emily Monea, "The High Cost of Unintended Pregnancy," CCF Policy Brief 16 (Brookings Institution, 2011), www.brookings.edu/research/papers/2011/07/unintended-pregnancy-thomas-monea.

71. Brooke Winner, Jeffrey F. Peipert, Qiuhong Zhao, Christina Buckel, Tessa Madden, Jenifer E. Allsworth, and Gina M. Secura, "Effectiveness of Long-Acting Reversible Contraception," *New England Journal of Medicine* 366, no. 21 (2012): 1998–2007.

72. Gold, Sonfield, Richards, and Frost, "Next Steps for America's Family Planning Program."

73. J. Joseph Speidel, Cynthia C. Harper, and Wayne C. Shields, "The Potential of Long-Acting Reversible Contraception to Decrease Unintended Pregnancy," *Contraception* 78, no. 3 (2008): 197.

74. Ibid.; see also United Nations, Department of Economic and Social Affairs, Population Division, *World Contraceptive Use 2012* (POP/DB/CP/Rev2012).

75. Lawrence B. Finer, Jenna Jerman, and Megan L. Kavanaugh, "Changes in Use of Long-acting Contraceptive Methods in the United States, 2007–2009," *Fertility and Sterility* 98, no. 4 (2012): 893–97.

76. Jacqueline E. Darroch, Susheela Singh, and Jennifer J. Frost, "Differences in Teenage Pregnancy Rates among Five Developed Countries: The Roles of Sexual Activity and Contraceptive Use," *Family Planning Perspectives* 33, no. 6 (2001): 244; Tessa Madden, Jenifer E. Allsworth, Katherine J. Hladky, Gina M. Secura, and Jeffrey F. Peipert, "Intrauterine Contraception in Saint Louis: a Survey of Obstetrician and Gynecologists' Knowledge and Attitudes," *Contraception* 81, no. 2 (2010): 112–16.

77. Kaye, Suellentrop, and Sloup, "The Fog Zone," p. 40.

78. Ibid.

79. Speidel, Harper, and Shields, "The Potential of Long-Acting Reversible Contraception to Decrease Unintended Pregnancy," p. 198.

80. These costs are based on those reported by Planned Parenthood; see www.plannedparenthood.org/health-topics/birth-control/iud-4245.htm. According to Dr. Jeffrey Peipert at the Washington University Medical School in St. Louis, the full cost, including insertion and follow-up, is higher. Personal conversation, December 27, 2013.

81. Sendhil Mullainathan has coined the term "behavioral hazard" to talk about the opposite of "moral hazard." People who succumb to behavioral hazard do not use a highly effective service or treatment because of its up-front costs. Requiring a co-payment is one way to prevent moral hazard (by giving patients a stake in any decision to seek health care); but requiring a co-payment could

increase behavioral hazard by discouraging the use of highly effective forms of care. Women who opt out of using birth control, particularly methods that have high up-front costs, may be demonstrating behavioral hazard. Given the high cost both to women and to society of the failure to use birth control, subsidies or rewards for birth control use could be good policy. Sendhil Mullainathan, "When a Co-Pay Gets in the Way of Health," *New York Times*, August 11, 2013, sec. Business Day.

82. Other methods include the transdermal patch, the contraceptive vaginal ring, and depot medroxyprogesterone acetate (DMPA). Gina M. Secura, Jenifer E. Allsworth, Tessa Madden, Jennifer L. Mullersman, and Jeffrey F. Peipert, "The Contraceptive CHOICE Project: Reducing Barriers to Long-Acting Reversible Contraception," *American Journal of Obstetrics and Gynecology* 203, no. 2 (2010).

83. This insight was provided to me by Dr. Jeffrey Peipert in a personal conversation on December 27, 2013.

Chapter 7

Winston Churchill is quoted from a speech, London, November 5, 1919.

1. Pamela Haag, *Marriage Confidential: The Post-Romantic Age of Workhorse Wives, Royal Children, Undersexed Spouses, & Rebel Couples Who Are Rewriting the Rules* (New York: HarperCollins, 2011), pp. 22–23.

2. "There are regions in our own land, and classes of our population, where the birth rate has sunk below the death rate. Surely it should need no demonstration to show that wilful sterility is, from the standpoint of the human race, the one sin for which the penalty is national death, race death; a sin for which there is no atonement; a sin which is the more dreadful exactly in proportion as the men and women guilty thereof are in other respects , in character and bodily and mental powers, those whom for the sake of the state it would be well to see the fathers and mothers of many healthy children, well brought up in homes made happy by their presence." Theodore Roosevelt, as quoted in Elaine Tyler May, *Barren in the Promised Land: Childless Americans and the Pursuit of Happiness* (Harvard University Press, 1997), p. 61.

3. Claudia Goldin and Lawrence F. Katz, "The Power of the Pill: Oral Contraceptives and Women's Career and Marriage Decisions," *Journal of Political Economy* 110, no. 4 (2002): 730–70.

4. David Willetts, *The Pinch: How the Baby Boomers Took Their Children's Future—and Why They Should Give It Back* (London: Atlantic, 2011), p. 13.

5. Isabel Sawhill and Quentin Karpilow, *A No-Cost Proposal to Reduce Poverty and Inequality*, CCF Policy Brief 51 (Center on Children and Families, Brookings Institution, January 2014).

6. Jonathan V. Last, *What to Expect When No One's Expecting: America's Coming Demographic Disaster* (New York: Encounter Books, 2013), p. 2.

7. Ibid., p. 154.

8. Sarah Blaffer Hrdy, *Mother Nature: Maternal Instincts and How They Shape the Human Species* (New York: Ballantine Books, 2000), p. 311.

9. The biological factors include "endocrinal priming during pregnancy, physical changes (including changes in the brain) during and after birth; the complex feedback loops of lactation; and the cognitive mechanisms that enhance the likelihood of recognizing and learning to prefer kin. *But almost none of these biological responses are automatic.*" In humans, "maternal investment in offspring is complicated by a range of utterly new considerations: cultural expectations, gender roles, sentiments like honor or shame, sex preferences, and the mother's awareness of the future." Ibid., p. 378.

10. Liza Mundy, "The Gay Guide to Wedded Bliss," *The Atlantic*, June 2013, www.theatlantic.com/magazine/archive/2013/06/the-gay-guide-to-wedded-bliss/309317/.

11. Compulsory sterilization laws were targeted at the "unfit," including the poor, the feeble-minded, the mentally ill, criminals, sexually promiscuous women, and later women of color, especially those on public assistance. They were enacted by many states and found to be constitutional by the Supreme Court in 1927 when Justice Oliver Wendell Holmes infamously wrote "three generations of imbeciles is enough." Shockingly, Hitler is said to have modeled the Nazi experiments with eugenics on a program in California. For a history of this and other developments in the long history of attempts to control fertility in the United States, see May, *Barren in the Promised Land*.

12. Adam Thomas and Emily Monea, "The High Cost of Unintended Pregnancy," CCF Policy Brief 16 (Brookings Institution, 2011), www.brookings.edu/research/papers/2011/07/unintended-pregnancy-thomas-monea.

13. Parents under 25 at a child's birth are much more likely to be "weak parents" than those over 25. Richard V. Reeves and Kimberly Howard, "The Parenting Gap" (Brookings Institution, 2013), www.brookings.edu/research/papers/2013/09/09-parenting-gap-social-mobility-wellbeing-reeves.

14. Melissa S. Kearney and Phillip B. Levine, "Reducing Unplanned Pregnancies through Medicaid Family Planning Services," CCF Policy Brief 39 (Brookings Institution, 2008), www.brookings.edu/research/papers/2008/07/

reducing-pregnancy-kearney; Isabel Sawhill, Adam Thomas, and Emily Monea, "An Ounce of Prevention: Policy Prescriptions to Reduce the Prevalence of Fragile Families," *The Future of Children* 20, no. 2 (2010): 133–55.

15. Mia R. Zolna and Laura Lindberg, "Unintended Pregnancy: Incidence and Outcomes among Young Adult Unmarried Women in the United States, 2001 and 2008" (New York: Guttmacher Institute, 2012).

16. Melissa S. Kearney and Phillip B. Levine, "Media Influences on Social Outcomes: The Impact of MTV's 16 and Pregnant on Teen Childbearing," Working Paper w19795 (Cambridge, Mass.: National Bureau of Economic Research, 2014).

17. Isabel Sawhill and Joanna Venator, "Reducing Unintended Pregnancies for Low-Income Women" (Washington: Hamilton Project, 2014).

18. This social marketing campaign coincided with Iowa's expansion of Medicaid family planning services in 2010 and a huge increase in funding for family planning clinics starting in 2007, so we cannot conclusively attribute this whole effect to the social marketing campaign. However, it should be noted that the decline in pregnancies accelerated during the campaign. Whereas the percent of unintended pregnancies dropped from 46 percent to 45 percent between 2007 and 2009, it dropped from 45 percent in 2009 to 41 percent in 2011. Sally Pedersen, "Iowa Initiative to Reduce Unintended Pregnancies," Webinar presented at the Department of Health and Human Services, www.hhs.gov/opa/pdfs/11-26-12-iowa-initiative-transcript.pdf; "Reducing Unintended Pregnancies in Iowa by Investing in Title X Clinics" (Bixby Center for Global Reproductive Health, 2012), www.philliberresearch.com/files/Reducing-Unintended-Pregnancies-in-Iowa-by-Investing-in-Title-X-Clinics.pdf.

19. Leslie B. Snyder, Mark A. Hamilton, Elizabeth W. Mitchell, James Kiwanuka-Tondo, Fran Fleming-Milici, and Dwayne Proctor, "A Meta-Analysis of the Effect of Mediated Health Communication Campaigns on Behavior Change in the United States," *Journal of Health Communication* 9, no. 1 (Supplement, 2004): 71–96; David R. Holtgrave, Katherine A. Wunderink, Donna M. Vallone, and Cheryl G. Healton, "Cost–Utility Analysis of the National Truth® Campaign to Prevent Youth Smoking," *American Journal of Preventive Medicine* 36, no. 5 (2009): 385–88.

20. Christine Dehlendorf, Kira Levy, Rachel Ruskin, and Jody Steinauer, "Health Care Providers' Knowledge about Contraceptive Evidence: A Barrier to Quality Family Planning Care?," *Contraception* 81, no. 4 (2010): 292–98; Cynthia C. Harper, Maya Blum, Heike Thiel de Bocanegra, Philip D. Darney, J. Joseph Speidel, Michael Policar, and Eleanor A. Drey, "Challenges in Translating

Evidence to Practice: The Provision of Intrauterine Contraception," *Obstetrics & Gynecology* 111, no. 6 (2008): 1359–69; Tessa Madden, Jenifer E. Allsworth, Katherine J. Hladky, Gina M. Secura, and Jeffrey F. Peipert, "Intrauterine Contraception in Saint Louis: A Survey of Obstetrician and Gynecologists' Knowledge and Attitudes," *Contraception* 81, no. 2 (2010): 112–16.

21. Personal conversation with Dr. Jeffrey Peipert, December 27, 2013.

22. Emma Green, "Why Is It Hard for Liberals to Talk about Family Values?," *The Atlantic*, July 2013, p. 2, www.theatlantic.com/politics/archive/2013/07/why-is-it-hard-for-liberals-to-talk-about-family-values/278151/.

23. Isabel Sawhill, "Twenty Years Later, It Turns Out Dan Quayle Was Right about Murphy Brown and Unmarried Moms," *Washington Post*, May 25, 2012.

24. Michael Wald, "Beyond Child Protection: Helping All Families Provide Adequate Parenting," in *Improving the Odds for America's Children: Future Directions in Policy and Practice*, edited by Kathleen McCartney, Hirokazu Yoshikawa, and Laurie B. Forcier (Harvard Education Press, 2014).

Index

CPSIA information can be obtained at www.ICGtesting.com
Printed in the USA
LVOW11s0524020316

477405LV00001B/1/P